SINS OF THE FATHER

Tracing the Decisions that Shaped the Irish Economy

CONOR McCABE

First published 2011

The History Press Ireland
119 Lower Baggot Street
Dublin 2
Ireland
www.thehistorypress.ie

British Library Cataloguing in Publication Data.
A catalogue record for this book is available from the British Library.

ISBN 978 1 84588 693 6

Typesetting and origination by The History Press
Printed in Great Britain
Manufacturing managed by Jellyfish Print Solutions Ltd

CONTENTS

ACKNOWLEDGEMENTS

Special thanks to:
Donagh Brennan; my nephews Kevin and Jack Cleary; John Cleary; Ronan Colgan and the staff at The History Press Ireland; Rudi Deda; Ciarán Finnegan; Daithí Flynn; Colm Hall; Dr Brian Hanley; Dr Donnacha Seán Lucey; Donal McCarthy; Padraig Walsh McCarthy; Miriam Guillén Pardo; the staff of the National Library of Ireland and in particular Gerard Kavanagh; my brothers Aiden, Niall, Paul and Gerard, and my sisters Kathleen, Nora, Sandra and Siobhan; and Joanne Walsh.

INTRODUCTION

There have been more than a few attempts to explain why the Irish banking crisis developed the way it did, and the argument that it was due to a breakdown in moral standards is quite a popular one. The journalist Fintan O'Toole was explicit in this regard when he wrote in 2009 that, 'the absence of a sense of propriety, of restraint and of right and wrong' on the part of the bankers 'was not just obnoxious, it was economically disastrous.'[i] *The Irish Times* talked of a 'frightening lack of morality' within Anglo Irish Bank, the most indebted of the Irish institutions, and how the actions of its chairman 'cast a shadow over the ethical culture of the bank he ran for most of the past 33 years.'[ii] The newspaper's senior business correspondent, Arthur Beesley, said that the directors of Irish Life and Permanent inhabit an 'ethical cocoon in which the sense of right and wrong is at odds with standards in the outside world', while the economist Brian Lucey talked of the immorality of the government's actions in pouring money into Anglo Irish Bank in a desperate attempt to keep it going as a business concern.[iii]

Yet, the banking crisis in Ireland was not caused by pockets of immorality in an otherwise reasonably well-functioning system. The ruthless pursuit of profit is not personal; that is the way business works. And what is condemned as immoral in times of crisis is often praised as savvy and pragmatic in times of prosperity.[iv] Similarly, there is nothing particularly unique about the ethical cocoons of Irish bankers, their frightening lack of morality, lack of restraint or sense of propriety. This was a worldwide financial crisis, after all, not a regional or a Celtic one. In other words, it was not the implosion of speculative debt but the ability to transfer that debt wholesale onto the shoulders of the State which marked out Irish bankers as a step above their worldwide contemporaries.

The decision by the Irish government on 30 September 2008 to guarantee almost all the liabilities of six Irish financial institutions was not an economic decision but an exercise in power. 'The deeper truth exposed by the present crisis,' wrote the journalist and politician Shane Ross, 'is that Ireland harbours more powerful forces than Fianna Fáil.'[v] And while this is true, the purpose of this book is not to show that banks and property developers are indeed powerful in Ireland but to explore why that is the case. What is it about the Irish economy that has made financial and property speculation a core activity and not, say, fisheries or gas? Why were builders and insurance salesmen fêted as entrepreneurs, while indigenous exporters outside of agriculture and tourism struggled to find support? How did this situation arise, and how deep are its roots?

Put as concisely as possible, the type of business activities which dominated the Irish economy in the twentieth century – cattle exports to Britain and financial investment in London; the development of green-field sites and the construction of factories and office buildings to facilitate foreign industrial and commercial investment; the birth of the suburbs and subsequent housing booms predicated on an expanding urban workforce – saw the development of an indigenous moneyed class based around cattle, construction and banking. These sectional interests were able to control successive government policy, much to the detriment of the rest of the economy, which had to rely on whatever scraps it could pick up from quasi-committed multinationals and government-funded grants and tax breaks. In 2008 the construction and banking sectors of that class closed ranks in order to protect themselves from oblivion, resulting in the bank guarantee and the creation of the National Asset Management Agency.

The power to do that did not develop overnight. In order to find the reason why that class was able to wield such influence at such short notice, we are going to have to dig. This book sets out a historical analysis of the events of September 2008 in order to achieve that objective.

History provides a canvas wide and deep enough to enable us to see the economic and political mechanisms, the machine itself, in motion. By looking at the way the Irish economy actually works – the deep structures and investment strategies – the government's response to the banking crisis, despite its inherent insanity, starts to make sense. The logic behind it reveals itself. It is still deeply shocking, but it was not the result of a few bad apples.

The plan of the book is, hopefully, straightforward enough. There are four chapters dealing with the development of the Irish economy, and one chapter on the crisis itself. It starts with housing, as the subject is saturated with so many myths and half-truths that it demands a factual analysis. There is no Irish property-owning gene. It is not part of our DNA. Home ownership outside of rural areas is a relatively new phenomenon. Chapter Two deals with cattle, as it is simply impossible to discuss the history of the Irish economy without discussing beef and live exports. Up until the 1980s, cattle was to Ireland what the car industry was to Detroit and, although the Irish Free State gained partial independence in 1922, its economy, via the cattle industry, remained intertwined with that of the UK.

The structural problems related to that situation – an independent country with a regional economy – had an influence on the so-called Whitaker/Lemass revolution in the 1950s and the superficial industrialization of the Irish economy in the decade which followed in its wake. Ireland imported foreign industry as a substitute for indigenous industrial growth. This is also the period when we see a new type of Irish businessman – the speculative builder and financier – come to the fore. The banking system is opened up and liberalized. By the late 1980s foreign industrial investment has stalled. The government decides to extend its low corporation tax rate to financial as well as industrial exports. The International Financial Services Centre is born. Ireland becomes a tax haven, with minimum regulation and oversight. By the time the last of the barriers to speculative financial trading are lifted in the US, Ireland is more than ready to take the world's money. In 2008 the veneer of cheap credit suddenly fades, leaving the shaky edifice of the Irish economy exposed.

It is hoped that these five chapters will shine a light on the reasons why Ireland has the businesses it has, and why banks and speculators wield so much power and influence. It is only by acknowledging the facts of our situation that we can even begin to attempt to do something about it. This book is presented as a small contribution to that process.

1

HOUSING

A lot of what we consider to be normal and natural about Irish housing dates from the 1920s. The first garden suburbs were built during this time, with significant subsidies to private builders backed up by a government policy that promoted home ownership above tackling the tenements and slums. It was a policy which favoured the middle classes and the higher-paid, skilled members of the working class.[1] However, while suburbia can be traced back to the turn of the last century, it took decades for this type of planning to become the norm. Issues such as cost, distance, work and community all acted against these moves towards the periphery. In other words, there is nothing natural about suburbia. There is nothing normal about living significant distances from one's place of employment, even if it is normal to us today. The semi-detached with a garden and a fence was not an organic or spontaneous development. As with so many things regarding large-scale societal development, it began with an idea and was pushed through by government, through the use of incentives and the elimination of alternatives.

In 1898, an English civil servant produced a book entitled *Tomorrow: A Peaceful Path to Real Reform*, in which he described his vision for the cities of the future. His name was Ebenezer Howard and his publication proved to be quite popular. It was quickly followed by a second edition, which he called *Garden Cities of Tomorrow*, the name by which it is commonly known today. Throughout the nineteenth century, the apparently insurmountable problems of urban sprawl – poverty, dirt, disease and crime – were subject to a multitude of official reports and parliamentary enquiries. Rural dwellers were regarded as stronger and healthier than their urban cousins who, it was believed, suffered from both physical and moral decay. Cities were depraved and corrupt, while the countryside was honest and noble. However, it was seen as well-nigh impossible to have an industrial society without urbanisation. It was unfortunate, but the stench and decay of the modern city were simply part of the sad but necessary price of progress. Its extremities could be tempered, but never eradicated.

Howard thought otherwise. He wanted to merge the benefits of the city with those of the countryside through the creation of satellite towns of no more than 30,000 people and 1,000 acres, each surrounded by an agricultural green-belt of 5,000 acres and 2,000 people, and linked to the main metropolis by quick and efficient public transport. This 'town-country' fusion would offer the individual and his family such opportunities for employment and personal advancement as available in any town, while also providing the benefits of fresh air and bright sunshine via the city parks and nearby countryside. He wanted to show how, in his 'town-county' cities, 'equal, nay better, opportunities of social intercourse may be enjoyed than are enjoyed in any crowded city, while yet the beauties of nature may encompass and enfold each dweller therein'.[2] Over the next sixty years, Howard's vision of 'garden cities' mutated into the suburbs of today.

It is not a coincidence that the dominant form of housing in modern Ireland, i.e. one-family occupancy with a garden in suburbia, can be traced back to a small book by an English reformist. When it came to housing and planning, Ireland frequently looked across the sea to Britain, and this influence was present in Irish newspapers, journals and pamphlets, as well as official reports, planning committees, and architectural design. From the 1880s onwards, the House of Commons passed legislation which gave a notable amount of Irish rural labourers 'high-quality, low-cost social housing and also created a social housing sector which was precociously large for its time'.[3] These acts, along with the 1890 Housing of the Working Classes Act, provided the underlying framework for much of social housing schemes which were built post-independence.

The reason for this advancement in rural housing was not altruistic but political. The Irish Parliamentary Party used land reform as a tactic in its campaign for self-government. The transfer of land ownership from landlords to farmer-tenants led to demands for a similar franchise on the part of agricultural labourers, who were excluded from land reform, but who were too much of a social force to be ignored by the Parliamentary Party. From 1883 to 1906, some 20,000 agricultural labourers' cottages were built by local authorities.[4] Construction rose to new levels after the introduction of the 1906 Labourers (Ireland) Act.[5] By 1922, an estimated 50,582 cottages had been completed under the various Acts. This accounted for about 10 per cent of the total rural stock. By way of contrast, during the same period only 8,861 dwellings had been completed by urban councils. This was despite the fact that Ireland's rural population was declining while its urban population was increasing.

The Irish Free State inherited a rural social housing system and a body of planning laws and design ideas from the British administration, but very little in the way of actual, constructed, urban social housing. Whatever was needed to address the needs of the towns and cities, the Irish government was going to have to work out for itself.

FROM INDEPENDENCE TO 1932

> '[We] wish to resuscitate the speculative builder ...'[6]

On the eve of the First World War, around 29 per cent of Dublin's population lived in slum conditions. This included not only the majority of unskilled labourers, but also a significant proportion of the city's skilled (or artisan) workers. In 1923, the Cork Borough Restoration Committee said that the city needed at least 2,500 houses. The same year, the Limerick Housing Association called for the immediate construction of

3,000 houses and that all rented accommodation be subject to medical, sanitary and structural tests. 'The housing conditions in Limerick,' it said, 'are a perpetual crime against humanity.'[7] Two years earlier, it had been reported that of the seven members of a family who lived in one room of a tenement in the city, three had died of influenza, 'and for a time living and dead were together in the one small apartment'.[8] The Irish Minister for Justice and Foreign Affairs, Kevin O'Higgins, told the Dáil on 12 June 1923 that, 'We are confronted with a serious situation in regard to houses; it is a disease in our social system.' These sentiments were echoed by W.T. Cosgrave at a meeting of the Rotary Club at Clery's Restaurant, Dublin in 1924. 'At no time in the history of this country was there greater need for the provision of housing for all classes of the community,' he said, adding that he knew 'of no service in the State that demanded a greater amount of co-operation and sacrifice in order to achieve something towards the desired end'.[9]

It was clear that the housing problem was of such a scale that it could not be solved without significant government assistance. The manner of that assistance, though, was a matter for debate.

At the same Rotary Club meeting where Cosgrave spelt out the seriousness of the housing problem, he also discussed the government's preferred solution. *The Irish Times* reported his conclusions:

> Looking around the country he knew of no better platform than that of the Rotary Club from which to deal with this subject. They [the government] had discovered during the last few years that neither municipalities, nor local authorities, nor State organisations were in a position to deal alone with the housing problem. They had come to the conclusion – and he thought it would be subscribed to by all who had knowledge of the conditions – that if success in this matter were to be achieved it must come through private enterprise; that is to say, commercial enterprise.

Cosgrave's speech was praised by *Irish Builder and Engineer*, which wrote that 'it was gratifying, in these days of socialism, to find the head of State disassociating himself from the foolish notions that some have, that the whole of such vast problems have only to be made a government concern to be solved'.[10] And the President's comments echoed those of his cabinet colleague Ernest Blythe, who said in June 1923 (as Minister for Local Government) that 'we believe, in general, more houses could be got for the money available by subsidising private builders than by subsidising local authorities'.[11] It was a rare occasion of a government minister publicly stating that he wanted *less* money for his department.

Cumann na nGaedheal planned to reduce the level of construction undertaken by local authorities, and instead divert public funds to private builders (via grants and tax breaks) in order to answer the State's housing needs. The party argued that it was doing this because public services were inefficient and incapable of delivering value for money. The contradiction of a private sector that needed public money in order to deliver an 'efficient' service was never teased out by Cosgrave, Blythe, and the rest of the ministers.

The government not only moved to divert funds from the local authorities; in a number of cases it shut them down completely. The official reasons ranged from the over-charging of business rates to financial irregularities on the part of councillors. However, the councils which were disbanded had on them a strong Sinn Féin and anti-Treaty presence. Dublin City Council, for example, had passed resolutions calling for the inspection of jails, the release of Civil War prisoners, and their examination by the Corporation's medical officer.[12] Dublin Corporation Council was dissolved in May 1924 by order of Seamus De Burca, Minister for Local Government, who was satisfied, having heard the evidence of an inquiry into the council, 'that the duties of the Council of the County Borough of Dublin are not being duly and effectually discharged by them'.[13] Cork Corporation was suspended the same year, with P. Monaghan appointed as commissioner. Monaghan said, 'The Corporation was a business concern, to be run on business lines, with a definite programme of work to be done in a definite time and for a definite amount of money.'[14] He told the people of Cork that although he was a Dublin man, he had their interests at heart, and was better positioned to answer their needs than the elected representatives from their communities.

There may have been other reasons for the suspension of the local authorities. In January 1924, Thomas Johnson, leader of the Labour Party and the official opposition in the Dáil, told the House that:

> … there appears also to be an intention to remove any control which local authorities may have in the past intended over the layout of sites: that where something in the nature of a town plan was decided on by a local authority, it is now suggested that all those decisions shall be set aside, and that anyone will be allowed to build a house anywhere, in any fashion, subject to the final decision as to the design of the house by the Minister for Local Government. I think that is a defect, and I think that there ought to be, in the minds of Ministers, some general plans and that the policy of *laissez-faire* in house-building should not be allowed to continue.[15]

For the next six years, the administration of the capital, including the social housing programme, was in the hands of three government-appointed Commissioners.

The Housing (Building Facilities) Act was passed by the Dáil in April 1924. It provided grants of between £60 and £100 to anyone building a house for their own use, for sale, or for rent. It also offered remissions on local authority rates. The maximum selling prices were £270, £300 and £450, for three, four and five-roomed houses respectively. An additional Housing Act was passed in 1925, which expanded on the themes of speculation and owner-occupancy.

Although these Acts applied to all urban local authorities, most construction took place in Dublin and Cork. Cathal O'Connell, in his book *The State and Housing in Ireland*, explains why:

> The modest level of housing activity which these Acts stimulated was limited to Dublin and Cork – big local authorities who could raise money through bond issues on the stock exchange. This is illustrated in the figures for house completions. Fully 80 per cent of all local authority building by local authorities was carried out by Dublin and Cork Corporations. Because the Local Loans Fund, the mechanism

> used to finance local authority infrastructure projects, did not extend to housing schemes, smaller local authorities who wanted to proceed with schemes had to borrow funds from commercial banks who were very reluctant to lend money for such 'unproductive' purposes.[16]

The majority of houses built under the Acts was done so not by speculative builders but by owner-occupiers. This was the type of *laissez-faire* construction that Johnson had warned about, and the local authorities had opposed before their suspension.

Nevertheless, future owner-occupiers as builders of their own homes, using whatever sites they could and lacking any sense of town planning, was seen as a positive outcome by the government. The argument was that this process would free up the quality rented accommodation previously occupied by the now property-owning middle classes. These vacancies would eventually filter down to the slums, allowing those who could afford the rents to move up the housing chain. The problem was one of congestion, the government said, and the 1924 Act would help to relieve this.

For that to happen, though, populations would have to have remained absolutely static. The moment that more people entered the equation – through births, the continued migration of thousands from rural to urban areas, and by people starting families of their own – the spurious symmetry of housing which is freed up for those at the bottom by those at the top, is gone.

The government's plan also required that the housing problem itself did not exist. They maintained that it was not housing that was the problem, but the lack of better housing for the middle classes which was causing the bottleneck within the slums. It was as if the need for housing was akin to a tram queue, one that no new passenger ever joins, but which is made shorter by those at the top buying cars and becoming transport-occupiers instead. Yet, this was the logic: middle-class people and property speculators, building and selling houses with public money, will make life better for those in the tenements and slums.

The reason why local authorities were excluded from the Act was all too clear to Richard Corish, the Labour Party TD for Wexford. On 25 January 1924, he spoke in the Dáil in relation to the Housing Bill:

> The President has suggested here, on more than one occasion, that the reason that prompted him to take this matter out of the hands of the local authorities was that the houses would cost too much money if they were built under their jurisdiction. I do not know whether that argument is correct or not. I do not believe it is correct, because I do not see why the local authorities, whose members represent the people, would squander money to the extent suggested by the President. The only inference to be drawn from the President's statement is that the money would be squandered. I have yet to learn that any private builder will take as much interest in the working classes as a local authority. I do not think the President is going to accomplish what he proposes to set himself to do under this Act, by handing over the building of houses entirely to private builders. This, to my mind, is an invitation to private people to become speculators, without due regard to the fact that these houses are wanted for the housing of the working classes.

In the words of one historian, the Housing Acts of 1924 and 1925, by emphasising owner-occupation, tended 'to favour the middle classes, rather than the working classes, for whom the housing problem was so severe'.[17]

The First World War, the War of Independence and the Civil War had all dramatically curtailed building activity in Ireland. By the time hostilities had ceased in 1923, it had been almost ten years since Ireland had seen relatively normal levels of construction. The drop in new housing affected the middle classes, and it was this shortage rather than the horrendous slum conditions in Dublin, Cork, Limerick and Waterford that the Free State government made its priority. 'One might as well try and live in an aeroplane,' said one Dublin Corporation barrister, summing up the middle-class dilemma, 'as to get a vacant house in Dublin.'[18] The Housing Acts were one element of this strategy, while the other was the construction of suburbs.

'NOTHING GAINED BY OVERCROWDING'

In 1914, Dublin Corporation commissioned a study for a proposed garden city at Marino from the respected town planners Raymond Unwin and Patrick Geddes, both of whom were admirers and colleagues of Ebenezer Howard. Their original plan called for 1,100 houses with a density of twelve per acre, green paths and a complete separation of traffic and pedestrians.[19] A further plan was commissioned in 1918, this time from the City Architect, Charles McCarthy, with final permission given in 1920. This was for 530 houses, construction of which did not begin until 1922 due to the post-war political upheaval.

Marino was Dublin Corporation's first garden suburb. By the time the final tender was completed in 1927, the scheme had expanded to include Croydon Park and consisted of 1,283 five-roomed houses with a density of twelve per acre. Although it was social housing, the entire scheme was tenant-purchase. On 21 May 1925 the Dublin Borough Commissioners invited 'applications from persons of the working classes, employed or resident in the City of Dublin, for the purchase of houses at Marino under the Corporation house Purchase Scheme'.[20] There were 258 houses available in this first batch and the prices ranged from £400 to £440.

The Corporation received 4,400 applications for the first phase, of which a shortlist of 414 was drawn up. The houses were earmarked for married couples with at least four children, but of the 414 families shortlisted, not one had fewer than six children.[21] A deposit of £25 was also required, but the Borough Commissioners – who, since the suspension of the Corporation Council in 1924, had the final say in all applications – stated that 'preference, however, will be given to intending occupiers who are prepared to deposit the whole or a substantial portion of the purchase money'.[22] Each applicant had to be able to meet the minimum weekly repayments of 15–16*s* a week. Such financial barriers meant that the Marino scheme was out of the range of the majority of Dublin's working class.

In March 1927, tenders were advertised for the erection of 128 three-roomed houses, seventy-seven four-roomed and sixty-one five-roomed in the fields behind St Patrick's Training College, Drumcondra. This was the first time that Dublin Corporation had tendered for three-roomed houses and as with Marino, the scheme was tenant-purchase. Prices went from £230 for a mid-terraced three-room, to £460 for a semi-detached five-room, with the Corporation offering forty-year loans at 5¾ per cent for part or all of the price.[23] The weekly cost to the purchaser ranged from 9–17*s* a week, depending on house size. On its completion in 1929, the scheme consisted of 535 houses: 211 three-room, 144 four-room, and 180 five-room.

Dublin Corporation began construction on Donnycarney in 1929, which, upon its completion, comprised 421 houses of four rooms each. Prices ranged from £300 to £380, and again were offered to married couples with four or more children. Similar prices and offers were made with regard to the first section of the Cabra area scheme at Fassaugh Lane. The Corporation had also begun construction on 484 houses in Emmet Road, Inchicore, with prices ranging from £300 to £440.

In September 1926, the Cork Commissioner announced at a meeting of the city's Rotary Club that he 'proposed to raise a loan of £100,000 Corporation Stock, to be expended on the building of 200 new houses in the city'.[24] The houses were built on land behind Evergreen Road and to the side of Curragh Road, and followed the construction of 158 houses at Capwell. As with the Dublin housing schemes, the Cork houses were for purchase only. During this time, one ninth of the population of Cork City lived in tenements. Mr Monaghan was following Dublin's lead by providing 'affordable' housing for those in secure employment with relatively high wages, as a means of combating the problems of the tenements and slums.

Between 1924 and 1929, the Dublin City Commissioners sanctioned the construction of around 2,436 houses, almost all of which were sold by tenant purchase.[25] The price of the houses, and the cost of the loan repayments in the form of weekly rents of 9–17*s* a week, meant that the effect of the new houses on the city's slums and tenements was negligible.

The Free State's policy of owner-occupancy was applied to schemes completed before 1924. Over the next ten years, all of Dublin Corporation's suburban cottages – a total of 4,248 dwellings – had been sold to tenants.[26]

Prior to independence, Dublin Corporation's housing policy was primarily concerned with providing 'cheap dwellings for unskilled labourers in central districts'.[27] However, there was a significant body of opinion which opposed this policy. In early 1916, both the Citizens' Housing League and the recently formed Dublin Tenants' League (headed by William Larkin, brother of Jim) argued that garden suburbs were the only solution to the city's slums. This was broadly in line with the social ideals of Ebenezer Howard and the Garden City movement. Post-independence, the Free State government took on board a lot of the architectural ideals of Howard – twelve houses per acre, with gardens, and schools and shops as part of the layout – while pushing to one side the social, economic, and cultural arguments which underpinned his work.

The entry of Fianna Fáil into the Dáil in 1927 changed the dynamic somewhat, and in 1929 Cumann na nGaedheal passed a Housing Act which provided some relief to the majority at the end of the scale. This was followed by the 1931 Housing Act which placed slum clearance centre stage. It provided for 'the clearance of unhealthy areas, the demolition and repair of unhealthy houses, the compulsory acquisition of land, and the assessment of compensation'.[28]

These objectives were given a further boost in 1932 with the Fianna Fáil-sponsored Housing (Financial and Miscellaneous) Act, which enabled local authorities to fund slum clearance on the type of scale demanded by the problem. The legislation stated that preference be given to families living in one-roomed dwellings, where either:

(a) one or more members of the family is or are suffering from tuberculosis; or
(b) one or more members of the family, exclusive of the parents, has or have attained the age of sixteen years; or
(c) the dwelling has been condemned as being unfit for human habitation.

The Act also required that 'the Minister [for Local Government] shall not make any contribution under this section towards the expenses incurred by local authorities in the provision of houses in respect of which grants have been made by him under the Housing Acts, 1925 to

1930'. Fianna Fáil were not just building upon the 1931 Housing Act, they were making a clear break with Cumann na nGaedheal's policy of housing the middle classes and more 'respectable' working classes.

1932 TO 1948

The majority of the working class could not apply for Cumann na nGaedheal's house purchase schemes. The structural deficiencies within the Irish economy would not allow it. The type of employment needed to sustain a universal owner-occupancy policy simply did not exist. Fianna Fáil recognised this, and set out not only to provide housing for those at the lower end of the wage scale, but also to create the type of economy which would sustain an urban population and limit the drain from rural society. It introduced a series of tariffs and incentives to bolster local industry, and returned to building flats in central locations and houses for rent rather than purchase.

Under the various Housing Acts, local authority housing (as opposed to local authority building grants) was earmarked for the working classes in the towns and cities and agricultural labourers in the countryside. The 1908 Housing Act, which was the legislative baseline for all Irish Housing Acts until it was repealed in 1966, provided a definition of 'working classes'. It read:

> The expression 'working classes' shall include mechanics, artisans, labourers, and others working for wages, hawkers, costermongers [street sellers], persons not working for wages but working at some trade or handicraft without employing others except members of their own family, and persons, other than domestic servants, whose income in any case does not exceed an average of thirty shillings a week, and the families of any such persons who may be residing with them.

The Dublin Housing Inquiry, which sat from 1939 to 1943, having considered popular and official views of 'working classes', took the view that the phrase covered:

> All classes of adult persons in receipt of an average weekly income not exceeding the highest wage rate of a skilled tradesman. We naturally exclude persons who have substantial reserves of property or capital, even if their current wage income would otherwise qualify them. We also exclude those persons obviously belonging to a higher economic category whose current earnings may be low owing to terms of apprenticeship, training, instruction, probation, or similar conditions.[29]

Despite the inquiry's best efforts, it could not come up with an actual figure for Dublin's working class based on income, because in the early 1940s the Revenue Commissioners did not have this information. Instead, it had to rely on the 1936 census reports for occupations, and through this criteria, it came to the conclusion that working-class households constituted 75 per cent of the capital's families.

In terms of housing, the problem was not that 75 per cent of Dublin's households were working class, but that under Ireland's economy the wages were so low as to make the provision of housing for the working class on a private, profitable basis virtually impossible. As we have seen, houses tended to be built by their future occupiers, and where speculative construction did take place, it was not uncommon for the houses to be sold to landlords rather than to owner-occupiers. Private housing on a scale necessary to address the needs of the working population was unthinkable under the Irish Free State's low-wage, export-led, agrarian-based economy.

However, in order to qualify for a local authority house or flat, it was not enough to be a member of the working classes; you had to be able to pay the rent as well.

The available pool of rent payers had an influence on loan floatations. The ability of prospective tenants to pay rent affected the terms and conditions of the construction loans. Most local authorities believed that one fifth or more of income on rent was too heavy a demand on the tenant, as such levels of payment undermined the householder's ability to feed and clothe his or her family. As such, public housing rents were often less than this ratio. These so-called 'uneconomic rents' were possible only through substantial rate and State subsidy. Even with this, families with very low incomes were often passed over in favour of families with enough of an income to pay corporation rents after the family's physical needs had been met.

The housing schemes of Crumlin, Cabra, North Lotts, Terenure and Harold's Cross dominated the 1930s. Between 1932 and 1939, Dublin Corporation built 6,019 cottages for rent, of which more than half were in Crumlin. By way of comparison, just 229 were built by the Cumann na nGaedheal government in the previous eight years. Fianna Fáil also returned to providing flats in central locations. In 1931, the City Architect was instructed to 'construct a three-room model flat, the expenditure not to exceed £30, so that a clear idea may be gained of the class and extent of the accommodation which a dwelling of this type will contain'.[30] The largest schemes centred on Cook Street, Hanover Street, Railway Street, Popular Row and Mary's Lane. Between them they accounted for almost 70 per cent of the 1,619 flats built between 1933 and 1939.

The scale of the 1930s housing schemes can be seen by the fact that in the forty-four years prior to 1931, Dublin Corporation had built 7,246 dwellings, 78 per cent of which were houses.[31] This figure was doubled over the next eight years.

The 1946 census is the earliest we have which gives a breakdown of owner-occupancy in Ireland. Of the 662,654 private dwellings recorded that year, 348,737 (or 52.6 per cent) were either owned outright or were being purchased by the householder. There were 31,173 dwellings which were occupied rent-free, leaving 282,744 (or 42.7 per cent) which were rented. However, these national averages were by no means uniform across the State. In Kildare, owner-occupancy stood at 38 per cent, while in Mayo it was 86.2 per cent. There was also a significant difference between rural and urban areas. Cork County Borough (i.e. Cork City), for example, had a home-ownership level of only 13.2 per cent. Similar levels were recorded in the county boroughs of Waterford (13.6 per cent), and Limerick (13.8 per cent). In Dublin City, owner-occupancy stood at 23 per cent, while in Dún Laoghaire it was 30.8 per cent.

Even where offered, home ownership was not the automatic choice for working-class families. In 1923, the Labour Party noted that with home ownership as the only solution offered to the housing problem, 'workers are being compelled to purchase their homes and [are] saddled with the cost of maintenance'.[32] Twenty years later the Dublin Housing Inquiry noted that 'many tenants did not want to buy a house, but used the only means at their disposal of getting a house. If similar accommodation could have been got on renting terms most of them would have preferred it.'

The policies of the local authorities which placed garden suburbs on the edge of the cities were at odds with the practicalities of working-class life. It was remarked at a meeting of the Civics Institute that 'it seemed to be impossible to induce people to go outside the city (i.e. to newly built suburban areas), even if dwellings were there for them'.[33] Families were allocated houses by the Dublin Corporation, but were done so on an individual basis. In other words, families, not communities, were moved to the garden suburbs. Often there was little public transport available, and the houses were quite a distance from where people worked and socialised. There were few shops, and even fewer pubs. The families that moved to Crumlin in the 1930s were saddled with an increased cost of living. In 1940, Jim Larkin told the Government Housing Commission that up to '20 per cent of the tenants in the Crumlin area were living below starvation level'.[34] His evidence was collaborated by Dr C. Hannigan, Crumlin, who told the Dublin Board of Assistance in May 1940 of a case of:

> ... a man and his wife and eight children, whose income was 25 shillings a week, out of which rent and light absorbed one-half a week. The children were sent to an outside school so as to get the benefit of the midday free meal. The diet of the family consisted of bread and tea.[35]

The corporation's policy of building large numbers of three-roomed houses in Crumlin was at odds with its allocation policy which gave precedence to the largest families: 'Almost 70 per cent of the families who were allocated Corporation housing from 1934 to 1939 had more than six members, yet only 39 per cent of the houses built at Crumlin South had four rooms.'[36] The 'garden cities' plan for Crumlin in the 1930s was as far from Howard's original idea as the Marino and Donneycarney schemes of the 1920s, albeit in different ways. Whereas Cumann na nGaedheal took the aesthetics of garden suburbs and privatised it, Fianna Fáil built more, with fewer rooms, and made them for rent. The idea of the garden suburb as an interconnected community of work, shelter, education and leisure, was as elusive as ever. In the words of Máirin Johnston, author of *Around the Banks of Pimlico*, 'housing schemes gave [the people] houses, but it stripped away the fabric of their lives'.[37]

The scale of construction, however, was entirely new. From 1898 to 1948, over 100,000 dwellings were constructed by local authorities, and a further 80,000 by private citizens and speculative builders with public financial assistance. Yet, 65 per cent of these dwellings had been constructed during Fianna Fáil's tenure in government, '53,000 by the local authorities and 66,000 by private persons under the Housing Acts, 1932 to 1946'.[38] Fianna Fáil had promised to build flats and houses for the working classes, and to a large degree it had kept its promise.

The war years greatly curtailed construction, due to a shortage of manpower and materials. In January 1948, the Department of Local Government circulated a White Paper on housing, and estimated that approximately 100,000 new dwellings were required, of which 60,000 were needed to house the working classes. A general election was held in February 1948 which was lost by Fianna Fáil and led to the formation of the first Inter-Party government. It also led to a change in emphasis in housing policy.

1948 TO 1959

The Irish Times printed an editorial in July 1948 entitled 'White Collar Dwellings'. It welcomed the news that Dublin Corporation was extending the issuing of loans to builders and potential owner-occupiers under the Small Dwellings Acquisition Act:

> Faced by the exigent need to make some provision for those who are not rich enough to pay for the type of homestead that seemed to be

> within reach ten years ago, or poor enough to qualify for the tenancy of a Corporation cottage, Ministers, as we believe, are justified in their decision to extend to the fullest possible measure of assistance to those who are able and willing to contribute towards the solution of their own problem of housing.[39]

The formation of the first Inter-Party government in February of that year saw the return of Cumann na nGaedheal (now renamed Fine Gael) to power for the first time in sixteen years and the resetting of owner-occupancy as a cornerstone of housing policy.

The policy was not to restrict house prices in order to accommodate affordability, but to use government money to chase after rising prices. 'Even the most modest type of dwelling for the average wage-earner and his family is likely to cost something not far short of £2,000,' wrote *The Irish Times* in its July editorial, 'a figure which represented the pre-war cost of modern villa residences for comparatively wealthy people.' Yet, instead of embracing the logical conclusion – that as free-market speculators and private builders cannot provide affordable housing, it's probably best not to leave such a fundamental societal need in the hands of those who cannot provide it – the government began to once again subsidise private builders with public money in order to make housing purchases 'affordable' for the middle classes.

Two years previously, *The Irish Times* criticised the policy of rehousing 'thousands of families ... at the public expense' while there were 'hundreds of citizens' who could buy their own homes 'if only they can buy them on reasonable terms, and thus can do without State or local bounty'.[40] The fact that these 'reasonable citizens' needed as much State assistance to buy their homes as the thousands of families who needed State assistance to rent their homes, was conveniently ignored not only by *The Irish Times* but by a government which saw subsidised private ownership and private construction for the middle class as acts of citizenship, and subsidised rents for the working class as 'a public expense'. This idea of ownership as citizenship, and rent as scrounging, would eventually shed the language of class which enveloped it during this period, but none of the class dynamics from which it gained its energy and direction.

The first Inter-Party government allocated £580,000 to private building in its 1948 Housing Act, and by 30 June 1949 the Department for Local Government had approved 6,292 grants. The majority of these grants – 4,247 – were for housing in rural areas. The Department's Minister and Fine Gael TD Michael Keyes told the Dáil that:

> ... private enterprise could make a very valuable contribution to the solution of the housing problem. And it was, therefore, desirable that any uncertainty as to future policy in the matter of grants should be removed, so as to allow full scope to persons intending to plan for the building and reconstruction of houses within the next two or three years.[41]

He was speaking on the occasion of the Dáil debate on the Housing (Amendment) Bill, 1949, which proposed to triple the amount of government spending on private house construction from £580,000 to £1,750,000, and to allow grants for the building of new houses for letting and the reconstruction of existing housing in rural areas. Private landlords would now receive public money in order to provide private rented accommodation.

The private ownership of a house was often put forward as a panacea for all of society's ills. Not only would the promotion of home ownership save the local authorities money in the long run, it would also bring stability and good sense to a family. In 1952, the Labour Party senator, James Tunney, told a meeting of Dublin County Council (of which he was chairman) that 'I am a firm believer in private ownership, because it makes for better citizens, and there is no greater barrier against communism.'[42] He went on to say that 'where all the necessary conditions regarding repair have been complied with, the tenants should be compelled to purchase, unless they could show very good reason for not doing so'. The Educational Building Society (EBS) stated at its annual general meeting in 1956 that it was carrying out 'important social work' in 'promoting a property-owning people'.[43]

The social arguments for owner-occupancy were raised once again in 1957, by the Bishop of Cork, the Most Revd Dr Cornelius Lucey. 'The man of property is ever against revolutionary change,' said Dr Lucey at a Confirmation ceremony at Monkstown, County Cork. 'Consequently a factor of the first importance in combating emigration and preventing social unrest, unemployment marches, and so on, is the widest possible diffusion of ownership.'[44] Dr Lucey raised these points as he believed that 'ownership [of property] is neither valued nor favoured among us, as it should be'.

In 1962, a UN team of housing experts, including Charles Abrams, came to Ireland to compile a report on urban renewal. They were suitably impressed with the government's initiatives, and wrote that Ireland was undertaking 'one of the largest slum-clearance and public-housing programs in the world in terms of population, has emptied many of the central slum areas of Dublin, and is now proceeding with renewal legislation designed to replace slums with non-residential as well as residential land uses.'[45]

One year later, the Minister for Local Government, Neil Blaney, announced his 'home for every family' housing policy. He amended legislation so that allocation for local authority housing 'would not be determined by whether a person was by definition an agricultural labourer of a person of the working classes, but primarily by his need for housing'.[46] 'This,' he said, 'would unequivocally admit to eligibility for the benefit of State and local authority facilities all persons in need of housing, including old people, small farmers, widows and other special categories whose needs had not been adequately served under existing legislation.' Whether it was Blaney's intention or not, his Housing Bill of 1963 added to the view that local authority housing should be the housing of last resort.

In February 1966, the Fine Gael TD Mark Clinton put forward a motion during Private Members' Time in the Dáil, 'urging the government to facilitate the provision of tenant-purchase schemes for Corporation tenants in Dublin, Cork, and other municipalities'.[47] Mr Clinton said that such a move would show that 'the government was alive to the interests of citizens who wished to better themselves'. This idea was given its fullest expression in the Fianna Fáil government's Housing Act of 1966, which allowed local authority tenants in urban areas to purchase their houses. It took as its model the 1936 Labourers' Act, under which almost 80 per cent of the 86,931 labourers' cottages had been sold to tenants in the twenty-eight years since its inception. During the same period, 6,393 urban dwellings had been sold to tenants.[48] This figure dramatically increased over the next twenty-five years.

In 1971 there were 112,320 local authority rental housing units in the State, which amounted to 15.9 per cent of the total households. By 1981 this figure had dropped to 111,739, and now constituted 12.4 per cent of total households. Yet, there were 64,170 new local authority units completed between 1971 and 1980. The State was selling its public housing stock to its tenants quicker than it could build it. The amount of households in urban areas in 1981 that either owned their property or were buying their house from a local authority was 65.6 per cent. In 1961 that figure was 37.9 per cent. The tenant-purchase scheme had been heavily utilised, and resulted in 'waves of heavy selling of local authority housing.'[49]

Purchase prices for local authority housing were typically extremely favourable to tenants. The tenant-purchase scheme implemented by Dublin Corporation in the late 1980s, for example, entitled discounts on the market value of housing of up to 60 per cent. The consequence for Irish social housing was that by the early 1990s, of the 330,000 dwellings built by local authorities over the previous century, some 220,000 had been sold to tenants, which amounted to one in four of the homes in private ownership in Ireland by that time. They were thus a major contributor to the overall tenure revolution and in particular were the dominant means of access to home ownership for the urban and working classes.

Home ownership reached its peak in the early 1990s, with 74.5 per cent of all households in urban areas, and 81 per cent of all households nationwide, listed as owner-occupied or occupied free of rent.[50] What had been paid for collectively, had been sold off individually. The *de facto* privatisation of Irish housing meant that the need for a house was now replaced by the need for a mortgage. The banks, building societies and mortgage brokers were the unchallenged gatekeepers to securing a home.

By the end of the 1960s, there was an estimated housing need of 59,000 – with unfit houses of 35,000 and overcrowding of 24,000.[51] The

State would need to build 9,000 dwellings a year, with projections for the mid-1970s at 11,500 a year 'to meet the loss of dwellings through obsolescence, etc., and to provide for increases in numbers of households'. It was reported that with increased prosperity, local authority housing was no longer a priority, and that the majority of housing would be produced by private builders and other agencies.

1971 TO 1987

In the 1970s the State, having already secured the legislative framework to privatise urban local authority housing, now undertook to privatise house loans. It is during this decade that government strategy moves towards assisting families with mortgages, rather than assisting families with houses. It was a crucial development. The government was funding prices, and those prices were being set by builders and estate agents, often in collusion with building societies and banks. Ireland's property market was soon dictated almost exclusively by speculation. It was not how much money people earned, but how much credit they could secure, which set the bar for prices. It led to the bizarre situation where Irish people were paying twice for the same house. The Irish taxpayer had to pay to fund the grants and exemptions to make private housing 'affordable'; then, the same taxpayer had to go out and buy a mortgage for a house, the price of which had increased precisely because of the grants and incentives which the taxpayer was funding in the first place. Yet, by the start of the 1980s, this had become normal and 'common sense'.

The idea of a house as a speculative product, not just for builders but for owner-occupiers, also gathered momentum throughout this decade. 'One of the oldest ghosts in the residential market was laid this week by Mr Edmund Farrell, chairman of the Irish Permanent Building Society,' wrote *The Irish Times* in February 1973, 'when he revealed that the purchase of a new home is not necessarily the biggest single lifetime investment – simply because the average building society mortgage has itself a lifetime of only about ten years.'[52] The article explained that:

> The significance of this information is considerable, and it does much to explain the frenzy of activity both in the residential market and in the £150 million Irish building societies' movement. If the average mortgage is 'turned over' once in a decade, the average man can buy not one, but two or three different homes in his working life.
>
> What is emerging – trendwise, as the Americans put it – is a housing requirement that sensibly fluctuates with the homeowner's personal needs. In the early stages of a man's married life, for example, his space requirements are relatively small ... later with an increased family, our subject can move to a three-bedroom house in a suburban estate, close to schools and probably to a shopping centre. As the family gets bigger, there can be yet another move, possibly to a four or even more bedroomed house, depending upon the finance that's available. And finally, to complete the circle, as the children grow up and move away to start their own housing-cycle, the parents can sell the family home and buy a flat closer to town and its infrastructural centre ...
>
> And, most important point of all for the saver and investor in the housing market as it is and will be for the foreseeable future, a hefty profit is made by the seller at each point in the cycle.

The privatisation of housing cured not only social ills and moral fickleness, but, according to *The Irish Times* and the building societies, it also settled all your financial upsets and indigestions. In September 1973 the paper told its readers that property was the perfect 'hedge against falling money values'.[53] Property was moral-proof, future-proof, and inflation-proof.

The reality was that as the decade progressed, prices increased and mortgages of twenty-five and thirty years' duration became the norm. A householder may change house, but rarely was it after having completed his payments on a ten-year mortgage. Not only that; this fantasy world of full employment and eternal growth – where people swap houses like shoes for slippers – never materialised. Indeed, within eighteen months of the *Irish Times*' strident pronouncement of the dawn of the Four Property Stages of Man, the Irish economy was in recession.

At the start of 1974, in a statement which would become all too common thirty years later, the president of the Irish Auctioneers' and

Valuers' Institute, Mr Anthony Morrissey, said that the drop in house sales was due to a lack of lending in the economy. Building societies and local authorities weren't making loans available to house buyers, and this was leading to a downturn in the market. The solution was more credit. The government needed to act to save the construction industry. 'Restrictions and preconditions on building society financing must have a negative effect on the property market and on the chances of achieving national housing targets,' said Morrissey. 'A more lasting solution must lie in the further assistance of the [building] societies by the government or by the provision of house finance at realistic levels and in large quantities by the government itself either directly or through some agency.'[54]

One year later, the Minister for Local Government and Labour TD James Tully issued a statement pointing out the problems with providing mortgage assistance rather than actual housing. 'One basic problem which these people overlook,' he said, 'is that, in the ultimate, additional subsidies can come only out of taxation and must be met by the community at large, including those who are not yet fortunate enough to have a house of their own.'[55] From 1971 to 1974, Irish building societies' assets had grown from £80 million to £200 million, yet they still claimed the poor mouth and received a government-backed loan of £5 million in the autumn of 1974 to help them over this particular credit crunch.[56] By the autumn of 1976, the building societies had assets of over £350 million.

The building industry, for its part, maintained that the loan limits under the Small Dwellings Act – a maximum of £4,500 – and the lack of loans from the building societies were the reasons behind the large lay-offs and the subsequent rise in unemployment. 'Nothing short of an injection of about £20 million in loans would be needed to prevent a running down of the industry in the immediate future', said a spokesman for Abbey Homesteads, one of the largest builders of houses in the Dublin area.[57] The construction industry employed around 80,000 people nationwide and had an annual turnover of £400 million, with housing accounting for some 40 per cent of that business.[58] A slowdown in construction, of any kind, would be a disaster for the economy. 'House-building should be given priority over most other areas of economic endeavour', said

The Irish Times, quoting an anonymous group of builders, 'And within the housing sector, the most beneficial sub-sector is that concerned with private dwellings.'[59] In May 1975, Daniel McInerney, deputy chairman of McInerney Properties Ltd, said that 'beside being a great social need, housing in Ireland was a leading industry and was like the motor industry in America. When building boomed, the nation boomed.'[60] These new houses had to be built, regardless of whether there were people willing or able to buy them.

Certainly there was no shortage of new private houses being built. In 1974, there were 19,510 dwellings completed, almost double the amount which were completed in 1971. This was independent of local authority completions, which was 6,746 in 1974 and 4,789 in 1971. Nor was there any let-up in prices. In 1970, the average new house cost £5,261; by 1975 it had almost doubled to £10,438. Prices continued to increase throughout the 1970s, despite two years of recession. In order to meet the 'affordability' crux, the government requested the major banks operating in Ireland enter the residential mortgage market. The Minister for Finance, Mr Richie Ryan, announced in the June 1975 budget that Bank of Ireland (BOI) and Allied Irish Bank (AIB) had both agreed to make £40 million available to house purchasers over the next two years. They were followed by the Ulster Bank and the Northern Bank in August 1975, when it was announced that they intended to extend finance for house purchase.

In the first six months of their entry into the residential mortgage market, BOI and AIB approved 1,415 home loans totalling £12.5 million. Previously, the major banks had limited their involvement with home-buyers to short-term or 'bridging' loans. Their entry into the mortgage market was tentative and slow – the banks tended to focus on higher earners, of which in Ireland there were comparatively few. This changed in the 1980s, as tax incentives and government grants developed in scope and ambition, and by 1987, Irish banks had secured around 43 per cent of the mortgage market. At the same time, the building societies accounted for around 34 per cent of all mortgages. They were soon helped in no small measure by the decision to cancel the involvement of local authorities in mortgage lending. In October 1987 the Minister for

Environment, Pádraig Flynn, announced details of a new government incentive in which building societies would undertake 'up to £70 million worth of mortgage lending next year which would more usually have been done by the local authorities'.[61]

This was the final part of the overall assault on local authority housing initiatives, the last major obstacle to the privatisation of the housing and mortgage market. Up to then, local authorities were still able to grant mortgages under the Small Dwellings Act, which had refocused itself mainly towards low-income households. The 1987 Act gave the building societies full access to this final outpost of State involvement in what had become the option of first and last resort in securing a home: a mortgage. The very idea of public housing itself was severely undermined in 1984 after the introduction of the £5,000 Surrender Grant Scheme, which directly led to the further ghetto-isation of local authority estates. And as with the 1987 Act with followed it, the Surrender Grant Scheme was primarily geared towards the needs of lenders and speculators during those recessionary times.

'... THE REPORTS OF THE EXTENT OF THE PERCEIVED PROBLEM HAVE BEEN GROSSLY EXAGGERATED'[62]

The Surrender Grant Scheme was introduced in October 1984 as part of the coalition government's programme 'Building on Reality, 1985-1987'. It provided a grant of £5,000 to local authority tenants to entice them 'to buy private homes and surrender their existing homes to the county council or corporation'.[63] When the grant was added to other available government grants and incentives, eligible tenants 'could have up to £10,000 at their disposal to acquire a dwelling in the private market'.[64]

The scheme had two objectives. Firstly, it made available local authority housing without the need to build additional stock. The quality of housing would be maintained as families would be moving out of the estate rather than buying within the estate. People would, in effect, 'trade-up' with the government's help. They would swap their well-built local authority house for a presumably better-built, and much more desirable, private-sector house. Secondly, the scheme would give a boost to the private house-building sector, as it would generate 'a new source of demand from local authority tenants transferring into private ownership'.[65] It was seen as a win-win situation. The local authorities would get freed-up houses for £5,000, while the private sector would get customers for their empty units, of which there were thousands on the edges of Irish towns and cities across the country. The mid-1980s saw the first sustained drop in property prices since the foundation of the State, and the government duly rose to the occasion and guaranteed those speculators a steady stream of sales. And as with so many win-win scenarios, the reality turned out to be somewhat different.

The Housing Finance Agency, which administered the grant, reported an 'enthusiastic response to the scheme' in 1985, and predicted that 'around 1,000 tenants may avail of it' that year.[66] In June 1986, the Minister for the Environment, John Boland, told the Dáil that 'from its inception until 31 March 1986, 6,321 applications have been received by local authorities, 4,347 have been approved, and 2,790 have been paid'.[67] As a consequence, 2,200 dwellings were made available within the local authority housing stock – 'a significant contribution' the Minister said, 'to the housing of nearly 12,000 applicants by local authorities during the year'. He pointed out that, 'as over 40 per cent of the grant recipients have purchased new houses, the scheme is of considerable benefit to the building industry also'. In conclusion, he was 'pleased at the way in which the scheme has widened the opportunities for home ownership for so many people, and enabled them to house themselves in dwellings of their choice'.

During Dáil questions, the Fianna Fáil TD for Dublin North, Ray Burke, asked the Minister if he was 'aware that the view of the sisters and priests serving in the west Tallaght area, in the parishes of Brookfield, Fettercairn and Jobstown, is that the scheme as it operates at present has a totally unintended consequence in that it is producing a ghetto … ?' A fundamental flaw in the scheme was coming to light. It was not tenants in decent housing and settled communities who were availing of the scheme, but 'relatively well-off tenants who were living in the poorest segments of the stock who took up the £5,000 grant most enthusiastically'.[68] Those who had jobs were being replaced by those on the housing list who had none – a situation which accelerated the marginalisation of public house estates.

At the same time, the tenants who bought houses under the scheme were not fully informed of the true costs of home ownership. The housing advice agency Threshold found that many of the grant recipients were not informed of the level of costs involved 'in transferring from a situation where the rents were subsidised and maintenance costs covered by the landlord to one where all costs fell on the shoulders of the householder'.[69] Threshold also found local authority compliance with the private sector in the operation of the scheme, with grant cheques 'frequently paid to third parties (usually builders) thus speeding up the transfer of tenants from their local authority houses to their new private houses'.[70] The unrealistic expectations of costs and subsequent repayment difficulties saw a number of transfer tenants evicted from their new homes, or brought to court over arrears. By 1994, around 55 per cent of the grant recipients in Cork City had mortgage arrears of two years or more, while the communities left behind slipped further into decay.

The National Economic and Social Council (NESC) found that the uptake for the scheme was concentrated in the worst-off local authority estates. In Dublin, 75 per cent of recipients came from three areas: Darndale, Ballymun and Tallaght. Many of those who qualified for the scheme were working and were active in the local community. The scheme upset the balance in these areas between working and non-working tenants. Ray Burke told the Dáil in 1986 that on the Fettercairn estate in Tallaght, 177 families had left under the scheme, and were replaced by 95 households that were welfare dependent. In Brookfield, also in Tallaght, around 12 per cent of all households had left under the scheme. There were 100 single-parent families on the estate, and unemployment stood at 65 per cent. A similar trend took place in Jobstown, where 177 families had left and where the unemployment rate stood at 61 per cent. The scheme had intensified the polarisation of Irish housing between public and private, and had greatly added to the association of local authority estates with social problems. Tallaght was a long way from Marino, in more ways than one.

In March 1987, the Minister for Finance, Ray McSharry, announced the termination of the scheme. This was done because of financial concerns, and not the social damage it had inflicted. No alternative funding for public housing was given, which meant that 'housing lists would grow at a time when no extra housing was being provided'.[71] The true benefactors of the Surrender Scheme were builders and estate agents, who were quick to lament its demise. The minister's cut in funding 'could not be justified', they said. 'The scheme was more than self-financing in releasing valuable assets for use by local authorities and virtually eliminating housing waiting lists.'[72] There *was* money for housing, but it was focused on making mortgages 'affordable' and building costs 'realistic'. The Irish government was spending tens of millions a year in grants and tax breaks in order to make efficient the dynamics of the mortgage industry. By 1987, with public housing a by-word for social deprivation, the only real option open to new households was the private sector, either through the rental sector or house purchase. 'The withdrawal of political commitments to the welfare state initiated by the New Right in the 1970s [had] all but permeated the entire political spectrum.'[73] The long-cherished dream of both *The Irish Times* and Catholic bishops, of a nation of semi-detached owner-occupiers docile with mortgage debt, was all but complete.

1987–1997

The creation of the Irish Financial Services Centre in 1987 was an integral part of the new developments in the Irish economy. A revolution was underway. Banks were becoming 'one-stop shops' for financial services, and the Irish government played its part by changing the rules and allowing building societies and insurance companies to compete with high-street banks in the areas of personal and business loans. The competition within the Irish mortgage market was already well established, but in 1988 it became even more intense, as Irish Life joined forces with Irish Intercontinental Bank to form UK and Irish-based mortgage corporations, while 'Ulster Bank, having concluded a deal with the Prudential to use its 330 sales force to sell Ulster Bank mortgages in the north is now looking for similar partners in the south.'[74] The government had changed corporation tax rates in the 1987 budget, along with tax breaks for Irish banks working within the mortgage market, and both Irish Intercontinental and Ulster Bank saw these changes as an opportunity 'to obtain [mortgage market] share essentially through product innovation and service'.[75] These 'innovations', these new financial products, saw banks selling credit in an economy which was producing little else by way of merchandise and more by way of services. By 1998 around 80 per cent of all goods exports were being produced by about 8 per cent of the workforce, while in the rest of the economy these financial innovations were being used to fuel speculation in one of the least-productive economic activities: property.

In the first three months of 1988, the Irish mortgage market grew by 20 per cent, a large part of which was due to the transfer of local authority lending to the building societies. The 1987 initiative gave the building societies £75 million in business overnight, as well as complete access to the previously untapped, low-income mortgage market. It saw total loans issued by building societies increase by 104 per cent in 1988 to £532 million, up from £260 million the previous year. By way of contrast, bank mortgage lending during 1988 increased by a relatively modest 25 per cent. Overall, there was also an increase in house prices. In Dublin the average price for a new home rose by 20 per cent, with second-hand house prices up by 9 per cent. Outside the capital, the price increases were around 9 per cent for both new and second-hand homes. This was at a time when Ireland's unemployment rate stood at over 16 per cent, emigration was at its highest for decades, and the number of new houses sold actually fell by over 6 per cent.[76] It also took place in the wake of severe budget cuts which were initiated by the Minister for Finance, Ray McSharry. When interviewed on the rise on house prices, despite a drop in demand and the continuing recession, the director of the Construction Industry Federation, Michael Greene, cited a rise in building costs, adding that 'quality had also increased over the period'.[77] As with so much which relates to housing and construction in Ireland, the reasons behind the price hikes had more to do with tax breaks and financial investment than the modest dreams of first-time buyers or the fictional high standards of self-regulating builders.

'IT'S A GODSEND FOR THE WEALTHY, A REAL HAVEN'[78]

In March 1988, Ray McSharry reintroduced Section 23 reliefs on rental properties. It was listed under Section 27 of the Finance Act but retained its name from 1981, when it was first introduced as a stimulus for investment in construction. *The Irish Times* reported that the government's decision to bring back the section provided a 'tax efficient outlet for investors and a valuable shelter for people with existing rental income'.[79] The maximum relief available was essentially the purchase price of the property less the cost of the site.[80] The scheme was announced as a short-term measure to help what was seen as a flagging construction industry, and was due to run from 27 January 1988 to 31 March 1991. It would allow investors to construct and/or purchase flats and town houses, with a floor area of no more than ninety square metres each, in designated areas in towns and cities – including large sections of central Dublin – and to offset construction costs and rental income against income tax. Its main purpose, however, was not to provide housing or rental accommodation. The reason for the scheme was to provide tax relief for investors. The fact that this was done via construction should not disguise the fact that this was a legal procedure for the avoidance of tax.

The scheme was not exclusive to the income from the rental property in question. The exemptions went to the company or individual who availed of the scheme, and the building costs were offset against all of the client's existing rental income, subject to the maximum relief allowable. It allowed investors 'to obtain tax-free rental income from the new units they buy and from any other new or old property they own (or subsequently may buy in the State) whether it is commercial, industrial or residential, until all the relief is used up'.[81] The tax allowances meant that as a financial investment, property could provide 'gross return [of] around 17 per cent, with the additional attraction of a potential capital gain over ten years'.[82] Property, once again, was providing a tax shelter for investors, and not surprisingly, investors responded with energy and enthusiasm. For their part, builders almost immediately increased the price of properties, 'with the tax relief in mind in much the same way that first-time buyer housing grants were previously absorbed'. A property and price boom had begun, fuelled not by wider economic activity within the State – that is, by wages, employment and demand from below – but by investors looking for tax relief and seemingly safe investments.

By the end of 1988, *The Irish Times* was reporting a 24 per cent increase in building starts in Dublin, while in Galway the increase stood at over 50 per cent. During the months of September and October, around £20 million worth of new homes were sold, and according to one Dublin auctioneer, 'a healthy chunk of that was sold to investors availing of the tax advantages contained in Section 23 (now Section 27)'.[83] The fact that investment, not jobs and wages, was driving demand could be seen by the nature of the sales. *The Irish Times* found that prices at the lower end of the housing market remained 'all but unchanged with the middle and upper areas deriving the greatest benefit from the boom'.[84] It reported that around 60-70 per cent of all sales of new homes in the affluent areas of Dublin 4 and Dublin 6 were to investors under the Section 23 tax relief scheme.

The nature of the late 1980s property boom – its subsidy by government incentives via mortgage grants and the creation of tax havens – was of particular concern to the governor of the Central Bank of Ireland, Mr Maurice Doyle. In November 1988 he gave a speech at the annual dinner of the Master Builders' Association, where he pointed out the dangers of Section 23 concessions, mortgage interest relief, subsidised local authority housing, and first-time buyer grants:

> The arguments for so much subsidisation – direct and indirect – of the housing market, which looked reasonable at a time of free-spending high inflation, high marriage and birth rates, high interest rates and domestic rate charges looks rather different against a background of belt-tightening all round, low interest rates, low household formation and no rates.[85]

In May 1989, the journalist Maev Ann Wren argued that 'the flow of money into house purchase may be limiting funds for other more productive purposes'. She pointed out that in 1988, 'financial institutions lent nearly £300 million more to homeowners than two years previously ... At the same time the amount of money being invested in new machinery and equipment for productive purposes grew by just over £200 million.'[86] Wren noted that while government borrowing was down, personal borrowing by way of mortgage debt was increasing. Not only that, the rise in house prices gave homeowners the feeling that they were wealthier as a result. 'The financial institutions regard [this "wealth effect"] as real,' she said. 'They are prepared to offer people new higher mortgages on their homes to finance spending on other things, and in this way the rise in house prices might be passed on in a rise in other prices.' However, none of this 'wealth effect' was down to actual productive economic expansion, but to the influx of speculative capital into the housing market via incentives such as Section 23 and first-time buyer grants. Wren was describing the formation of a bubble. She concluded that unless action was taken to deflate the 'wealth effect' – by a property tax, for example, which would serve to remind people that property price increases are a cost to the economy, not a boon – Ireland was in danger of substituting its government debt crisis for a personal debt crisis. Over the next twelve years, Wren's concerns would come to fruition.

In January 1991, the government announced a two-year extension of Section 23 relief. By December of that year, over 15 per cent of all new homes in Dublin had been bought by investors under the scheme. The investment aspect of the scheme – property as a tax write-off – was underlined by the accountant and tax specialist Kieran Corrigan in an interview with *The Irish Times* in January 1992. He said that 'Section 23 is particularly suitable for people who already own other rental properties [as] very often people in this situation can claim immediate relief for all of the allowable cost of the Section 23 property.'[87] Any interest on loans raised to purchase Section 23 properties was also tax-deductible. 'This is very advantageous,' he said, 'as the taxpayer will receive a deduction for the capital cost of the property as well as the interest cost.' Not only was the cost of construction subject to tax relief, so was the interest on any loan raised to fund construction. This was a boon to both banks and builders, as it made money cheap to borrow without any loss to the banks and building societies, as well as making construction itself an act of tax avoidance. The government was subsidising both speculative borrowing and speculative construction. The fact that prices kept on rising meant that these public subsidies went directly into the pocket of the lenders, builders and speculators. The Irish people, recently denied access to local authority mortgage lending and placed in impossible queues for housing, had no option but to turn to the publicly subsidised entrepreneurs for what is a basic human need. There was nothing entrepreneurial about Section 23. It was simply the transfer of public money to private hands with construction as the conduit. The apartments were built whether they were needed or not. What mattered most was the tax relief which came with the apartment.

There were around fifty Section 23 housing schemes under construction in Dublin in 1992. The properties ranged from one-bedroom apartments in Temple Bar and Bolton Street, to the leafy surroundings of Shrewsbury Park, Ballsbridge, where two-bedroom houses with turret-shaped living rooms and double-glazed conservatories went on sale for £140,000 – over three times the price of the inner-city apartments. Other areas covered by the scheme included Donnybrook, Dalkey, Sandymount, Killiney, Sandycove, Blackrock and Monkstown.

The chairman of the Society of Chartered Surveyors, Mr Thomas D'Arcy, gave a speech at its annual dinner in February 1993, in which he urged the continuation of the scheme, as it had been 'a major factor in stimulating residential development and rejuvenating significant areas of the inner city'.[88] And having praised a government scheme which gave tax breaks for the construction of apartment blocks for speculative purposes in the most opulent areas of the capital, Mr D'Arcy took time to criticise the 'scandalous and needless waste of resources' on public-sector civil engineering projects. He also looked forward to the EC's Cohension Fund, which was due to come on stream later that year and which would lead to 'further significant spending' and provide a real boost to the construction industry. He noted that the urban renewal scheme, of which Section 23 was a key element, 'had generated over

£800 million in private sector development, although it had led to a proliferation of commercial development and a disappointing level of residential development'. Yet, regardless of whether the properties constructed were offices or houses, the fact remained that a large proportion of financial investment in Ireland was going into property, not actual, indigenous, exporting businesses, which was one of the areas of development which the Irish economy desperately needed. The idea that £800 million poured into property was a non-productive and essentially wasteful form of investment was lost on Mr D'Arcy and his audience of charted surveyors. And slowly but surely it was being lost on the rest of Irish society as well.

In January 1994, *The Irish Times* carried an article by Kevin Warren, a financial advisor. 'If you are fortunate enough to have some cash on deposit you are unlikely to get a yield greater than 5 per cent per annum after tax,' he said. 'In the current era of low inflation there is no prospect of improving on this yield for the foreseeable future.' Help was at hand, though. Warren pointed out that the government's urban renewal relief scheme, which incorporated Section 23 and was due to open for investment that year, was 'a welcome boost to the hard-pressed construction sector,' and that 'investors are likely to focus on property in the new designated areas on which they can claim capital allowances'. [89] The government launched the scheme in July. 'Providing for the growth of urban communities is the bedrock on which urban renewal in the true sense is built,' said the Minister for the Environment, Michael Smith, at a ceremony in Dublin Castle. 'I want to see people moving back into town, families growing up in town, communities living in town.'[90] The government's vision for urban renewal, though, did not include schools, hospitals, fire stations, transport or parks. It was not a community-directed plan. Its focus, once again, was on creating commercial and residential property tax havens for investors, and hoping for the best.

In November, the mortgage finance company Irish Life Homeloans launched a new product aimed at first-time buyers. It was called the Super-Flexible Mortgage and it offered the prospective buyer 'complete control of how and when the loan is paid back'.[91] The way people were living and working was changing, they said – 'the way we spend our money, how we marry and have children, and the decisions we make about where we live' – and this new mortgage reflected these new times. The scheme, of course, was not about empowerment, or offering complete control, or reflecting the changes in the way we lived. It was about expanding the market for home loans. The flexibility was about widening the mortgage net and financing the purchase of the houses and apartments produced under the Section 23 scheme. All that was new was the marketing, which received a significant boost that year with the creation of a new and much-cited phrase.

On 31 August 1994, the international investment banking group Morgan Stanley produced a review of the Irish economy and stock market, the title of which ended up as a label for an era. The report was called 'The Irish Economy, a Celtic Tiger' and the phrase was coined by Kevin Gardiner, a UK economist who worked for the group at that time. It said that although the Irish stock market was one of the smallest in Europe, it had 'some of the most exciting prospects of all' and that 'the [stock] market, particularly the banks, [were] undervalued'.[92] It concluded that 'Ireland's longer-term potential for higher EPS [Earnings Per Share] growth than the European average in both real and nominal terms assures it of an overweight position within the Morgan Stanley model portfolio.'[93] The newsletter recommended a 'buy' for Bank of Ireland shares, and a 'hold on AIB. It had an immediate effect, with ten pence added to Bank of Ireland's share price overnight. Morgan Stanley's 'extraordinary bullish thirty-page report' was out of step with the thoughts of Dublin dealers, but the rise in prices was more than welcomed.[94]

Although the Morgan Stanley report referred to the financial services centre and the share value of banks in the Irish stock exchange, the phrase 'Celtic Tiger' was soon picked up by Ireland's politicians as a handy by-word for national economic recovery and government-led forward thinking. The Taoiseach, Albert Reynolds, referred to it on a trip to Australia. 'Seemingly An Taoiseach was attempting to draw a parallel with the growth economies of south east Asia,' wrote *The Irish Times*, 'in the hopes of wooing more foreign investment into the burgeoning financial services sector.'[95] The newspaper was quite dismissive of the claims of both Morgan Stanley and Albert Reynolds, seeing in the phrase a 'picturesque imagery' devoid of actual economic substance. It noted the high level of unemployment and saw the boasts of growth as nothing more than fancy accounting:

> The problem is that much of the welcome activity is seen by many as illusory, being confined to financiers and other shufflers of paper. Abstract 'paper' growth has yet to make an enduring impact on unemployment, the Republic's most pervasive economic problem. Until that happens here those filing into labour exchanges can be forgiven for regarding the 'Celtic tiger' as more of a paper tiger.[96]

Meanwhile, the march into property carried on.

The strong level of institutional investment in property was borne out by Jim McMahon, associate director of the Investment Bank of Ireland (IBI), who said in October 1994 that the bank 'uses investors' funds to purchase office, retail and industrial sites', including 'outlets in Dublin's main shopping areas such as Grafton Street and Henry Street, in suburban shopping centres and along Cork's Patrick Street.' He described these retail premises as 'very secure investments … suitable for pension funds'.[97] AIB, for its part, also invested in retail, industrial and office property, and for reasons mainly due to the IFSC, property speculation and the Morgan Stanley report, the Irish economy was attracting attention from overseas investors. The *Irish Times* journalist Justin Comiskey wrote that it was assumed that Ireland would experience 'growth rates of between 5 and 6 per cent for a number of years to come [and] as property values generally rise on the back of an improving economy, it is easy to appreciate the sense of anticipation which many property investors are now experiencing'. Furthermore, Ireland was now dubbed the Celtic Tiger 'by overseas investors'. A single report by Morgan Stanley, one treated with surprise and scepticism by Irish share traders less than two months previously, had now become plural in authorship, and objective in its assessment.

The urban renewal tax havens and increased international investment in Irish banking fuelled greater demand (and supply) for mortgages and loans. *The Irish Times* reported in 1994 that the previous year '7,700 new home buyers injected £516 million into the Dublin housing market'.[98] It noted that around 25 per cent of these sales were under Section 23 tax relief, and that nearly 3,100 of the purchases were apartments. Overall, there were 16,230 home loans approved that year, which was an increase of 25 per cent on the figures for 1993. House completions – and here 'house' includes apartments as well – also increased by 25 per cent. This had an effect on the unemployment figure, which dropped to 14 per cent, having been at over 15 per cent for the previous two years.

The amount of financial investment surrounding the construction industry, including land speculation as well as commercial and residential completions, meant that by the end of 1995 the two largest companies on the Irish Stock Exchange were AIB and Bank of Ireland. Financial shares had 'come of age' and were continually outperforming industrial shares such as those of Smurfit. International financial corporations were investing in Irish banks, which were investing in property, which was being subsidised by the taxpayer, who were buying the houses with finance provided by the banks, the shares in which were rising due to investment via international financial speculation. And due to this hermetically sealed universe, mortgages just kept on rising.

At the same time, almost 40 per cent of all private rented dwellings were in receipt of rent allowance. It cost the government £115 million (€146 million) in 1999 in payments. Ten years previously, that figure was £6.1 million (€7.7 million).[99] By 2005 it had risen to an estimated €380 million.[100] The State had gone from a policy of eradicating slum dwellings in the 1930s, to actively subsidising private landlords and sub-standard dwellings. The expansion of the private rental market was official government policy. It was, after all, one of the criteria for Section 23 relief. The Irish State had encouraged the expansion of landlordism. It had privatised public housing so that the funding which would have gone to local authorities now went to private individuals and businesses.

In the 1990s, the banks and building societies changed the criteria from householder's income to household income. This meant that a mortgage application could be based on two incomes. Almost overnight, financial institutions could double the amount they could demand for a mortgage. By the time the Rainbow Coalition government left office in June 1997, the average house price was around £80,600 (€102,400), over five times the average industrial wage of £15,211 (€19,318). This was the highest wage:house price ratio since 1980, and a serious danger to the health of the economy. The reason was affordability. In 1967, the Department of Local Government issued a booklet entitled, 'A House of Your Own'. It said that when buying a house, 'the amount which you borrow should not be more than the 2½ times your annual income (excluding overtime, bonuses and the income of your wife and of any grown-up children'.[101] The building societies usually limited loans to an amount which ensured that mortgage repayments were between 20 to 25 per cent of the person's income. The reason for such a criteria was to allow the household to maintain itself while meeting repayments. In normal times, the wage:house price ratio of 1997 would be seen as a sign that a bubble had formed in the property market, but these were not normal times. The Irish State was deep into a period of financial exuberance surrounding construction, armed with little more than a bag of myths and a tiger for a sound bite.

1997 TO 2010

> 'It reminds me of Islington in the 1980s'[102]

The relationship between house prices and Irish wage levels lost any sense of reality under the 1997 Fianna Fáil/PD government. Soon, house prices were close to eight times the average industrial wage. 'In today's property market place couples at least have an edge because they have two incomes', wrote *The Irish Times* in February 1998. 'Single people need to be earning unusually high incomes to purchase even apartments, much less houses.'[103] And despite numerous warnings, the government, with Charlie McCreevy as Minister for Finance, continued to stimulate the property market via tax relief. One such example was the Rural Renewal Scheme, which covered all of the counties of Leitrim and Longford as well as certain areas in counties Cavan, Roscommon and

Sligo. The scheme was intended for commercial, owner-occupied, and rental residential properties, and was one of three urban and rural rental schemes which formed part of the 1998 Finance Act.

Under the terms of the scheme, 50 per cent of capital expenditure could be used as tax relief for both owner-occupiers and lessors of the buildings constructed or refurbished under the two schemes, 'with the remaining 50 per cent being written off at 4 per cent per annum over the next thirteen years'.[104] McCreevy wanted to give 100 per cent tax relief on capital expenditure, but this was rejected by the EU Commission, who gave belated permission for the scheme in June 1999. There were other dissenting voices closer to home. The Chief Executive of the Western Development Commission, Mr Liam Scollan, said that it had 'not been thought through and appears to be more appropriate for Temple Bar than Carrick-on-Shannon'.[105] Both the Development Commission and the Heritage Council pointed out that almost half the schools in Leitrim and Roscommon were in danger of losing teachers due to falling numbers. They said that 'the area is in desperate need of people, yet [the Rural Renewal Scheme] will do nothing to encourage owner-occupancy but will assist developers who build for the rental market'.[106] These sentiments were in line with those of the Department of Finance, which also raised serious concerns, all of which were ignored by the Minister.

In 1999, the Department of Finance produced a tax strategy group paper on the urban and rural renewal schemes. It was critical of the fact that the objective of the scheme was to provide tax relief for investors, with construction once again the conduit rather than the actual objective. It also questioned the desirability of providing investment incentives via tax relief during a time of high economic growth. What encouragement does expansion need when expansion is already taking place? According to the report:

> ... the majority of the beneficiaries of property tax relief schemes are high-net worth individuals or corporate investors. The introduction of further tax incentive schemes even in times of exchequer surpluses does not assist the policy of continuing to lower tax rates and widen

> the base from which taxes can be levied. The possibility that tax incentives for property development have contributed to the emergence of asset price inflation cannot be discounted. Such reliefs may not be the most appropriate and cost effective way of promoting the development of an area or promotion of an undertaking given the present economic climate with record growth and increasing construction costs.[107]

The strategy group had highlighted the tax relief measures as a serious flaw within the scheme. However, the whole point of the scheme was to create a tax haven for investors and developers. And as this was the intention, it was no surprise that the Minister and the government declined the group's advice and allowed the scheme to run its course, with devastating results for the affected towns. The Shannon area was about to drown in a sea of concrete and decking. As to who would benefit from such an outcome, on that the strategy group was quite clear: high net-worth individuals and corporate investors.

From 1999 to 2006, a total of 6,452 housing units were constructed in Leitrim. The 2006 census showed that the number of households in the county had risen by 1,547 since 2002. Almost 22 per cent of all housing in Leitrim was vacant. A similar pattern occurred in Longford, with 5,842 houses built under the scheme up to 2006, a household increase of only 1,736, and a vacancy rate of 22 per cent. Overall, the census found around 216,000 empty housing units in the State – this did not take into account holiday homes, of which there were 49,789. Fifteen per cent of all housing in the country was empty. In 2010, the website Life After NAMA, which is run by academics based at NUI Maynooth, concluded that there were 302,625 empty housing units in the State, and again this figure was exclusive of holiday homes.[108] Large swathes of Ireland, entire communities, were being used solely as tax avoidance by investors, who had been encouraged for decades to do so by successive Irish governments.

By 2007, it was obvious that the Irish property bubble was about to burst. In an article for *The Irish Times*, the UCD economist Morgan Kelly wrote that 'the question is no longer whether the Irish property market will have a soft landing or a hard landing but what kind of hard landing it will have'.[109] He pointed out the high level of vacant houses in the State, and that 'almost none of the 70,000 or so new units built this year have been sold'. His was a pessimistic, yet entirely realistic, assessment of the situation, and as such was roundly criticised and dismissed by the economic experts who were brought in to undermine any realistic attempt to understand the true dynamics of the Irish economy. The chief economist with IIB Bank, Austin Hughes, said that 'the proportion of unoccupied dwellings here is slightly below the EU average' and that 'a surge in spending power that made ownership of holiday homes and accommodation for children at college almost commonplace is one element in this rise in so-called "empty" homes'. In July of that year, the Taoiseach, Bertie Ahern, told a conference of the Irish Congress of Trade Unions that he was fed up with those who spoke of serious problem within the Irish economy. He said that 'sitting on the sidelines, cribbing and moaning is a lost opportunity. I don't know how people who engage in that don't commit suicide, because frankly the only thing that motivates me is being able to actively change something.' Fourteen months later, the Irish banks would need the largest bail-out in the history of the Irish State, and the property market was on its slide towards disaster.

The 2002 census contained an interesting statistic. Irish owner occupancy levels had dropped in the 1990s, from a high of 79 per cent in 1991, to 77 per cent ten years later.[110] By 2006, owner-occupancy stood at just under 74 per cent. In EU terms, Ireland was eighteenth in home-ownership levels, out of twenty-nine nations listed by Eurostat.[111] Ireland was bucking European trends with a declining level of home ownership, yet the popular narrative has Ireland with the highest rate of home ownership in Europe and, unlike the rest of Europe, obsessed with owning their homes. It does not matter that seventeen other countries – Spain, Italy, Greece, Portugal, Norway, Cyprus, Malta, Iceland, Latvia, Romania, Lithuania, Poland, Bulgaria, Estonia, Hungary, Slovenia and Slovakia – all have higher rates of home ownership than Ireland or that the EU average rate is 76 per cent. Never let the facts get in the way of a story.

On 8 June 2006, *The Irish Times* printed a report by John Holden which perfectly reflected the blend of dinner-party philosophising and lazy assumptions that has come to characterise so much of the public narrative on Irish housing. He stated that Ireland, 'at 77 per cent has one of the highest rates of home ownership in Europe,' that 'home ownership is by no means an international preoccupation,' and that 'the Plantation, Land Wars, and the famine years are certain to have had some impact on every Irishman wanting his own plot'. He made the argument for a historical obsession with land after interviewing P.J. Drudy of the Centre for Urban and Regional Studies, who said that Irish people buy their dwelling as 'there is not great incentive to get into private rental accommodation. The standard is not good enough, particularly at the lower end, and the rents are as high as average mortgage repayments.' Michael Dowling of the Independent Advisers' Federation said that 'Irish people have seen the returns on property and so continue to keep the market buoyant' and that 'other European cultures are less interested in property [as an investment]. They tend to invest more in business and enterprise.' Professor Musterd of the University of Amsterdam told Holden that home ownership in Europe isn't all related 'to a history of oppression or landlessness'. All to little avail. The factual myths and pseudo-historical analysis carried the day.

Later that year, the Chief Executive of the Irish Bankers' Federation, Pat Farrell, said that Ireland's home-ownership level stood at 82 per cent, and that the EU average was 63.5 per cent (75 and 66 per cent respectively). He went on to say that the growth in wages was a key factor in driving the demand for housing, and that any curtailment of prices and 100 per cent mortgages would be against the national interest. In 2009, the deputy editor of *The Irish Times*, Fintan O'Toole, said that '87 per cent of Irish households own their own homes, compared to an EU average of 61 per cent.'[112] These myths and made-up figures were bandied about as if they expressed some profound truth about the Irish people, even though the home-ownership figures related not to the island of Ireland but to the twenty-six counties. Not only was owner-occupancy part of the Irish gene, apparently so was partition.

Yet we have seen that it took decades to convince the urban working class that home ownership was one of their innate desires. In the end it was the privatisation of urban public housing in the 1960s and '70s which led to the rise in home-ownership levels, going from 25 per cent in urban areas in 1961 to over 75 per cent in 1986. By then, a private mortgage was effectively the only route open to families who needed a house, and public housing had become a by-word for poverty and violence. The middle classes had won. It had taken seventy years, but Ireland had become 'respectable'. It had become a nation of homeowners, living mainly in suburbs with a modicum of facilities and infrastructure, the likes of which would have horrified Ebenezer Howard.

However, housing cannot be explained simply in terms of itself. It is both a social necessity and an economic activity. Its development in Ireland in the twentieth century cannot be separated from these two spheres. The key elements of the official narrative of the banking crisis and property collapse – that Irish commercial and residential property prices lost all contact with value and demand and by doing so crippled an economy, and that the Irish State must nationalise those losses while protecting the rights of private property – are not the result of the need for housing in the cities. But this is the way that the banking crisis is explained; that 'we lost the run of ourselves' and 'we all went crazy' with buying houses. The Irish housing market recorded its highest ever level in 2007, with the average price for new and second-hand houses at €322,634 and €377,850 respectively. These figures dropped by between 5 and 7 per cent in 2008, and by October 2010 the average price had dropped below €200,000 for the first time in eight years. At least 150,000 Irish householders were now in negative equity. Yet in 2007 the median wage in Ireland – that is, the 50 per cent mark – was €25,000 before tax, and €29,000 for those in employment for more than one year. At the height of the boom, Irish property prices were between eleven and fifteen times the median wage. Where was the money coming from? And why was this actively encouraged by successive governments via national economic policy?

The myths which saturate the subject of housing in Ireland, the false histories and pop psychologies, the sheer laziness of analysis which is brought to bear on the topic, these have been the concerns of this chapter. It has been an attempt to give an overview of the actual development of housing in Ireland over the past ninety years based on the facts, and not fantastical assumptions such as an Irish property gene which dates back to the famine, but only in the twenty-six counties, and is somehow different and unique to similar patterns of home ownership in the rest of Europe. However, a picture of what happened, no matter how factual it may be, is not an explanation of why things happened. We have to look at the Irish economy, its history and dynamics, in order to make sense of why the Irish housing market and subsequent property bubble turned out the way it did, and why the bank guarantee and NAMA were pushed through as solutions, with total disregard to the predicted effects and consequences. And in order to get to grips with the economic development of Ireland in the twentieth century, to tease out the dynamics which surrounded government policy, we need to go back to agriculture and the livestock exports which dominated the Irish economy until the 1970s, when foreign investment and industrial exports finally took over. No more glib and easy answers. No more mythical DNA. We need to look at how the machine worked, and why it worked the way it did.

2

AGRICULTURE

The popular narrative of the Irish economy in the twentieth century has the State as inward-looking and protectionist until the arrival of Whitaker and Lemass to positions of leadership in the late 1950s, which propelled the country into the modern era. The details and complexity of the story may vary from teller to teller, but essentially that's the tale.

But Ireland was always part of the modern era. Its role was to provide agricultural produce for the industrial centres of Britain, and this was done mainly in the form of live cattle exports. The domestic economic power blocs which developed on the back of that export trade resisted almost all attempts at either reform of that trade, or the development of other forms of trade which might jeopardise their income. The lack of a sufficiently strong industrial base to combat the self-interests of the ranchers and cattle exporters had a profound effect on the development of Ireland in the twentieth century. The Whitaker/Lemass initiative in the late 1950s and early 1960s centred on the development of a 'third way' for the Irish economy.

Instead of creating export-led industries which would have lessened the State's reliance on Britain and countered the economic power of the live cattle exporters, Whitaker/Lemass decided on the importation of fully developed, and foreign-owned, companies which would give

Ireland an industrial presence without any of the pain of self-development. However, the main boost to the Irish economy was not so much the new factories, but the construction of these new factories – the majority of which, especially the pharmaceuticals, did not source their raw materials from Ireland. Furthermore, the development of secondary industries surrounding the transplanted factories was neglected to almost a criminal degree. Builders and contractors, land speculators, banks and financial institutions, import and export service providers – these were the main beneficiaries of the Whitaker/Lemass revolution.

What we see in the 1960s and early 1970s is the development of an indigenous industrial class which is adept mainly at providing financial, building and port services, rather than actual goods.[1] An economic model such as this, which is overly reliant on construction as its base, is a recipe for boom/bust disaster, and that, unfortunately, has been the Irish experience for the past forty years.

THE RISE OF THE GRAZIER

> 'The grazier lives at ease, and the poverty in the district is a disgrace to human nature.'[2]
>
> *John Quin, Esq., land proprietor, County Wicklow, 1847.*

Speaking in the Dáil in 1922, the Cumann na nGaedheal TD J.J. Burke said that agriculture was 'the rock on which our economic structure rests ... the one sound and staple thing in the present welter of commercial uncertainty and insecurity'.[3] The Free State's economic links were such that in 1924, Britain and Northern Ireland accounted for 98 per cent of the total export sales of £51.58 million.[4] Agriculture accounted for 86 per cent of that figure. Live cattle export sales that year mounted to £17.2 million, or 35 per cent of the total amount.[5]

According to the 1926 census, there were around 25,000 graziers in the Irish Free State at that time.[6] Their status and income were dependent on the exportation of live cattle to Britain, and they did everything they could to protect that trade, often at great expense to the rest of the country. In the eyes of the rancher, the natural business of Irish agriculture was pasture. It was God's will that Ireland was such a lush and green country. Cattle fattening was the natural order of things; the best utilisation of Ireland's blessings. It was providence that made Ireland the way it was, and it was simply providence that ranchers were able to make millions from such opulent blessings. At the same time, it was an unfortunate providence that consigned those not provident enough to be cattle ranchers to poverty and emigration. God had blessed the Irish, it seems; he just hadn't blessed all of them.

Yet, no matter how green the grass grew, no matter how flat the fields were, there was nothing natural about the Irish live cattle trade. It was a modern industrial assembly line, one which stretched for hundreds of miles, from the smallholders of Sligo to the slaughterhouses of Deptford, and one for which the cattle ranchers supplied the raw material. The graziers did not produce beef. They did not produce shelf-ready products. They exported livestock to British fatteners and slaughterhouses, and it was there that the products which ended up on the kitchen table were made. This system of production had deep historical roots – so much so that almost all attempts to disentangle the Irish economy from such a lopsided relationship as one which saw calves on grass as the *ne plus ultra* of agricultural and industrial ambition, were completely frustrated up until the 1950s, at which stage the importation of foreign industry was put forward as the seemingly perfect partner to the livestock business.

Although not a straight line by any means, the first hints of this assembly line can be seen as far back as the early 1700s. This does not mean that the move to open up Ireland to foreign investment in the 1950s was caused by the Cromwellian invasion and the Battle of the Boyne – that is not how history works; it's not a game of pool where one event hits off the other causing it to move. Rather we need to go back to the 1700s in order to observe how deep the roots run of the 'middleman' or comprador class in Ireland, as well as those of the grazier – as deep, in fact, as the factory owner in England. This is not surprising, as they are interrelated, albeit in a highly unequal way. In historical terms, to mangle a phrase, England's opportunity was Ireland's difficulty, never the other way around.

In 1687, Sir William Petty suggested that Ireland should be a cattle ranch for Britain. That year he published *A Treatise of Ireland*, in which he proposed the transportation of a million people from Ireland to the UK, where they would live 'in a more cultivated country, and in more elegant company and variety of entertainments', leaving 300,000 behind as herdsmen and dairywomen to help 'breed and feed 6 million of beefes [*sic*] of 3-years-old a piece'. The reasons for this were not just economic. Petty wanted:

> ... to cut up the roots of those evils in Ireland, which by differences of births, extractions, manners, languages, customs, and religions, have continually wasted the blood and treasure of both nations for above 500 years; and have made Ireland, for the most part, a diminution and a burthen, not an advantage, to England.[7]

His plan was never implemented – at least not in the way that he envisioned – but three key elements did remain up to the middle of the twentieth century: to Britain, Ireland was a source of trouble, a source of labour, and a source of food. The idea that it was the job of Ireland to provide for England was one that proved stubbornly resistant to the passing of time.

The defeat of the Irish confederate forces and subsequent Cromwellian settlement (1649–62) saw an upheaval in Irish land ownership. The soldiers of the New Model Army who fought during the campaign were given land as payment for services. 'Adventurers who had helped to finance the military campaign in Ireland,' writes the historian Donald Woodward, 'soldiers, and those who bought them out, replaced many of the previous landowners.'[8] It should be noted that the change in land ownership did not mean dispossession for the majority of Irish people, simply because the majority of Irish people were not landowners. The Cromwellian settlement meant a change in ownership, but it also meant a change in landlord, and with this a new dynamic enters Irish social and economic life.

Most of these new landowners did not cultivate the land themselves. They were, after all, soldiers, not farmers. 'Owing to the uncertainty of their possessions and, perhaps, lack of ability,' writes Woodward, 'they mostly confined their activities to stock raising and letting land at high rents to the Irish.' A lot of the new landlords were absentee, and so they relied on Irish agents to let the land and administer their affairs. These intermediaries, or middlemen, became a significant presence in Irish agriculture, often letting vast tracts of land from English-based landlords, and then subletting that land to Irish tenants. These rents needed to be paid with coins, and so for the tenant-farmer the rearing of cattle became a commercial necessity. Cattle was soon a cash crop for the payment of rent, and by the late 1660s the new landowners were claiming that cattle exporting was their chief trade.[9] Pastoral (or livestock) farming required less effort and less commitment than tillage, and was 'much better fitted to the condition of men who were consigned to a fugitive property'.[10] They invested little time in fattening, preferring to breed livestock for quick export, the trade in which 'was so flourishing that it seemed scarcely worthwhile to spend money in fattening in order to procure good meat and dairy produce for sale abroad'.[11]

The Cromwellian settlement had a profound and long-lasting effect on Irish society. In the words of the geographer, William J. Smyth:

> [The period] from the 1690s up to the 1760s, can be described as a critical formative phase in the making of the modern [Irish] landscape and society. From the perspective of the landlord, his townland administrators (the head-tenants or 'middlemen') and their urban allies (the merchants, estate agents and solicitors), this phase was one of infrastructural development, while from the viewpoint of the occupiers of the land, this phase was one of reorganisation and often displacement – all consequent upon the greater commercialisation of a predominantly pastoral economy and the related expansion of the enclosure movement. This latter process involved the creation or enlargement of compact grazier farms on the lowlands and the commercialisation and privatisation of the former communally-held upland areas where both older cooperative systems in landholding and, in some instances, clustered settlements were broken up. By the 1770s then, the skeletal framework of the modern landscape of compact enclosed individual

> farms with large fields geared mainly to pastoral pursuits was generally established.[12]

The land displacements, the new landlords, the creation of a middleman class, the attractiveness of low-labour but high-yield cattle farming, and the tenants' need for cash to pay rent: these were the long-term developments.

The influx of cattle from Ireland was such that the English parliament twice passed laws banning its importation – in 1667 and 1681. The effect was a short-term depression in Ireland, followed by growth in the food trade and the shipment of beef to the Continent. It also led to a shift from cattle to sheep. Over the next eighty years, Irish capital developed trade in provisions, dairying and wool production. According to a contemporary writer:

> ... after some years [of the Cattle Acts] Ireland found a way of salting, barrelling and exporting beef. So that in lieu of exporting 70,000 head of live cattle to England at 40 shillings a head, which cost England all but £140,000 and which they manufactured afterwards and had all the hides and tallow [rendered beef fat] into the bargain, Ireland now exports that beef to the value of £20,000 and butter worth £200,000 more; about 3,000 raw hides to England, 70,000 raw hides to France and Spain, and about £70,000 worth of tallow.[13]

The 1667 and 1681 Cattle Acts had the effect of turning Ireland into a producer, not just of livestock, but of goods as well. New markets opened up in Europe after the signing of the Treaty of Utrecht in 1713 and the ending of the War of Spanish Succession. The continued influence of the graziers was such that in 1735 the Irish House of Commons moved to exempt pasture from tithes.[14] In 1759, Irish cattle, beef and butter were allowed once again into the UK. 'Landlords increasingly let their land to graziers who cleared them of small tenants and turned the land over to pasture', writes the historian Michael Beames. Within two years, 'the pressure for new pasture was strong enough in the province of Munster to tempt graziers into enclosing lands previously understood to be commons. It was these enclosures which sparked off the earliest Whiteboy disturbances.'[15] A conflict of interests was emerging between grazier and smallholders and localised class antagonisms were breaking out, often with violent repercussions.

The picture of Ireland at the time is a complex one, as there is a strong regionalism to Irish agriculture. Most of the grazier holdings were in 'Meath, Westmeath, Offaly, parts of Kilkenny, Roscommon, parts of Galway and Sligo'.[16] At the same time as the commons enclosures, Ireland went from being an importer to an exporter of corn. After the 1820s, though, with the end of the Napoleonic Wars, the reopening of Europe to Britain, and the rise in cattle and sheep prices, pastoral farming became decidedly more attractive than tillage. However, it was with the repeal of the Corn Laws in 1846 and the devastating effects of the famine that the advance of grazing gathered an unstoppable momentum and transformed the face of the country.[17]

1849–1924

'The ranches were created by filling the emigrant ship.'

Senator J. T. O'Farrell, 3 August 1923.

The post-famine years saw a dramatic rise in grazing and cattle production. The land clearances in the wake of the evictions, death and emigration which surrounded the period sped the move towards livestock which had been taking place since the 1780s. 'The whole trend of the markets in pre-famine decades was to favour cattle and sheep and to place tillage at a competitive disadvantage', wrote Ray Crotty. 'Had more capital been available, almost certainly this would have gone into increasing stocks of the now more profitable cattle and sheep rather than into investment for tillage.'[18] The repeal of the Corn Laws in 1846, 'which had protected grain-growing from competition with imported grain' meant that 'grain was no longer profitable … and landowners changed the focus of their enterprise to grass'.[19] As Ireland was a full part of the UK, and had been since the 1801 Act of Union, its exports to Britain were categorised as domestic and as such severely affected by the change in law.

However, in order to make grazing profitable, more land was needed for livestock. 'There are no such thing as graziers on a small scale', as James Quin pointed out in his evidence to the House of Commons committee on land in Ireland.[20] Evictions reached their highest level during the years 1847 to 1850, while by 1851 an estimated quarter of a million had already emigrated – including between 15 and 17.5 per cent of the population of the rich grazing lands of Meath.[21] By 1869, the number of sheep in Ireland was double the 1847 figure, while the amount of cattle had increased by 50 per cent to just over 3 million. Petty's vision of a depopulated Ireland filled with livestock no longer seemed so far-fetched.

By 1870, Irish cattle production had reached a national organisational structure which would remain relatively unchanged for the following eighty years. There was a strong geographical dimension to the process, one which reflected the division of labour.

> The breeding, rearing and fattening of cattle was divided fairly systematically among the eastern, western and southern provinces. Munster contributed the main proportion of the store cattle, though fattening was also carried out in the rich grazing lands of Limerick and Tipperary; Connaught reared a large share of the cattle, while Leinster concentrated mainly on fattening the animals – cattle and sheep – from both provinces.[22]

The different stages of cattle production – rearing, grazing, fattening, and shipping – were undertaken by different groups of farmers with different-sized holdings. The historian Fergus Campbell gives a succinct overview of the process which is worth quoting in full:

> [The] smallholders were the 'breeders' who reared the young calves and bullocks that were the basis of the Irish cattle industry. They then sold their cattle (typically when aged between one and two years)

> to the 'grazier', who kept them for a further period of between six months and two years. He then sold them as 2- or 3-year-olds to the 'fattener', who grazed them on the rich grazing lands of counties Kildare, Meath and Westmeath. Most of the land of Connacht was insufficiently rich to 'fatten' cattle and usually this part of the process took place on the large grazing farms of Leinster. Finally the 'fattener' sold the finished cattle to the 'shipper' who exported the cattle to the fairs and markets of England and Scotland.
>
> The smallholders had insufficient land to raise themselves above the role of 'breeders' in the Irish cattle industry. If they were to improve their standard of living, they would have to rear a larger number of cattle for sale at a more advanced stage of development. This would require capital, better-quality land, and a certain amount of expertise. The least available of these commodities was grazing land: the primary source of income in an agrarian economy devoted to the sale of cattle.[23]

Although the 1880s were dominated by the Land League and the campaign for ownership, the smallholders of the south and west were well aware that a simple transfer of title (from tenant to owner-occupier) would not in itself lead to a transformation of the inequalities inherent in the system of production as outlined above. The Land League itself was:

> ... above all a class alliance of the rural bourgeoisie, the middle and poor peasantry, and the agricultural proletariat ... The large and middle farmers were looking for rent reductions, the smallholders of the West were looking for land redistribution, while the labourers of the South were contemplating at least a general strike for better wages.[24]

It is important to recognise that the Land League did not change the economic system of production in Ireland. After the Land Acts were passed, instead of renting an uneconomic farm which was often little more than a feeder for graziers, a smallholder was now securely tenured and paying a fair price for an uneconomic farm which was often little more than a feeder for graziers. As Paul Bew has observed, 'there was a widespread awareness [among smallholders] that their land – even if rent-free – could not support a family and that they needed more land'.[25]

The key to breaking this poverty trap was the redistribution of grasslands and a move to tillage in order to make small to medium-sized farming tenable. The needs of the small farmer to make a living, however, were at odds with the needs of the grazier to make a profit, and this clash of interests between the class of graziers and the class of small farmers and labourers, came to the fore when the Land League's nationalist and anti-landlord campaign, the glue which held these opposing forces together, became unstuck with the passing of the Land Acts.

On 31 March 1907, a crowd gathered in the little village of Elphin, County Roscommon to hear the United Irish League organiser, C.W.P. Cogan, speak in protest against 'grazierism and grabberism' and to make an appeal 'to the people to stick together until the graziers were driven from the ranches of North Roscommon'.[26] It was part of a wider campaign for land redistribution, rather than the simple purchase of current holdings. The 1903 Wyndham Land Act allowed almost 200,000 Irish tenant farmers to become owner-occupiers, but despite the moves to encourage landlords to sell untenanted lands, the MP for North Westmeath, Laurence Ginnell found that after three years of the 'greatest Land Act ever passed, ranchers' cattle [were] still grazing over evicted lands, and young people [were] still emigrating from the neighbouring uneconomic bog holdings for want of land to live upon, while the parts of the Act purporting to have provided for them remained a dead letter'.[27] A campaign of protests, rent strikes and cattle driving followed the passing of the Wyndham Act and lasted from 1904 to 1908. It became known as the Ranch War, the object of which was to 'harass and demoralise the graziers; eventually, it was hoped, such men would surrender their land to the surrounding peasantry, rather than have their lives made a misery'.[28] The limited success of the 1904-8 campaign was due in no small part to the fact that the smallholders 'were dependent on [the graziers] to buy the cattle which paid their rent'.[29] The system of production had a lock on the lives of the small holder, with disciplined, united action – a difficult momentum to sustain – their only effective weapon.

The production of livestock for export to Britain had other, less high-profile effects. In terms of cattle, the dominant breed in Ireland was the Shorthorn. It was originally developed in Britain and introduced to Ireland in the 1820s as a dual-purpose breed – that is, suitable for both beef and dairy production. By 1860, Ireland was 'the centre of excellence for Shorthorns'[30] and by the 1880s it had replaced the Old Irish Cow. Yet the 'dual-purpose' tag was a bit of a misnomer. The Shorthorn was bred primarily for its beef, not its milk. In 1921, the Commission of Inquiry into the Resources and Industries of Ireland produced a report on stock-breeding farms. With regard to the Shorthorn it had this to say:

> It is a fact that the pedigree Shorthorn is constitutionally and naturally a beef and not a dairy cow. The expression 'dairy Shorthorn' is, in fact, somewhat of a contradiction in terms. As a consequence, the attempt to change its natural line of development in the effort to obtain milk from her is large quantities is, in the words of one capable witness, 'a fight against nature'. The statement is made that very heavy milking Shorthorns lose health, develop udder troubles, or fail to breed.[31]

This was not, by any means, a revelation. It was well known that dairy farmers needed a specialist breed in order to compete and grow. 'Shorthorns have not been bred during the past decade on milking lines,' stated the Armagh Agricultural Committee in 1910, 'and are, therefore, to a large extent, unsuitable for a country that, as years roll by, finds itself drifting deeper into the dairy industry.'[32]

The system of cattle production, however, was such that the 'feeder' farmers who produced calves did so primarily for the ranchers. Dairy farming was almost an afterthought. The Irish dairy industry found itself flanked by livestock export business on one side, and those 'feeder' farmers who needed to sell beef calves on the other, and it lost out as a result. The number of milch (milking) cows in Ireland hardly grew during the years 1851 to 1911, while the total number of cattle during the same period increased by almost 70 per cent.[33] For all intents and purposes, Irish breeders produced only one thing: beef calves destined for Britain. Everything else – tillage, dairying and people – came a very distant second.

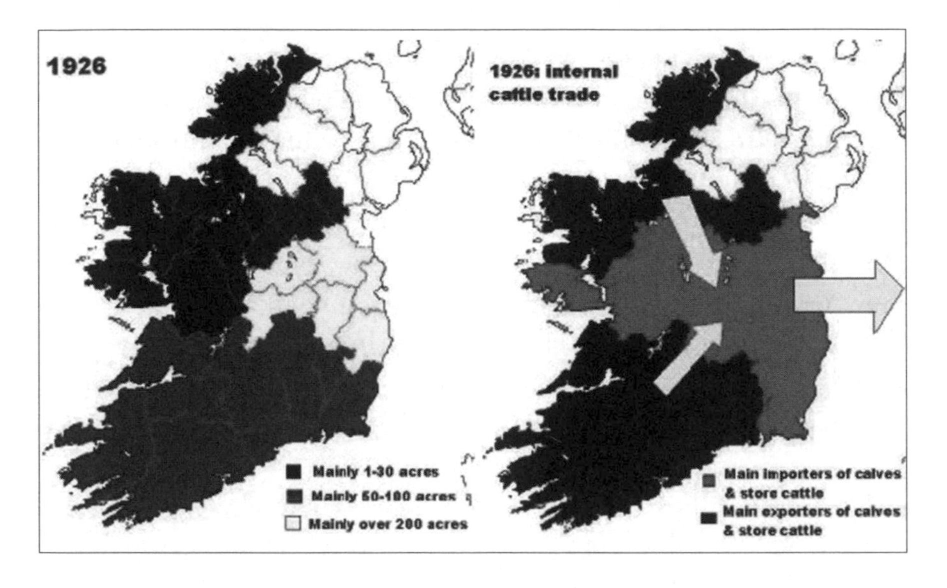

The subsumption of small farms into larger holdings – a process which had been accelerated by the famine – coupled with the declining power of the landlord class, saw the consolidation of both economic and societal power into the hands of wealthy farmers and their familial networks. For them, government was the next logical step. As William J. Smyth puts it, 'By the 1880s, the urban kinsmen of such [wealthy] tenant farmers played a vital link role in the legal, ecclesiastical, journalistic and trading spheres … [and] their descendents were to dominate the structures and ethos of the newly independent state between the 1920s and the 1960s.'[34]

1924 TO 1957

In January 1924, the Minister for Agriculture, Patrick Hogan, wrote a memo to his cabinet colleagues in which he emphasised his opinion, that 'national development in Ireland for our generation at least is practically synonymous with agricultural development'.[35] It was a view shared by the rest of the government. It was also accepted by Hogan and the cabinet that 'agricultural development' meant a continuation of the status quo, i.e. the livestock trade with Britain and the subordination of all other economic activities to that trade.

The bias towards beef-producing cattle stock, instead of specialisation in dairy and beef breeds, for example, was also held by the Department of Agriculture. In the 1920s it published its criteria for the register of non-pedigree dairy cattle. It accepted for registration only those cows which upon inspection were found to be of 'good conformation, short-legged, well-ribbed and deep in body'. The reason it favoured non-pedigree dairy cattle of such dimensions was because 'the dairy farmer is to a large extent also the breeder of store cattle ... and it is essential that his cows as well as being deep milkers should be of a type calculated to produce good store and beef animals'.[36] This was despite the findings of the Report on Stock-Breeding Farms in 1921, as noted above, which saw the dairy Shorthorn as 'a fight against nature'. This did not stop Hogan telling the Dáil in January 1924 that it was the dairy farmers who were the kingpins:

> The raising of grass-fed beef though an extremely important part of the industry, is at present small – it is a by-product of the great dairy industry. Anyone who knows anything about farming knows that, and as the dairy industry gets more and more efficient, as I hope it will, the less stores and the less grass-fed beef you will have in the country.[37]

This was simply a lie on the part of the Minister. The promotion of the 'dual-purpose' Shorthorn and the bias towards beef calves, 'encouraged dairy farmers to breed as much for beef as for milk, thereby lowering yields. Inevitably, the greater profitability of the beef trade ensured a bias towards beef characteristics.'[38] And as already noted, from the 1860s onwards, the total number of dairy cattle remained almost static. The growth in cattle occurred in beef-producing stock for export.

The promotion of the livestock trade to Britain was also justified with a 1920s version of trickle-down economics. According to George O'Brien, professor of economics at UCD and a personal friend of Hogan, the Minister believed that it was important to help graziers and exporters achieve greater profits because the more they consumed in goods and services, the more the rest of the economy would benefit:

> The farmers being the most important section of the population, everything that raised their income raised the national income of the country. Prosperity amongst farmers would provide the purchasing power necessary to sustain the demand for non-agricultural goods and services, and it was useless to encourage secondary industries unless the primary industry was in a position to purchase their products. The principal aim of agricultural policy in the Free State should therefore be the maximization of the farmers' income, and not, as in certain other countries differently situated, the provision of food for the urban population or the solution of the unemployment problem.[39]

For Hogan, 'the lawyer son of a senior Land Commission official', the ordinary farmer was 'the 200 acre man'.[40] In order to address the needs of this class, he 'urged curbs on local government spending to reduce taxes on farmers, advocated cutting the wages of local authority road workers to prevent pressure on farm labourers' wages, pressed for lower tax levels to increase competitiveness, and urged that farmers be compensated for cost increases consequent on protection'.[41]

For its part, the Free State government held true to these trickle-down principles by cutting services to the working classes while providing a helping hand to the graziers and livestock exporters, as well as urban middle-class house buyers (as we saw in chapter one). It undertook to encourage industry only insofar as such measures entailed no negative change in ranchers' incomes. The senior officials in the Irish civil service, particularly those in the Department of Finance who had served under the British administration, 'emphasised a tradition of financial austerity and avoidance of government intervention. A largely conservative party advised by a thoroughly conservative administrative elite resulted in economic orthodoxy.'[42] The government's economic policies favoured graziers and livestock exporters but 'offered little to those facing emigration or inadequate living standards'.[43]

In October 1924, six months after the government had passed the Housing Act which gave purchase subsidies of between €60 to €100 to middle-class households, the Minister for Industry and Commerce told the Dáil in a debate on unemployment and welfare assistance that 'there are certain limited funds at our disposal. People may have to die in this country and may have to die through starvation.' This was in response to the documented accounts of starvation which were coming in from around the country. In January 1925, Dr Brian B. Crichton, who had a long association with the Coombe and Rotunda hospitals, told the Rotary Club that 'a child's chances of life in the City of Dublin are worse than were the chances of a soldier in the trenches during the Great War'.[44] He said that women often came to him to the clinic but 'instead of medicine, he often gave a note to some philanthropic organisation to enable them to get food'. The same month, the Clare Health Board was informed of a man and his wife who lived near Kilmikil, who had died of starvation and neglect. The relieving officer had found the woman 'lying in a corner of a filthy and verminous room, covered only by a dirty rag. The man was also in a deplorable condition, weak and hungry.'[45] In another case, a doctor visited a house in 'New Hall, near Ennis, and found two old people living in a terrible condition of filth. They had been eating portions of the carcase of a calf, which was lying in the kitchen.'[46] In Longford, two married women were charged with stealing potatoes from the mental asylum garden. 'I took the potatoes for my children, who are starving at home,' said one of the women. The judge said that from his knowledge no one need starve in Longford. When the defendants' lawyer asked the judge had he read the report in the local newspapers about cases of starvation, the judge replied, 'Yes: and I saw it contradicted.'[47] It was increasingly clear that Cumann na nGaedheal was protecting the financial self-interests of the class it represented, while the rest of the nation could, quite literally, starve.

In terms of the economy, the government's plan to keep things as they were ignored the obvious fact that they weren't. The island had been partitioned into two separate political entities, with the twenty-six-county Free State now responsible for its own fiscal affairs. Yet, the approach of Cumann na nGaedheal and the senior officials within government was to behave as if Ireland remained a regional economy within the UK. The problem was that the type of financial redistributions and shared costs which regions could expect while part of a greater national economy were now all but gone. (One example of this was the social housing fund set up under the 1919 Housing Act, which allocated grants and loans to local authorities to build sanitary accommodation for the urban and rural working classes. With the War of Independence and subsequent partition of the island, that funding stream was now shut off for the twenty-six counties.)

Ireland was now a nation-state. 'Fiscal separation from the UK meant that Irish exports to Britain of protected commodities became subject to British import duties, and all imports into Ireland became dutiable at the same rates as goods imported into Britain.'[48] But instead of working towards the creation of a national economy with an independent fiscal policy and actual agricultural products for export (not just livestock), the Irish government took to protecting the relatively small percentage of farmers, financiers and administrators who made a comfortable living from the structural deficiencies of the Irish economy, while consigning the rest of the population to poverty and emigration. In real terms, this meant the continuation of 'free-trade' in livestock and finance, while finished products were subject to tariffs and quotas. The three government-appointed commissions set up to examine the economy – the Commission on Agriculture (1924), the Fiscal Inquiry Committee (1923) and the Banking Commission (1927) – all decided in their majority reports that things should remain as they were, that 'Ireland would maintain parity and financial links with sterling, produce food for Britain, and retain a free-trade industrial sector.'[49]

The conservatism of Cumann na nGaedheal did not stop with economics. Divorce was banned in 1925, while in 1926 the Department of Justice under Kevin O'Higgins set up the Committee on Evil Literature. Its purpose was to consider 'whether it is necessary or advisable in the interest of the public morality to extend the existing powers of the State to prohibit or restrict the sale and circulation of printed matter'. It was followed by the Censorship of Publications Act (1929), which sought 'to make provision for the prohibition of the sale and distribution of unwholesome literature'. The Irish Free State may have wanted its economy to remain petrified in a pre-partition wonderland, but it had definite views on the morality of its citizens, and on this it took a more vigorous course.

Not all sections of the government were happy with the continuation of the status quo. In April 1924, the Cumann na nGaedheal TD for Cavan, Seán Milroy, told the weekly meeting of the Dublin Rotary Club that:

> [The people of the Free State] had been told that any departure from the old fiscal regime which they had inherited would jeopardise, if not seriously injure, Ireland's foreign trade. Anyone who had studied that foreign trade knew that it was uneconomic – largely an export of foodstuffs and raw material. [Milroy] asked those who opposed Protection to cease talking about theories and to take cognisance of the realities.[50]

Officials in the Department of Industry and Commerce also urged the use of tariffs as a means of economic and industrial development. The tasks which the Free State needed to undertake in order to turn itself from a regional to a national economy, it was unwilling to carry out. There was an ideological element to this, with free trade invariably put forward as the solution to Ireland's economic problems.

In June 1923, the Fiscal Inquiry Committee was established to examine the fiscal situation for industry and agriculture and to report on any changes needed to foster growth. It was chaired by Timothy Smiddy, professor of economics at University College Cork and economic advisor to Michael Collins in the lead-up to the Treaty negotiations. (He would later serve as the Free State's Minister in Washington.) Despite the fact that the overwhelming majority of those who gave evidence called for protection, the Committee concluded that high wages and a lack of skilled labour, and not the uneven 'free-trade' links with Britain, were undermining the growth of native industry. The historian Mary E. Daly notes that 'there was no minority report, so the message of free trade and the priority afforded to agriculture and export industries was not challenged'.[51]

The argument that tariffs would add to the cost of agricultural production – as was made not only by the Fiscal Inquiry Committee but also by the graziers' supporters in Cumann na nGaedheal – ignored the important fact that fertilizer and agricultural machinery made up the bulk of important agricultural producer goods; the rest was home produced. The main cost for a grazier was the purchase of young stock, which almost invariably came from small farmers, and 'this cost was the income of the small farmer who had reared the stock'.[52] Yet the call for tariffs was made with regard to consumer goods. Any widening of import duties would have hurt a graziers' pocket – were he to continue to buy imports – but not necessarily his profit. As the historian J.J. Lee put it:

> ... dogmatic free traders cleverly succeeded in confusing all farmers' purchases with farming 'costs'. There was no immediate reason why protection on consumer goods should have directly and sharply increased famers' costs of production, as distinct from cost of living. The convenient confusion between famers' consumer purchases and producer purchases was a shrewd propagandistic *non-sequitur*.[53]

The idea that the consumer power of well-to-do farmers and graziers should be protected at all costs made no economic sense to a country with the type of structural deficiencies such as those of the Irish Free State.

One contemporary commentated on the fact that 'close on forty Irish manufacturing industries gave evidence before the Fiscal Inquiry Committee in support of protective tariffs, and each one of these, with one trifling exception, were prejudiced or damnified by the report, not upon the merits of each case, but upon general principles'.[54] The Dublin Industrial Development Association condemned:

> ... the non-judicial and extraordinary manner in which the great weight of evidence in favour of some form of protection was brushed aside by the Fiscal Inquiry Committee while all who abstained from tendering evidence were, for no very cogent reason, assumed to agree with the present system of free imports.[55]

The Fiscal Inquiry Committee, which included such free-trade stalwarts as Professor C.F. Bastasble of TCD, 'a survivor of the great days of Victorian liberalism when free trade was regarded by British economists as a religion rather than a policy',[56] had found that the solution to

Ireland's economic woes: put all your livestock and biscuits in the John Bull basket, and things will work out okay. The grand old sages of Irish economic thought, rather like the much-maligned insane, were staunch believers in doing the same thing over and over again in anticipation of a different result.

The early 1930s saw the Cumann na nGaedheal government forced to admit that its 'nothing to see here' strategy was not working and that the fundamental problems within the economy needed to be addressed. The economic downturn, the forced deflation brought on by the Irish currency's parity link with sterling, and the crash in agricultural prices all added to the calls for protection, some from within the agricultural sector, and by December 1931 there were tariffs on butter, bacon and oats. The favouring of middle-class incomes over economic development – in tandem with the housing grants, the standard income tax rate was cut from 25 per cent in 1924 to 15 per cent in 1927, while farm incomes were already exempt from income tax – had left the State in the unenviable position of borrowing more and spending less. 'Both taxes and expenditure fell marginally from 1926 to 1931,' writes Daly, 'though public debt rose from £14.1 million in 1926 to £29.3 million in 1931.'[57] The Fianna Fáil TD Seán McEntee said that 'the Churchillian principle which the Minister [for Finance, Ernest Blythe] had enunciated of meeting budgetary obligations by increasing the public debt ... was simply an inducement to undertax and overspend'.[58] The idea that tax breaks in lieu of structural change will save a shrinking economy has a half-life in Ireland that's greater than plutonium, and just as toxic.

'THE SMALL FARMER AND THE LABOURER ARE IN MORE NEED OF ASSISTANCE AND SUPPORT THAN ARE THE WEALTHY CLASSES'

Éamon de Valera, Sligo, 5 July 1930.

The Stock Market Crash and subsequent Depression saw governments across the world embracing protectionism with renewed vigour, and by the time Fianna Fáil came to power in 1932, Ireland was 'virtually the last predominantly free-trading economy in the world'.[59] The party initially formed a minority government with Labour Party support, but gained an overall majority after the snap election of 1933. It promised small farmers and urban workers significant changes and a positive difference to their lives. Policies included a campaign to encourage tillage; to break up the large grazier farms and destroy the rancher class; to divide the big farms among the small farmers and landless labourers; to introduce a general policy of protection; and to break the country's commercial dependence on Britain.

Seán T. O'Kelly was made Minister for Local Government and almost immediately began work on providing social housing for the working classes and agricultural labourers. Seán Lemass, as Minister for Industry and Commerce, was equally enthusiastic, and set about introducing a series of protectionist measures to encourage indigenous industry. Éamon de Valera, as Taoiseach, withheld land annuities to the British government and sparked a tariff war, which led Britain to place 20 per cent duties on all Irish livestock and livestock products, and de Valera, in retaliation, imposing duties on British coal. The tit-for-tat measures put a dent in Fianna Fail's limited economic reforms.

The most striking aspect of Fianna Fáil's economic policy, though, was not that the Free State had finally caught up with the rest of the world and was using tariffs to protect and encourage domestic industry, but that, having committed itself to tackling the structural deficiencies in the Irish economy via tariffs, it then decided to fight with one fiscal arm tied behind its back. There was no move to create an independent Irish currency, no move to establish a central bank, and no move to break the crippling parity with sterling. In addition, the 'bank rate remained at 3 per cent between June 1932 and August 1939 ... and though national debt rose, budgets continued to be balanced or nearly so'.[60] Furthermore, Fianna Fáil embraced protectionism as a means of creating industries which would produce for the needs of the Free State, and it alone, 'In de Valera's particular denomination of the tariff creed, the industries established were not expected to compete internationally, but were to service the home market.'[61] He saw 'little hope of establishing export industries, apart from food' and freely admitted that this particular brand of protectionism – great effort for little growth – would involve sacrifices. He simply counselled the people to 'forget as far as we can, what are the standards prevalent in countries outside this'.[62] Where this left the opening of letters from emigrants writing home, and sending money to boot, de Valera did not elaborate.

The move to impose tariffs, however, once taken, was quite robust. James F. Meehan, in his 1970 study, *The Irish Economy Since 1922*, noted that:

> ... at the end of 1931, the list of tariffs covered 68 articles including nine revenue tariffs. At the end of 1936 it covered 281 articles including seven revenue tariffs. These figures do not include a profusion of quotas and other restrictions. At the end of 1937 it was calculated that 1,947 articles were subject to restriction or control.[63]

Irish industry did expand as a result. The number of new industrial jobs generated between 1932 and 1936 was at least 40,000.[64] This increase in jobs, along with the substantial increase in house construction, meant that southern Ireland saw not only the first sustained growth in employment since the famine, but also a modest increase in prosperity in urban areas.[65] In keeping with the goal of national self-sufficiency, the government passed the Control of Manufactures Acts 1932 and 1934. These made it illegal for any business, unless it had been granted government permission to do so, 'to make, alter, repair, ornament, finish or to adapt for sale any article, material, or substance or any part of any article, material, or substance' unless at least 51 per cent of the nominal share capital and two-thirds of share with voting rights were held by Irish nationals. There was also an increase in the Semi-State sector, with the establishment of bodies such as Comhlucht Siúicre Éireann, Bord na Móna, the Industrial Credit Company, Ceimici Teoranta, Aer Lingus, the Irish Life Assurance Company, and the Irish Tourist Board.[66]

Concurrent with the move towards non-export protectionism was the campaign to encourage farmers to move from pasture to tillage, in particular, grain. 'A bounty was offered for calf skins, subsidies were introduced for wheat and sugar beet, import controls were imposed on sugar and tobacco, and relief was offered on rates in proportion to the amount of non-family labour employed.'[67] Wheat and flour to the value of around £7 million was being imported into the State and Fianna Fáil believed that it was time to redress this imbalance and make Ireland self-sufficient.[68] The Minister for Agriculture, Dr James Ryan, argued that increased tillage would see employment rise by as much as 50,000, with an extra £3 million in wages pumped into the economy as a result.[69] Again, the main idea was to create self-sufficiency in grain, as well as providing enough employment as to keep people on the land.

The results were mixed. There was increased production of wheat and sugar beet, 'but at the expense of other crops, not at the expense of cattle'.[70] A comparison between the 1926 and 1936 census shows that while the number of people engaged in agriculture dropped by 26,091 (from 670,076 to 643,985), the number of paid agricultural employees – as opposed to family members working on farms – increased by 1,998 (from 138,658 to 140,656). There was an increase of around 5,000 agricultural workers who didn't live on the farms they worked, but a drop of over 3,000 in agricultural workers who did. Ray Crotty notes that 'during the decade 1929-39, Leinster, the province with the greatest increase in tillage, showed the largest decline in agricultural employment. In Connaught, by contrast, where the decline in rural employment was very slight, there was a sharp fall in the tillage acreage.'[71] It seems reasonable to accept his conclusion that in terms of promoting tillage as a means of increasing employment, there is 'neither on a country nor on a provincial basis … any evidence whatever that wheat or sugar beet growing had this effect'.[72] Cattle production for export had a tendentious hold on all aspects of Irish agriculture.

Land redistribution was another key element of Fianna Fáil's plans to transform rural Ireland. The 1933 Land Act gave the Land Commission extra powers, while the amount spent on redistribution went from £2.7 million in 1931, to £7.6 million in 1936.[73] 'We may be told that a county is rich because of its profusion of grass,' said the Fianna Fáil TD for Meath, James Kelly, in 1932, 'but this merely gives us a wealth which cannot be diffused at present amongst our people. In fact, a large percentage of our poverty can be attributed to this cause.'[74] In this, Kelly was voicing an analysis which was central to the Ranch Wars, and was an underlying issue of conflict during the 1880s agitation.

In 1936, J.J. Waddell, the chief inspector of the Land Commission, argued that the minimum requirement for sustainable farming was 32.5 acres.[75] However, the size of new farms created by the government was limited to 22 acres, not enough to provide anything more than feeder farms for the ranchers, and certainly not large enough to threaten the system of production. Waddell cited the experience of the Rath Carn resettlement in County Meath, where families were given 20 to 200 acres each. 'Practically every family is sending members across the water to England' wrote Waddell, 'to assist the occupiers in living on these holdings and help to pay the annuity and rates, and to exist on them.'[76] However, any move to make small farmers economically self-sufficient would affect the supply of calves to graziers and fatteners – not because they would automatically switch to tillage, but because such redistribution would allow small farmers to fatten calves past the time which their present holdings would allow. The pressure to sell a calf after one to two years would lessen, and graziers and fatteners may be compelled to pay more for the product. The ranchers didn't just want small farmers to produce calves for them, they wanted *poor* small farmers who were not in a position to feed calves for much longer than a year.

By 1938, Fianna Fáil had all but abandoned the land annuities 'war' with the British. It is doubtful that Fianna Fáil ever really wanted to tackle the dominance of graziers. The reaction of Britain to the withholding of land annuities by de Valera ended up placing the issue of graziers within the wider remit of the party's tariffs policy – even though that policy was centred on creating a home industry for the home market. Fianna Fáil's tariffs were never about diversifying exports. In April 1933 the economist J.M. Keynes gave a lecture at University College, Dublin, in which he praised the merits of protectionism, much to the embarrassment of his hosts, but did so with the proviso that protectionism in an Irish context should be used to build up and diversify the economy – that Ireland's trade with Britain should be reciprocal in its nature. He criticised the idea of using protectionism to create industry for a 'self-sufficient' economy of such obviously limited size as the Free State.

Irish graziers were once again at the forefront of Irish economic policy. The structural problems remained in place. The Irish livestock export trade to Britain was not capable in itself of achieving economic wellbeing, but at the same time neither was the Irish political system willing to weaken the hold on exports which the livestock industry possessed. 'Again, following an iron precedent,' writes Roy Foster, 'the basic pattern of Irish agriculture showed little sign of change.'[77]

The plan which Fianna Fáil had for the Irish economy in 1932 was one which saw the expansion of tillage and redistribution of land as taking place alongside the cattle industry, not in conflict with it. The decision by the government to limit new farms created out of Land Commission acquisitions to 22 acres (later expanded to 25 acres) all but guaranteed that the old system of production remained in place – that is, small farmers as breeders, middle-sized farmers as fatteners, and graziers as finishers and exporters. 'It is most surprising that a Land Commission which for 30 years is committed to a policy of increasing the number of small farms' wrote the *Irish Farmers' Journal* in 1952, 'has never applied itself towards developing a system of farming that would give the 25 to 35 acre man a decent living.'[78] The purpose of the tillage campaign, it appears, was to make life on an uneconomic farm that bit more bearable by providing seasonal work for the small farmer and his family. Behind the rhetoric of tackling the 'old Imperialist policy' of 'making the country a ranch to provide cheap food for the English workers',[79] Fianna Fáil had consolidated that system by developing supplements to the income of small farmers and labourers, while bowing the head in deference to the primacy of cattle as the main cash crop. In May 1932, James Kelly told the Dáil that 'the ranching system [may be] a necessary adjunct to the production of beef … but the division of a larger holding into small holdings will not diminish its beef-producing capacity'.[80] Fianna Fáil wanted to develop a home market to sustain the working class and agricultural labourers, and to maintain an export market which would sustain the breeders and exporters. Yet it was not possible to square this economic circle, as in order to create an economy with employment levels high enough to sustain the population, the nature of the cattle trade needed to be changed. As Kelly noted, the livestock did not care if the grass and hay they ate belonged to a famer with 50 acres or 500 – but what Kelly failed to mention is that the problem was not so much one of an imbalance of livestock, but the fact that livestock were the end result. Ireland was still exporting its main raw material to Britain, not only because of the graziers and their hold on the economy, but also because livestock, particularly store cattle, was what Britain wanted.

The Irish government opened discussions with London in the immediate post-war years with regard to signing a new trade agreement. As part of the preparations, the British government requested a statement of agricultural policy from Dublin. To quote the historian Paul Rouse:

> [London] demanded, most pointedly: 'Has the Éire government the intention of ensuring that agricultural development takes place?' It asked what factors would retard expansion of production, what the fertiliser requirements would be, were there plans to specialise in agricultural industries such as canning, what other countries would Ireland look for markets in, and 'what effect will the policies proposed here have on the number of Irish workers coming to the UK?' Similarly, 'what evidence is there that the past apparently leisurely acceptance of improvements in technique, etc., by the Irish farmer will now give place to more speedy technical development?' The British missive wondered whether grassland and home-grown feed could be increased to improve stocking and to even out seasonality, and whether such increases would mean more fat rather than more store cattle. [It also asked] what policy as to concentration on beef, dairy and dual purpose cattle is being pursued? ... Why have cow numbers not increased in the last 30 years? ... it inquired what Ireland's preference for division on the export of her cattle would be between stores, fats, breeding stock and carcass or canned meats? ... Which products would Éire prefer to export? ... Will the import of feeding stuffs for bacon production be restricted as a matter of policy? Is it practicable to increase pig production from Éire's own soil?[81]

Éire may have been neutral during the Second World War, but in terms of its economy, the demands of Britain for Irish produce (as well as Irish labourers) took precedence.

Dublin responded with a report which assuaged the concerns of London, '[It] stated that substantial industrialisation was highly improbable and "the peasant character of the economy is evident from an analysis of agricultural equipment and of size of holding".'[82] In November 1947 an Irish delegation to London agreed that the 'total number of cattle to be exported from Ireland to continental countries as from 21 February 1948 will be the subject of consultation between the Irish government and the British Ministry of Food'.[83] The assertion in 1947 by G.D.H. Cole, Chichele Professor of Social and Political Theory at Oxford, that Ireland was Britain's larder, was a somewhat painfully accurate description of a State that would declare itself, with hollow importance, a Republic a year later.

'IN THE IRISH ECONOMY, CATTLE IS KING'

London's questions about Ireland's failure to modernise production in agriculture were not entirely without merit. The continuing preference for the dual-purpose Shorthorn over specialised beef and dairy breeds was a major factor in declining milk yields. As one commentator wrote in 1945:

> Ireland was about to spend another generation in Monte Carlo gambling with a dual-purpose to secure a high milk yield and a first-class butcher's beast. By the same breeding principles – by mating a thoroughbred with a Clydesdale [farm horse] – we should be able to win the Derby and plough the Rocks of Bawn.[84]

The use of chemical fertiliser was sporadic, and winter feeding the exception rather than the norm. 'So great were the structural flaws in the Irish dairy industry' writes Rouse, 'that the government was obliged to import New Zealand or Danish butter as Irish farmers found it more profitable to keep their low-yielding herds on subsistence rations through the winter months than to engage in dairying.'[85] James Dillon, who served as Minister for Agriculture from 1948 to 1951, told the

Cork County Committee of Agriculture in February 1950 that the Irish farmer, working in a free market, possessed all the skills and opportunities to make best use of his land:

> There may be a small minority of farmers who would like to have an inspector to wake him up in the morning, to dress them, to direct their daily work, and to tuck them into bed at night, but the vast majority of farmers of this country are well able to look after their own business, to make their own bargains, to hunt away from their gate anyone who seeks to exploit them, and effectively to make use of a profitable market when it is provided for them ... it is to these farmers I look for the efficient operation of the agricultural industry in this country.

Dillon's speech was not simply a populist piece of rhetoric aimed at a home audience – although it was certainly that – it also conveyed his ideological belief in individualised farming operations working in a free market as the pinnacle of efficiency; a view held by his party colleagues and, indeed, by many of the senior officials in the Department of Agriculture. Yet, as we have seen, there were serious structural inefficiencies within Irish agriculture – type of cattle bred, lack of fertilizer, diminishing dairy returns, antiquated machinery – and these were not going to disappear with a come-all-ye of 'dem feckers up in Dublin'. A year later, the Irish government commissioned a report into the reality of Ireland's economy and its possible future. It was compiled by the American consultancy firm Ibec Technical Services Corporation and entitled 'An Appraisal of Ireland's Industrial Potentials'. With no home crowd to please, its findings were a lot more sober than those of John Dillon.

Ibec began the report's section on cattle by stating, 'In the Irish economy, Cattle is King.'[86] It said that its 'examination of manufacturing activities in Ireland has brought into sharp focus the handicaps imposed by the relatively high prices of materials processed and the extraordinary degree of dependence upon imported materials'. Ireland needed to utilise its raw materials towards processing in order to increase jobs and income, and its greatest resources lay in agriculture. And within agriculture, it was the cattle industry, given its dominance, 'that deserves attention as a major source of potential processing activity'.

The authors found the country's dependence on livestock exports to Britain somewhat archaic in the post-war western world. 'The organisation of Ireland's cattle industry is exceptional in the degree to which its product is disposed of through export shipments of live cattle,' they wrote, 'and, consequently, in the meagreness of its meat production from cattle in Ireland relative to the size of its cattle industry.' It tried to uncover an economic explanation for livestock exports, but couldn't find one. It deduced that there was a 14 per cent margin on cattle exports, but that this compared badly 'with even the very low 43 per cent of additional value that was added to material costs at plant by Irish transportable goods manufactures in 1949'. Ireland was exporting cattle with comparatively little by way of jobs or profit to show for it.

Ibec held out a whole range of industries and products, if only Ireland took the decision to process cattle and not just export them. The report as a whole had a deep affect on Seán Lemass, who took to preaching from it. One can see why, as it positively bristles with energy and ideas for an Irish industrial future. As regards Ireland as a producer, rather than a supplier, the report had this to say:

> ... the initial processing alone in Ireland of live cattle worth £20 million would add £3.6 million of processing activity to the Irish economy ... There would be available on the Irish market an additional £3.5 million of hides (468,000 times 60 pounds time 30 pence per pound) for local processing which, since the fellmongery and leather category adds some 41 per cent in net product to the cost of materials, might contribute another £1.4 million of processing activity. This could make a substantial contribution also to Ireland's exchange position since Ireland's leather imports in 1949 (net of leather imports) amounted to £1.3 million. If the additional supply of leather from a domestic source was not of a suitable type to displace imported shoe leathers, it might be used substantially to increase leather manufactures of other types in Ireland. Estimating upon the analogy of Ireland's boot and shoe industry, in which the net product amounts to about 70

> per cent of materials costs, this could increase manufactures based on leather by £2.52 million, (£3.5 for hides and £1.4 for leather processing minus £1.3 imports times 7). Offal value should amount to at least £3 per beast, and that would provide another £1.4 million of raw materials for processing.

It would be another ten years, though, until the enthusiasm for Ireland's potential in Ibec's report would find itself reflected in government policy, but by then industrialisation through direct foreign investment, rather than by the exploitation of Ireland's agricultural and other raw materials, had become the preferred option.

In 1957 the Department of Finance produced a report which outlined what it saw as the structural deficiencies within the Irish economy, as well as possible solutions and a plan of action. It was published with modifications a year later and was called the 'First Programme for Economic Expansion'. As already noted, since the foundation of the Irish Free State in 1922 the dominant export had been livestock, the dominant breed the Shorthorn, and the dominant problem the promotion of both above all other options. 'First Programme', however, had a solution to these economic hurdles: more of the same, but this time with credit. 'A project to increase the cattle population by 300,000, with the emphasis on beef rather than milk production' wrote *The Irish Times*, 'is a feature of the government's five-year plan for economic expansion.'[87] The plan envisaged capital spending of up to £220 million and stated that 'the extra cows necessary if beef output is to be increased should, therefore, be of beef rather than dairy strain', which marked a definite, if belated, move towards specialised breeding, even if its call for 'beef rather than dairy' breeds gave the impression that cattle breeding in Ireland had ever been anything else. The report also stated that while 'the aim will be to secure greater access to Continental markets [our] trade relations with Britain, however, will remain a matter of prime importance and every effort will be made to foster their development'. There were provisions made for the development of a fish-processing industry, subsidies for phosphates for land fertilisation and reclamation, and a guaranteed price for millable wheat. The emphasis of the report was on agriculture – more specifically, cattle exports to Britain. The only contrast with previous economic policy was in the matter of credit. Ireland was to break with the idea of a balanced budget, and commit itself to running a deficit in order to facilitate growth.

The need to eradicate bovine TB in order to retain access to the British market was a major incentive behind the increased investment in cattle. Concurrent with this was the move to entice foreign investment to Ireland. Overall, though, the most significant change in Irish economic policy was in the attitude towards industry and industrial exports. 'While agriculture was our most important industry, and offered by far the greatest scope for expansion,' said Lemass at a meeting in Tramore, Waterford in 1957, 'it was very necessary also to foster the non-agricultural industries; and the only way to do that satisfactorily was by increasing the efficiency of our industrial organisation'.[88] The livestock industry was by no means over, but the day of placing everything on cattle exports to Britain was beginning to come to an end.

3

INDUSTRY

In August 2007, Danny McCoy, director of policy at the Irish Business and Employers' Confederation (Ibec), wrote an article for *The Irish Times* in which he outlined his opinion on the economic future of Ireland. 'Reflection should reassure us that the Irish economy remains in good health,' he said. 'The belief that Ireland's prosperity may be coming to a shuddering end does not stack up but a reality-check is nonetheless warranted.'[1] McCoy noted the decline in construction and the drop-off in consumer spending as evidence that domestic growth would slow in the last quarter of 2007. 'Yet none of these spell disaster for the economy,' he wrote, 'rather, they are signs of a welcome rebalancing of the economy. A rebalancing that we should cheer, not fear.' The main reason why we should not worry, argued McCoy, was exports. 'Ireland is a trading nation,' he said, 'and our prosperity is determined by our ability to sell our goods and services abroad.'

The strong performance of exports in 2006 and the first quarter of 2007 was offered as proof that whatever about the decline in domestic economic activity, a sustained growth in exports should see us right. The past was bright, the future brighter still. Ireland need only look after its exports, and the economy would look after itself. 'This economy is a better bet than anything on offer on St Ledger's Day,' said McCoy.

Twelve months later the Irish banking system was on the verge of collapse, swamped by billions in bad debts. In February 2009, the standardised unemployment rate breached 10 per cent for the first time since 1997. By December of that year, Ireland's national debt stood at €75.9 billion, or 65.6 per cent of GDP.[2] McCoy had gotten one thing right though. While merchandise exports stalled, service exports increased, and by the end of 2009 Ireland was the ninth largest services exporter in the world.[3]

McCoy's article was similar to others written in the months leading up to the 2008 crash, which were variations on the theme that exports will save the day. Yet, what is interesting about McCoy's analysis is not so much the mantra of exports, but the assumption that the exports are *ours*. A similar view was held by others. In February 2007, the economist and former Taoiseach Dr Garret Fitzgerald wrote, in criticism of Irish output, that 'during a period in which the volume of world trade has grown by one-third, *our exports of goods* have remained almost static'.[4] In June of that year the Minister for Enterprise, Trade and Employment, Micheál Martin, spoke in positive terms about how Ireland's two-way trade with China met the need 'for raw materials, parts and components to feed *our own manufacturing facilities*'.[5] In December, the then Minister for Finance, Brian Cowen, highlighted the fact that 'almost 40 per cent of *our* exports are services-based'.[6] Two years later, as Taoiseach, he said in relation to the government's economic strategy that 'as the world economy recovers and demand for *our exports increases*, there will be more people in jobs, and our tax revenues will rise'.[7]

Despite all the words of praise and, indeed, criticism of Irish exports, this sense of ownership was out of step with the facts on the ground. Since the 1970s, the majority of exports emanating from Ireland have been produced by multinationals; in 2008 they accounted for 88 per cent of all merchandise export sales. Yet the amount of people employed by IDA-supported companies in 2008 is only around 7 per cent of total employment.[8] These companies paid €2.8 billion in corporation tax in 2009, and direct expenditure in the Irish economy via payroll costs, Irish materials and services amounted to €19.149 billion. However, total sales amounted to €109.64 billion. Around 80 per cent of the money generated by IDA-supported companies completely bypasses the Irish economy. The profits are repatriated to the country of origin. In 2009, chemical products made up 51 per cent of all merchandise exports from Ireland, the bulk of which were made with imported materials. The chemicals come in via containers, and go out via containers. Irish economic policy has developed exporters, but not exports.

Given such a modest effect on the Irish economy – 7 per cent of total employment and approximately €2.8 billion in corporation tax – why is foreign direct investment constantly put forward as the prime objective of the State's economic policies and strategies? In 2009, employment among IDA-supported companies fell by 10 per cent, yet exports rose by 5.5 per cent.[9] Why is the promotion of such a business model, where the profits from 88 per cent of all exports leave the economy alongside the products, the central task of the three main Irish political parties?

The arrival of foreign capital in the 1950s saw not just the eventual development of export-led multinational industries on Irish shores, but also the expansion of Irish financial and commercial services which acted as intermediaries between the Irish State and these new investments. The acquisition of greenfield sites, the construction of factory and office space, road haulage, banking, and insurance – it was through these areas of commercial activity that indigenous non-agricultural business gained its commanding presence in Irish commercial and political life. The exports of multinationals in Ireland are lauded by politicians and bankers not because it is through these exports that Irish people make a living, but because it is by servicing these exporters that banks and commercial property developers make their profits. This is the key to understanding NAMA. The direct foreign investment which arrived in Ireland from the late 1960s onwards ends up sourcing very little of its raw material from Ireland. What they need they import, and what they produce they export. They are like stones skimming off the top of a pond, developing little of sustained substance in the local economy. But while they are based in Ireland, they need buildings and financial services. And for that, they need builders, accountants, bankers and lawyers. Here we see the structural weaknesses in the Irish economy which allowed something like NAMA to occur.

FROM CATTLE TO MERCHANDISE

The post-war Marshall Aid Plan for Europe set out 'to stabilize finances, liberalize trade, boost production, encourage a consumer society and thwart the extension of communism'.[10] From 1947 to 1957, Ireland received £46.7 million under the scheme. It was the first major foreign investment in Ireland since the foundation of the State, and it came mainly in the form of loans. Of Ireland's total allocation, only £6.1 million consisted of grants.[11] There were reasons for this. The perception in Washington was that Ireland had experienced a 'good' war. It had been neutral and had suffered relatively minor structural damage. Also, the country had large reserves of sterling, which it could use to offset its balance of trade with the USA. However, the Irish government was persistent and in 1949 received its first grant, which was for $3 million. This was given, in the words of Wayne Jackson, head of the State Department's British-Irish desk, in order to 'get the Irish off our backs, financially'.[12] The bulk of Ireland's Marshall Aid allocation was used, not to develop industry, but for land reclamation. Cattle and grazing still had a bind on the economy, but Ireland needed to develop new markets in the USA in order to address its trade deficit, and there was little chance of shipping live exports across the Atlantic. From at least 1949 onwards, 'increasing pressure was placed on the Irish to develop long-term sources of dollar earnings'.[13] The Ibec report of 1952 was part of this process.

Britain's demands that Ireland eradicate bovine TB, as well as the clear signals that it intended to continue to develop its indigenous livestock industry, were essentially the tipping points in pushing government policy towards industrialisation and export diversification. And while the government recognised that these developments had to take place, it was also clear that it did not want to address monetary policy and financial investment practices in the process. The need for indigenous investment, the breaking of the parity link with sterling, the widening of the tax net to include farmers and ranchers, and the establishment of a genuine central bank were all essential in order for the economy to develop, and all were fiercely resisted. Out of this resistance a 'new way' was flagged, which was the expansion of the economy through foreign investment. This became the means of industrialisation for Ireland; one which avoided the need to expand taxes, reform monetary policy, or in any way seriously challenge the status quo.

In January 1956, the Minister for Industry and Commerce, William Norton, undertook a tour of the USA in an effort to secure foreign investment for Ireland. Later that month, the Taoiseach, John A. Costello, said in a speech in Cork that 'it was the desire to increase investment, more particularly in export industries which prompted the government to send [the Minister] on a number of missions abroad to induce foreign capitalists to invest in such industries'.[14] The trip was a cause of some concern in Irish business circles, leading the government to offer reassurances. The Taoiseach told a meeting of the Federation of Irish Manufacturers in February 1956 that 'foreign industrialists … were to be encouraged to start factories here for the production of goods not already produced in Ireland, or which were being produced in insufficient quantity, and also, and perhaps more especially, for the production of goods for export'.[15] In August 1955, Norton had visited West Germany, where he stressed to German officials that 'Ireland's existing trade agreement with Britain allowed large varieties of goods to be imported into Britain from Ireland duty free and that Ireland had similar arrangements with Canada, Australia, New Zealand and South Africa.' 'Germans industrialists,' he said, 'would be able to export to these countries free of tariff if they set up plants in Ireland.'[16]

As with the Taoiseach in 1956, William Norton stressed that 'the object is not to encourage people to come in and compete with existing industries which are supplying the market, but to come in and make commodities which are being imported'. This move towards foreign investment was also pushed by the Organisation for European Economic Co-operation (OEEC), which said in its 1955 report on Ireland and Portugal that 'greater attention might be directed towards encouraging an increase of foreign direct capital investment in Ireland'.[17]

In October 1955, the Irish and American governments signed an agreement which allowed Ireland to take part in the United States Investment Guarantee Programme, which was set up to encourage production and trade by means of American foreign investment abroad. In November, the head of the Irish Development Authority (IDA), Dr James Beddy, said in Bonn, Germany, that Ireland 'was interested in the establishment of any and every industry'. He told a reporter that 'many towns, particularly in the West of Ireland, were willing to supply new industries with free building sites and grant them 33 per cent exemptions from rates for seven years'.[18] At a meeting of the Boston Chamber of Commerce in January 1956, William Norton said that Ireland had 'an intelligent and adaptable labour supply, an advantageous position for international trade, generous tax and import regulations designed to stimulate industry, easy conversion of Irish earnings into dollars, and stable political and economic conditions'. He added that 'capital directly invested may be freely repatriated at any time'.[19] Foreign investment as the path to economic and industrial growth was firmly at the heart not just of Irish government policy, but also of European and American policies as well.

The election of Fianna Fáil to government in 1957 saw a continuity in the pursuit of foreign investment. One of the first undertakings of the new Tánaiste and Minister for Industry and Commerce, Seán Lemass, was to amend the Control of Manufactures Act of 1932, which required Irish industries to be Irish owned. In July 1957 the Tánaiste said:

> Our industrial development has clearly reached the stage when export markets for industrial products must be the main target of future development ... We are approaching the end of the process of developing industry for the purpose of supplying home market needs and if we are to get from industry that increase in output and widening of employment opportunities which the country needs, it will be only by means of securing expansion of business into export markets.[20]

The amendment of the Act had been called for in 1955 by the American Ambassador to Ireland, Mr W.H. Taft, in a speech he made to the Cork Centre of the Association of Certified and Corporate Accountants. He said that the '51 per cent ownership and control law' which meant that Irishmen remained in charge of their own business 'was understandable ... but you are not apt to get capital investment in your own country unless you make concessions to foreigners'.[21]

Yet there seemed little that the Irish government was unwilling to do to encourage foreign capital. In April 1957, the Lord Mayor of Dublin, Councillor Robert Briscoe, went to New York to try to encourage American interest in Ireland. 'In the field of tourism, the fact that I, a Jew, am Lord Mayor of the largest city in a predominantly Catholic country' said Briscoe, 'has persuaded many to come to Ireland who otherwise would have avoided the country.' With regard to investment, at a business luncheon with 'about a dozen of New York's leading international bankers', Briscoe was asked about the legal restrictions on the repatriation in dollars of capital investment in Ireland. 'There were also inquiries about whether Ireland had, or would establish a free port – that is, a port at which goods passing through rather than remaining in the country could be landed free of duty', he said in an interview with *The Irish Times*. 'I explained that such a port was not necessary in Ireland because we permit companies to establish bonded warehouses on their own property for such duty-free merchandise.'[22]

Alongside the move to encourage foreign capital, the government also lifted export restrictions on Irish industries that produced for the home market. In 1958 it published the 'First Programme for Economic Expansion' which placed a primacy on increasing cattle exports and farm incomes. The new road that Ireland would walk was still paved with old assumptions. The expansion of agriculture 'was the key to future employment', said the Minister for Lands, Erskine Hamilton Childers. 'The consumption of meat was likely to rise in the next 20 years,' he said, and 'farmers who sold the greatest weight of beef per acre of land at the lowest cost and of best quality would benefit from this market, and employ thousands of extra people by buying more Irish goods.'[23] The idea that raising a ranchers' income would expand the entire economy was at the heart of Cumann na nGaedheal's 1920s economic policy. Similarly, the idea that grazing, rather than meat processing, would provide jobs for a new Ireland was equally stubborn to the vicissitudes of reality.

The real changes in policy as a result of Whitaker's plan were the measures to increase government borrowing and expenditure, and to allow indigenous Irish industry to export. In 1963 the government issued the 'Second Programme for Economic Expansion'. It stated that 'in the years following 1958 the task of raising productivity was made easier by the existence of under-utilized capacity,' and while 'there was little change in total employment ... output per worker rose by 5 per cent'.[24] This added to a modest increase in Irish GDP, which itself was aided by an increase in demand in the British economy. The government's decision to restart the housing programme helped to lessen unemployment and expand the construction industry. In terms of foreign capital and industrial expansion, however, it is with the signing of the 1965 Free Trade Agreement with Britain that Ireland became a prime site for foreign capital.

Despite the popular perception of Ireland as a closed, backward economy until the arrival of Whitaker and his economic program, the State had always had a relatively open economy. Even in the 1950s, the value of its imports and exports was between 66 and 70 per cent of GDP. The problem was the nature of those exports, and the destination. Ireland exported, but it exported mainly to Britain, and mainly livestock. The gradual rise in exports became a stampede after 1965, however, and by the early 1970s, merchandise exports exceeded livestock exports for the first time in the State's history. The Free Trade Agreement gave Irish-based German and American companies tariff-free access to British markets, and generous tax allowances for expenditures and repatriated profits. The idea that exports needed to be linked to the wider Irish economy in order to help expand that economy was slowly, and methodically, pushed to one side.

The change in the composition of exports reflected a change in the type of employment. There were fewer people working in agriculture and more people in services and industry. But the true growth in employment occurred not so much in export-led industry, which in employment terms remained somewhat modest, but in construction, banking, and administration – the indigenous areas of support for the foreign capital which arrived in droves in the lead-up to, and after the implementation of, the 1965 UK and Ireland Free Trade Agreement. Ireland experienced an export boom, but for the most part the jobs which were created were related to the dynamics of the local economy. The lack of a strong relationship between the new industries and Irish-sourced materials all but guaranteed a cap on industrial jobs growth. The main developments in Irish business as a result of foreign investment, took place in construction and services.

According to the census figures, there were 118,072 new jobs created between 1961 and 1971. These were almost completely absorbed by the loss of 115,772 jobs during the same period. During ten years of economic expansion and foreign investment, there were a total of 2,300 more jobs in 1971 than in 1961. Emigration had slowed during the decade, but had not stopped, and an estimated 135,000 people left the country during this period.[25] This was one third the rate of emigration in the 1950s, but it was not until the early 1970s that Ireland achieved net immigration. As late as 1965, *The Irish Times* reported:

> Gross National Product is up. Farm incomes are up. But what are these when they are set against an emigration rate still as high as 25,000 and an unemployment figure that one week last month was almost 56,000 and was down less than 400 on the same week in 1964?[26]

Irish industrial employment as measured by the 1971 census increased by 35,854, or 20 per cent, on the 1961 figure. This was mostly due to increases in the production of machinery, metal, plastics, chemicals, milk and meat products, and concrete. From 1960 to 1973 the IDA helped 418 establishments to set up business, of which 352 were in operation in June 1973, providing employment for 44,822 people.[27] It paid out £92.765 million in grants during that time, which represents a cost of £2,069 per job created.[28] Overall, 15.8 per cent of manufacturing jobs in 1971 were in grant-aided industries which had been established between 1961 and 1970. The largest increases, though, were in commerce, construction, professional and public service employment, banking and insurance. Growth in these areas accounted for 70 per cent of all new jobs, while manufacturing, the prime objective of government policy, made up the remaining 30 per cent.

The type of manufacturing establishments funded by the IDA were spread across all industries, including clothing, food, chemicals, toys, plastics, and heavy machinery. About 16 per cent of the successful enterprises were in meat, fish, dairy, biscuits and brewing – that is, industries which were based on Irish agricultural produce. The two largest industry groups, clothing/textiles and machinery/metal products, constituted nearly 55 per cent of all IDA-supported businesses, and were heavily reliant on imports for production. The new industries in terms of products and exports were based around chemicals, plastics and pharmaceuticals. These constituted 12.78 per cent of successful IDA-supported businesses, and somewhere around 5,000 jobs, but yet sourced very little of their materials from Ireland and so had little impact on secondary industry, except in the fields of construction and services. Of the 418 establishments which were grant aided during this period, 35 per cent were Irish, 20 per cent British, 18 per cent American, 14 per cent German, and 4 per cent Dutch. The remainder were either joint ventures or from other countries.[29] Despite the relatively high number of Irish ventures, the majority of exports came from foreign-owned companies.

When faced with the criticism that the IDA was 'bringing to Ireland industries using imported materials', the head of the authority, Mr J.J. Walsh, said that 'this was not entirely correct. Over £4 million had been given in grants to fifty projects based on home raw materials, mostly agricultural.' He went on to say that 'among the advantages of foreign investment were the benefits obtained from the research of the big foreign companies and the very high level of managerial expertise'.[30] This became a common response to criticisms levelled against IDA policy. The whole point of encouraging exports was to develop indigenous industry and help correct the balance of payments. Very quickly, within five years, the public stance was that foreign enterprise would develop managerial skills. Mr Walsh told *The Irish Times* in 1966 that 'given competitive costs, expanding international trade and an absence of serious restrictions on foreign investment in Ireland, our industrial growth could be stepped up to reach a situation where we would have full employment and emigration would be voluntary'.[31] The structural problems which came with that approach, however, were quite clear. In 1971, the *New Scientist* wrote that Ireland's 'industrial role is largely one of adding value to imported raw materials'.[32] The chances of anything but short-term growth under such an export model were minor.

By 1980, manufacturing accounted for 243,000 jobs – nearly a quarter of the working population. It was, in the words of *New Scientist*, 'Irish industry's finest hour', but at the same time the sector was still 'employing proportionally fewer people than any other comparable small country at industrial peak'.[33] 'We should have around another 100,000 engaged in industry if we were to have an industrial sector of the relative size of other small countries,' said Pádraig O hUiginn of the National Economic and Social Council in 1987. 'We will be unable to generate employment, growth and higher standards of living unless we develop an indigenous industrial sector comparable with ... other small economies.'[34] No matter how many times this was pointed out, the government and the IDA continued on with its splatter-gun approach to foreign investment, financing multinationals who opened factories of sorts in Ireland, but who had relatively little engagement with the wider economy. Why was such a short-term approach to industrial development able to continue for so long? Why were Irish government policy-makers obsessed with foreign investment regardless of whether that investment enhanced the medium to long-term objectives of sustained economic growth?

The responsibility for Irish merchandise exports had shifted decisively to multinationals, that was certain. However, the responsibility for servicing those multinationals was in the hands of Irish business interests. The State's role, in terms of economic policy, was not only to ensure the smooth interplay between these two dominant interests in Ireland, but to make sure the multinationals kept on coming. Servicing foreign-owned and import-heavy exporters, rather than developing an indigenous export sector, had become the economic and legislative focus of government. Pádraig O hUiginn, in his 1987 review of Irish industrial policy, noted that 'for nearly three decades, politicians of all parties have carried out similar policies of offering grants and tax reliefs to encourage manufacturing companies', with severely limited results for the growth of indigenous manufacture. He called for a review of the generous government grants, and 'suggested spending less on capital grants (worth £400 million a year) and tax relief (£800 million) and more on developing new products and managers' marketing skills to encourage indigenous industry'.[35] O hUiginn didn't seem to realise that the tax reliefs and capital grants were what Ireland's industrial policy was all about.

COMMERCIAL AND INDUSTRIAL PROPERTY

The influx of foreign capital in the late 1950s quickly had an effect on land and property prices. By 1960, there was a significant increase in demand for investment properties, 'particularly those secured by well-situated business premises'.[36] *The Irish Times* reported that 'there is ... a lot of money coming into the country for such properties from Continentals, mostly Germans, who have purchased a considerable amount of city business premises and, in addition, are keenly interested in acquiring good agricultural holdings and residential country properties, particularly near the sea'. The 352 IDA-grant-aided establishments which were operating in Ireland in 1973 occupied a total of 15.191 million square feet of industrial floor space, all of which had been built during the previous decade. It was a boon for Irish construction, alongside the residential property market, and saw employment in the sector increase by 42 per cent. By the end of the 1960s, the largest Irish company quoted on the Stock Exchange was Irish Cement. It was closely followed by Roadstone, which specialised in sand, gravel and quarrying. In 1970, the two companies merged to become Cement-Roadstone Holdings, under the chairmanship of former Taoiseach Seán Lemass. One of the directors was Desmond Traynor.

Whereas the demand for factory and office space was satisfied by the IDA and government incentives, the parallel influx of foreign capital into Ireland gave a huge boost to speculative building, which was a comparatively new phenomenon in Irish commercial property, 'The 1960s witnessed a rising scale of net capital inflows into the Irish economy, marking an expansion of foreign investment in industrial production, property and the national debt.'[37] Commercial property was seen as a safe bet. 'Property in general is accepted by an investor of either private or institutional funds as a first-class security', wrote *The Irish Times* in 1968. 'It has been always a hedge against inflation and it gives a certain status and a feeling of security to the small or individual investor.'[38] An unnamed auctioneer, given full and liberal space in its pages, told *The Irish Times* that 'there is not only £1 million, but several millions waiting to be put into good commercial property. If any of the office blocks was put on the market, it would be bought in a flash.'[39]

The 1960s saw a worldwide move towards intensive property speculation as investment, and Ireland was part of this trend. 'We became aware of the need for urban renewal in Dublin, following the pattern of other countries,' said Montague Kavanagh, managing director of the Irish property investment company, Hardwicke Ltd, in 1968, 'And we felt that were this to happen we, as an Irish company, should participate.'[40] Urban renewal for Dublin in the 1960s essentially meant the destruction of its Georgian heritage and the depopulation of the city area between the canals, to be replaced with office blocks, car parks and hotels – the Holy Trinity of Irish speculative building. And, as always with speculation, especially when government is providing grants and tax incentives to fuel it, there was an assumption that there were clients for the offices and buildings, and that the risk was in who would secure the business – that there was an actual supply and demand dynamic at play. The idea that the office tenants might not be there in the first place, and that government incentives rather than actual potential tenants and purchases might be fuelling the demand, was rarely entertained. 'Dublin, with an estimated 5 million square feet of obsolete or semi-obsolete office space, is a long way off letting saturation-point,' enthused one report, 'and surveyors, consultants, auctioneers and estate agents are confident of the long-term prospects'.[41] Within a year, there were reports of a 'slowdown' in the property market, and by 1974 the Irish commercial property market had recorded its first significant slump.

In 1969, despite all that had been said and written about property development in Dublin, 'only 12 new office buildings have been completed, offered on the market, and successfully let over [the previous] five-year period'. This moderate demand for office space did little to dampen speculation. The newspaper noted that around 1.5 million square feet of office space was planned for the foreseeable future, of which, 467,200 square feet was already under construction.[42] Into this breach came the government, and public money was used to absorb the speculative adventures of private investors. 'It is an acknowledged fact that the government has played a significant role in the office-letting market to date', wrote *The Irish Times*. 'In fact, lettings to the government or semi-state bodies make up roughly half of the new accommodation now occupied. If they withdraw from the market, the effect must be most significant.'[43] Government policy was both fuelling speculation and soaking up the result. It was promoting a phantom, using millions of pounds of public money to do so, almost all of which was ending up in the hands of private speculators, builders and investors. This was the unabashed transfer of public funds to private hands, with rent as the conduit.

The leader of the Labour Party, Brendan Corish, asked the Minister for Finance in 1969 for a breakdown of 'the location, the square-footage, the rent, the rates and the landlord of the individual office lots rented by each Department of State in Dublin and throughout the country'. The Minister replied that while individual rents were subject to commercial confidentiality, the total amount was €387,000 a year, on 207 properties, with an accumulated floor space of approximately 712,011 square feet.[44] The Irish government had spent millions of pounds via capital grants and tax breaks on stimulating commercial property ventures, not so that it could become a landlord, or even an owner-occupier, but a tenant. It did not buy these properties; instead it paid rent for them. The State had somehow decided that its interests were best served by being a lodger in its own country, and paying private landlords handsomely for the privilege. By the early 1980s, the public sector was 'a major source of the economic returns drawn by property interests associated with office development, [and] government and public bodies ... together occupy 60 per cent of the stock of rented space in office developments in Dublin'.[45]

The Fine Gael TD Gerald L'Estrange asked the Minister for Finance in 1969 why it was that his department could not reveal the actual individual property rents the government was paying for the use of these offices and buildings. 'Is there anything to hide?' he asked. 'Are they [the landlords] foreign speculators or members of Taca? What is the particular reason for not giving this House the information?' The Minister replied that he was shocked at the implication of impropriety. 'It is the business of the government, since we are spending the taxpayers' money, to get the best possible value for that money,' he told the Dáil. The confidentiality on rents was put forward 'for no other purpose than that'.[46]

LAND AND SPECULATION

> '... the pawgreasers and the Taca men are running one section of our country.'
>
> *Fintan Coogan, TD, 20 February 1968.*

In early 1962, it was reported that land in County Dublin was selling for up to £800 per statute acre, with farms in big demand; even 'poor land along the coast was selling at very high prices'.[47] Two years previously, the Parliamentary Secretary to the Minister for Justice, Charles J. Haughey, had bought Grangemore House in Raheny, County Dublin. It consisted of forty-five acres, and was sold in 1969 for a reported £204,000.[48] Land speculation, both within the city as well the surrounding green belt, was soon synonymous with the political culture of the 'Lemass era' and the 'Whitaker revolution'.

In February 1967, a group was formed in Dublin which set out to raise funds for the Fianna Fáil party. It called itself Taca, and its main focus was builders, speculators, surveyors, architects and businessmen. The main organiser of Taca was Charles Haughey. Its offices were on Amiens Street, at the same address as Haughey Boland, an accountancy firm run by Haughey and his friend Harry Boland. They were later joined by Desmond Traynor. It was an open secret that Taca was more than a fundraising organisation: it was about access to the corridors of political power. Kevin Boland, who was Minister for Local Government from 1965 to 1970, and responsible for local authority housing, recalled a 1960s Taca meeting where contributors to the Taca fund got to meet Fianna Fáil cabinet ministers, 'We [the cabinet] were all organised by Haughey and sent to different tables around the room. The extraordinary thing about my table was that everybody at it was in some way or other connected with the construction industry.'[49]

Writing in 1972, the journalist Rosita Sweetman summed up Taca in her book *On Our Knees*:

> You may wonder why the Fianna Fáil government doesn't do something about controlling the price of land, the building of houses and general accommodation problems in a city bursting at the seams ... If you're still sceptical, you might take a trip around the newer, posher estates being built on the outskirts of Dublin. The names 'Gallagher', 'McInerny' and 'Silk' will re-occur constantly on the billboards.
>
> Now if you dig a bit deeper you will discover that Mr Matt Gallagher and his brother are two of the biggest building/contractors in Dublin. And they're among the biggest contributors to Taca. And Taca is the fundraising section of the Fianna Fáil party.
>
> Without Taca, Fianna Fáil would go bankrupt in the morning. The eventual outcome of the situation whereby the government party derives a lot of its finances from such organisations as Taca, which in turn derives its finances from the capitalists, the speculators, means the government is in debt to such people.[50]

The level of speculation was such that in January 1971 the then Minister for Local Government, Bobby Molloy, set up a special committee to look into the price of building land. It was headed by Justice John Kenny and it presented its findings three years later, in January 1974. It became known as the Kenny Report, and its recommendations, to help curb the economic and social damages caused by land speculation, have never been implemented. In 2007, the Irish Green Party made the recommendations of the Kenny Report a key part of its election manifesto. This was shelved as soon as the party entered government. In this, the Greens were following Irish political precedent, as every party has made the same promise, and each one has dropped it on entering government. Nothing so became Irish politics and the Kenny Report, it can be said, as the manner of their leaving it to one side.

The Committee on the Price of Building Land was established under the following terms of reference:

> ... to consider, in the interests of the common good, possible measures for controlling the price of land required for housing and other forms of development; ensuring that all or a substantial part of the increase in the value of land attributable to the decisions and operations of public authorities (including, in particular, decisions and operations relating to the provision of sewerage and water schemes by local authorities) shall be secured for the benefit of the community.[51]

The committee found that from 1963 to 1971, the average price of 'serviced land [i.e. undeveloped land with water, sewerage and drainage services near it] in County Dublin increased by 530 per cent. In the same period the consumer price index increased by about 64 percent.' In one example of the type of profit to be made from speculation, the committee highlighted the case of sixty acres of land in Castleknock, County Dublin, which were sold for £67,000 in October 1964. 'In March 1965, the purchaser sold them to a finance company for £160,000 and so made a profit of about 140 per cent in a few months. Planning permission to develop the lands was granted to the finance company on 6 September 1968.' After five pages of similar examples, the committee pointed out that:

> These large increases in the prices of serviced and potential building land would not have taken place if the services (water, sewerage and drainage) had not been or were not intended to be provided by the local authority. If these were not available or were not likely to be provided in the near future, the price of the land would have been that for agricultural land.
>
> Therefore, the provision of the services by the local authority is largely responsible for the difference in price between agricultural land and serviced and potential building land and so, it is said, the community which provided the services has a legitimate claim to all the profit.[52]

This was a crucial point. Land speculators were able to make large profits not because of any improvements they made themselves to the land they had bought, but because of consequent public investment in the necessary infrastructure to turn agricultural land into building land – namely, the provision of water, sewerage, and drainage – all of which was paid for with taxpayers' money. The speculator need only sit and wait until the land was rezoned for development. The committee argued that this practice of 'betterment' of land by local authorities gave the taxpayer rights with regard to the rezoned land – they, after all, had paid for the 'betterment', not the speculators – and that remuneration through capped prices of land or increased taxation on land speculation was justified as a result.

The committee also found that large tracts of land surrounding various cities had been bought up by 'a number of large firms in the building industry'. In Dublin alone, 'they have acquired about 4,000 acres which they will presumably hold until services are provided'. It noted that local authorities had bought a pool of land surrounding the capital in order to release it for development once the price of land became too high. However, this policy was only undertaken after 1966, by which time the majority of speculative purchases had already taken place. In March 1967 the Dublin City and County manager, Mr Macken, wrote a report for the local authorities of Dublin City, County Dublin, and Dún Laoghaire, in which he outlined the problems caused by land speculation:

> The competition for land, even remotely available for development, has been so keen that even the public authorities (in cases where they have reached agreement for the purchase of land at high prices) find that builders and other speculators come in and offer a still higher price and in some cases have succeeded in prevailing upon the owner to sell to them rather than the local authorities.
>
> Even land for which drainage is not available at present has been purchased in the belief that when drainage becomes available the price of land will remain sufficiently high to ensure a profit to the speculator who believes that he will eventually obtain at public expense free main drainage and water facilities.
>
> These speculators feel that once they have bought the land at any price that that must be the minimum price they will get for it.
>
> The result has been that the price of undeveloped land has been inflated entirely out of its real value and the local authorities have had

> to pay exorbitant prices, even for land for the housing of the working classes.[53]

The local authorities were being charged via higher land prices for the improvements they made regarding water, sewerage and drainage – improvements which gave the developed land its speculative price in the first place. The developers did not have to do anything except squat and wait for rezoning to come their way. And for some at least, Taca was the road to rezoning.

The committee's main recommendation was to allow the High Court to designate areas which will:

> … probably be used during the following ten years for the purpose of providing sites for houses or factories or for the purpose of expansion or development and in which the land or a substantial part of it has been or will probably be increased in market price by works carried out by a local authority.

Once a designated area had been established, the local authority would have the right to acquire that land within ten years at its agricultural price 'plus some percentage of that value together with compensation for reasonable costs of removal but without regard to its development potential'.[54] The committee proposed that landowners should be given the price of the land at its current use value, plus 25 per cent. This percentage was, in their opinion, 'a reasonable compromise between the rights of the community and those of the landowners'.[55]

The committee also recommended that the rezoning of land for development purposes by local authorities should not in any way benefit speculators. In a particularly lucid section, it argued that:

> The foundation in principle of this scheme is that the community is entitled to acquire land at existing use value plus some percentage of it when it can be established by evidence that works carried out by the local authority have increased the price of the lands.

> This price however is also increased by the decisions of the planning authorities in their development plans at to the future use of the lands. Zoning may add a considerable amount to the price. *We do not think that an increase in price caused solely by decisions of the planning authority can be classified as betterment* [my emphasis].
>
> Legislation which provided that a local authority could acquire lands at existing use value plus some percentage of it when their price had been increased not by local authority works but by planning decisions only would, in our view, be unjust and probably repugnant to the Constitution.
>
> We therefore do not recommend that the designated area scheme should apply to lands in relation to which the sole cause of the increase in price is the decision of the planning authority as to their future use.

The committee also produced a minority report, which believed that 'open market value must continue to be the basic determinant of the price of land acquired for public purposes'.[56] It was signed by Michael J. Murphy and J.T. O'Meara, both government officials with the Department of Local Government.

The publication of the report in January 1974 was greeted with praise. The Minister for Local Government, Jim Tully, welcomed it. He said that the government agreed with its findings, and that they hoped to have 'the bones of the necessary legislation drawn up by the end of the year'. According to the Minister, 'if they did not stop speculation now they would never be able to stop it, as the problem was getting worse all the time'.[57] The *Irish Times*' journalist and local government correspondent, Frank Filfeather, said that the promised legislation would give 'a tremendous boost to the building of the three satellite towns west of Dublin at Tallaght, Clondalkin and Blanchardstown and the acquiring of property in central Dublin for housing purposes', as well as facilitating 'the construction of the motorways recommended in the £160 million Dublin Transportation Study, the new Liffey bridges and the proposed new rail lines'.[58] In an editorial entitled 'Looking to the Land,' *The Irish Times* warned:

> ... it may be assumed that those vested interests who have been fattening themselves on the status quo will react angrily against the findings of the Kenny Report, and will proceed to lobby with their experienced deviousness; they deserve no compassion and must be blocked off, together with any politicians who are over-sympathetic with their objectives of self-aggrandizement.[59]

The warnings of possible inaction were quite justified. Despite the positive soundings of Minister Tully, the reaction of the government to the Kenny Report was to shelve it. The two main recommendations – that the price of development land should be capped at the price of land plus 25 per cent, and that the act of recategorising land for future development should not be used as a payout for speculators – would have affected not only builders and speculators, but also the various politicians, banks and building societies who themselves profiteered from speculation and rezoning.

The Kenny Report has been cited and praised by every opposition party and sidelined and forgotten by every government since its publication. In February 2007, the then leader of the Irish Green Party, Trevor Sargent, highlighted the fact that his party had 'consistently called for the implementation of measures recommended in the 1973 [*sic*] Kenny Report, often in the face of opposition from Government parties'. He said that the 'persistent foot-dragging' in relation to the report 'has denied people access to homes; it has cost homeowners hundreds of millions of euro; and it has allowed speculators to profit at the expense of house-buyers and communities for decades'.[60] Four months later, the Green Party entered into a coalition government with Fianna Fáil, with a Green TD, John Gormley, as Minister for Local Government, and as such responsible for the implementation of the findings of the Kenny Report. Nothing was done. On 23 August 2010, NAMA reported that it had paid €6.12 billion for loans relating to land purchased for speculative purposes. This amounted to 22.5 per cent of all monies paid out up to that date. The Kenny Report, meanwhile, is out of print and off the agenda.[61]

MINERALS, GAS, AND OIL

In March 1956, the government passed an Act which granted tax exemptions on new mining activity. The previous year, a Canadian company, International Mogul Mines of Canada, had expressed interest in the copper mines of Avoca, County Wicklow, where, according to experts in 1955, there was 'a potential of copper ore valued at about £20 million'.[62] The government had entered into negotiations with 'mining concerns in Sweden and Canada to have the mines developed and operated as a commercial concern'.[63] These were successful, and Avoca was eventually leased to St Patrick's Copper Mines Ltd, a subsidiary of Irish Metal Mining Ltd, which itself was owned by Mogul Mines. At the end of 1955, the Minister for Justice, Mr Everett, told the annual dinner of the Wicklow Chamber of Commerce that the government hoped that soon up to 500 men would be employed at the mines. Everett said:

> No Irish industrialist need be in the least bit worried that his interests will be in any way impaired by foreign industrialists setting up here ... [The industrialists'] sole reason for coming here is that the kind of industry will be established for the manufacture and processing of articles which are not yet made here, and which we need, not only for ourselves, but for export as well.[64]

Mr V.B. Bjorkman, assistant manager of the St Patrick's Mines, Avoca, told the assembled guests that 'they – the Canadian experts – were satisfied that about eight million tons of ore were readily available [and that] full production was about 18 months away'.[65]

The 1956 Act, 'designed to compensate for high costs and the uncertainty of exploring for unproven resources',[66] was almost certainly written with the Canadians and Avoca in mind. In a speech given to the Dáil during the debates on the Mining Act, Seán Lemass, then in opposition, said that 'every deputy knows that this Bill has resulted from a bargain with one group in relation to a particular undertaking ... in so far as anyone outside the government service was consulted about this Bill, it was the Canadian groups interested in Avoca'.[67]

Northgate Exploration and Development Ltd of Toronto quickly followed Mogul to Ireland. In 1961, Northgate discovered large deposits of lead, silver and zinc at Tynagh, County Galway. The resulting increase in exploration in the wake of Tynagh resulted in significant finds, including the 80 million ton zinc-lead deposit outside Navan, County Meath, and the opening of five new metal mines.[68] By 1970, Tynagh was the largest producing lead mine in Europe. During the first five years of operation in Ireland (1965-70), Northgate recorded a net profit of $36,628,000 Canadian dollars. It also had control of the copper/silver/mercury mine at Gortdrum near Tipperary town; a 70 per cent direct interest in the Smelter Corporation of Ireland; a 10 per cent interest in the Anglo United Development Corporation, and a 10 per cent interest in Avoca Mines Ltd.[69] According to Kevin C. Kearns, 'Irish mining developments during this period are properly acclaimed largely as an achievement of Canadian expertise and enterprise.'[70] And it was Canada that was the net recipient of the value of these mineral deposits.

The benefit of this mining activity to the Irish exchequer was minimal, due to the tax breaks and the fact that the minerals were shipped directly out of Ireland and processed overseas. In terms of employment, from 1961 to 1971 the number of mining and quarry jobs in the State actually decreased by 149, although the 1971 figure was an increase of 564 on 1966 employment levels. The financial benefits of mining in Ireland were further eroded by the 1967 Finance Act, which brought changes in the law so that no tax was due on profits earned for the first twenty years of any mining operations begun prior to 1986. As most mines were reckoned to have an operating life of less than twenty years, this meant that the Canadian companies had been given Ireland's natural mineral resources, effectively, for free.

The tax changes were announced by the Minister for Finance, Charles Haughey, in the Dáil in April 1967:

> The achievements of [the mining] sector have been impressive and have contributed very satisfactorily to employment and export earnings … I am told that a great future expansion in exploration and

> development is possible and that additional tax incentives can generate a large volume of outside investment. I have accepted this argument.[71]

By way of explanation as to the tax holiday, he said:

> Many different types of allowances and incentives have been suggested but, instead of bringing in rather complicated new provisions, I have come down in favour of the simple decision to substitute for the existing reliefs a twenty-year period of complete exemption. I believe that Ireland now offers a very favourable sphere of activity to mining organisations and I hope they will not be slow to take advantage of this.

In his analysis of the Irish mining industry, Kevin C. Kearns said that 'in light of the successes resulting from the 1956 incentives many questioned the need and justification for augmenting the State's generosity to such a degree. There was, as one observer averred, "some mystery" surrounding the new concession.'[72] The tax holiday was eventually rolled back in the wake of the Navan find.

On 31 January 1968, the soils division of An Foras Taluntais completed a survey of east central Ireland which unearthed evidence of potentially significant quantities of lead/zinc/copper mineralisation in County Meath and north County Dublin. News of the discovery was presented in a paper to the Royal Irish Academy in June of that year, but the findings were not released until 30 June 1969.[73] On 25 July 1970, the Canadian-owned Tara Exploration and Development Company applied for a prospecting licence for an area of 18 square miles in County Meath; five months later the company's shares almost doubled in price when it confirmed that it had 'encountered zinc and lead mineralisation from 296 feet to 354 feet in the first drill hole in a new prospect' on the farm of Mr Patrick Wright at Nevinstown, about a mile from Navan.[74] It was soon obvious that this was a special find, and on 30 August 1971, the President of Tara Exploration, Michael McCarthy, announced that:

> ... the Navan ore body has clearly demonstrated its potential as a major world source of zinc and even at this stage of the development

> programme is can be said that the arrival of the Navan mine on stream will rank it as the largest zinc producer in Europe and among the four largest in the world.[75]

Contemporary analysis put the value of the Navan deposits at around £2 billion.

The news of the size and wealth of the find led to protests and public criticism of the terms of the 1967 Act. At a meeting of the Law Society in Trinity College in 1974, Mr David Giles of the Resources Protection Campaign pointed out that under existing law, all minerals in the State were owned by the State:

> There is no reason why the State should not retain its ownership of this fantastic potential for economic and social development and, while compensating the mining company for what it has already spent, use the profits from Navan to develop a smelter, metallurgical industries and humane system of social services.[76]

The opening of the mine was further complicated by counter-claims on the mining rights for the area. Eventually, in 1974, the Irish State took a 49 per cent interest in the mine, and agreed to accept royalties on the profits, not on the ore itself. The result was that Tara was able to extract million of pounds worth of ore from Navan and not have to pay a penny in royalties to the Irish government, who were fobbed off with profit warnings. In 1987, the Department of Energy requested royalties of £4.1 million on profits of £107 million.[77] This was rejected by the company and in 1989 the State sold its remaining share to the Finnish state-owned mining company Outkumpu for €50 million. One third of this amount was to cover back payments in royalties. Tara Mines was now fully nationalised, but it was Finland, not Ireland, that owned it.

Over 70 million tonnes of ore was extracted from Navan during the period 1977 to 2008. The current owners are New Boliden, a Swedish mining and smelting company. Annual ore production at Navan stands at 2.7 million tonnes, with yields of 200,000 tonnes of zinc metal and 40,000 tonnes of lead metal contained in concentrates. These are shipped out to either Boliden's smelters in Norway and Sweden or to other smelters in Europe.[78] There is no smelting facility in Navan, nor has there ever been one. The raw material was extracted and exported for processing, same as the cattle of Meath in 1968, the year the minerals were first discovered.

In 1989, the then leader of the Irish Workers' Party, Tomás MacGiolla, said:

> ... because of loopholes in the mining lease granted by the [1973-77] coalition government, Tara Mines has not paid a penny in royalties in almost 13 years of operation, despite the huge level of ore produced. The failure to ensure that a smelter was built has meant that huge quantities of raw ore have been exported and used to create jobs abroad, rather than here in Ireland.[79]

The servicing of exporters, rather than the production of exports: this was Ireland's way of utilising its natural resources.

'WE HAVE A LITTLE GAS, NOT VERY MUCH'[80]

Three Americans arrived in Dublin in March 1958 in order to set up an oil exploration business. They called it the Madonna Oil Company and, having hired the prominent Dublin legal advisors Arthur Cox & Co. of St Stephen's Green, they made contact with the Department of Industry and Commerce and its Minister, Seán Lemass, with a view to obtaining a licence to explore for oil and gas. 'When progress proved to be satisfactory, the company approached the Ambassador Oil corporation of Texas, with a view to selling the lease already negotiated.'[81] Lemass wanted a change of name before he would issue a licence, and in December the company became Ambassador Irish Oil Ltd. One month later, on 31 January 1959, it was granted exclusive oil and gas rights over 'the whole of Ireland, including the seabed and subsoil which lie beneath the territorial waters and the high seas under the control and jurisdiction of the Government of Ireland at this time or in the future, but not including the Six Counties'.[82] It was later revealed that Ambassador paid just £500 for these rights. Two years later, a two-thirds share in the lease was sold for £230,000.[83] In 1969 the Irish government renegotiated the 1959 lease with its then owners, Marathon Oil, who in 1965 had taken over Ambassador's activities in Ireland. The company was allowed to keep one third of Ireland's oil and gas rights, and got to choose which areas it kept and which it gave back. It kept the southern box, and in 1973 Marathon Oil confirmed that it had found commercially viable quantities of natural gas off the Old Head of Kinsale, County Cork. Having secured the rights for less than a quarter of a million pounds, Marathon Oil set about selling the gas back to Ireland at a cost which was estimated in 1977 to be £700 million.[84]

The renegotiation of oil and gas rights lead to a fresh round of speculation. Between April 1971 and January 1974, the Irish government issued fifty-nine non-exclusive petroleum prospecting licences, which allowed the holder to search for petroleum and natural gas on the continental shelf surrounding the Republic.[85] Each licence cost £610, which consisted of a £10 application fee, a £100 consideration fee, and a £500 yearly rental fee. Of the sixty-one companies which held the licences in 1974, only eight were Irish. The vast majority of the survey and exploration work, however, was undertaken by four companies who were themselves licence holders. These were: Western Geophysical; Delta Exploration; Continental Oil, and CCG. They worked on a subcontracting basis and sold the results of their surveys to the licence holders, who did not need to have any experience in oil and gas exploration in order to attain a licence. They merely needed to be 'competent persons' and have the necessary funds to 'purchase the technical competence' needed for exploration.[86] Nor did the government require of the licence holders that they actually explored for oil and gas. 'It was possible' wrote Paul Tansey in 1974, 'to spend £610 on acquiring a licence, undertake no expensive exploration work and hope that the non-exclusive licence will provide a passport to securing an exclusive licence'.[87]

The price of the licence was highlighted by Dr Seán O'Connell, a lecturer in Edinburgh University, at a public lecture in Monaghan in April 1974:

> It is maddening to see Britain selling off oil-blocks for exploration at figures of £1¼ million plus while one oil company held more than 100 such blocks belonging to Ireland. And it was almost ridiculous for a company which had got oil concessions from the Irish government to sell them to other companies.

He told the audience that 'the concessions given to the Marathon Oil Company were being constantly referred to in trade and scientific magazines as amazing, exceptional, and so on'.[88] In 2008, when Marathon Oil was sold to the Star Energy Group for $180 million, it had 100 per cent control of the Kinsale Head, South West Kinsale and the Ballycotton gas fields; 86.5 per cent interest in the Seven Heads field; and a 100 per cent interest in the company's gas-storage business. Net production from these fields was approximately 36 million cubic feet of natural gas per day. The total net proven reserves of gas was 62 billion cubic feet.[89] It had sixty-one employees and paid no royalties. Those employees paid more tax in Ireland than Marathon.

In 1977, Una Claffey of the Resources Protection Group pointed out in an opinion piece for *The Irish Times* that the terms and conditions of the non-exclusive licences saw some Irish businessmen 'set up front companies to give the impression of Irish involvement. [Then] without risking capital or having to prove technological expertise they carved a niche for themselves so that when it came time to allocate [exclusive] licences they were there to the fore.'[90] This approach was a variation on the property speculation of the 1960s and '70s: the purchase of large tracts of farmland surrounding Dublin and other cities which were then parked until government developmental policies regarding housing took effect and land ownership transformed into significant payouts. Speculation on land, oil, gas and mineral rights, rather than investment in actual economic activity, was one strand of the *modus operandi* of the modern Irish businessman – at least, those businessmen who had the ear of government policy makers. The position of the Irish businessman as an interface between foreign capital and the Irish State was the other. In 1967 it was announced that Gulf Oil Terminal (Ireland) Ltd were to build an oil terminal at Whiddy Island in Bantry Bay, County

Cork. The story of that terminal, the relationship between its owners, the government and the local population, in many ways came to typify the dynamics of the Whitaker revolution and the relentless pursuit of exporters over exports.

'GOD GAVE US BANTRY AND WE GAVE IT TO GULF OIL'[91]

On 6 May 1969, the Taoiseach Jack Lynch unveiled a statue of St Brendan the Navigator, 'frozen forever in beaten and brazed copper', in Wolf Tone Square, Bantry, County Cork, as part of the official opening of the Gulf Oil terminal at Whiddy Island. 'Now that the profitability and feasibility of such projects as this has been so satisfactorily demonstrated by Gulf,' said Lynch, 'it is the government's hope that this will encourage others to look at the natural advantages available for bulk trans-shipment not only at Bantry, but at other locations around our coast.'[92] The Taoiseach said that the government 'would be very pleased to assist industrialists concerned with industries such as petro-chemicals and refining and those who may be interested in the well-endowed facilities and advantages which such places as Bantry and Shannon Estuary have to offer, to make a full assessment of these facilities.' The P&Q liner *Orsova* later brought guests on a short trip around the coast. The journalist Karl Jones was on board. He observed a Gulf Oil executive leaning over the ship's rails and heard him say, 'Heck, why do some people think there's a company plot to turn this into a sludge tank. It is the loveliest bay in the world, and we aim to keep it that way.'

The crude oil terminal was situated on 350 acres which were purchased from local people on the island at a cost of £120,000, or just over £342 per acre.[93] There was no harbour authority for Bantry Bay and the county council's jurisdiction ended at the quays of Bantry itself. This meant that Gulf Oil did not have to pay any harbour or tonnage duties (which were estimated at £250,000 a year, had they been in place), nor was it answerable to any local authority.[94] The company planned to construct six tankers of 300,000 tons each – at that time the largest ships in the world. The move towards supertankers was to cut back on transport costs. However, these vessels were too big for European ports. Gulf Oil needed a storage facility which could accommodate the larger tankers, and from which smaller tankers could then transport the crude oil to the company's refineries in Europe. Hence the need for Bantry Bay and Whiddy Island. It was a short-term solution to Gulf Oil's transportation problems; Whiddy Island was viable until such time as European ports were able to accommodate the new supertankers, or an alternative arrangement was met. 'When Gulf identified Bantry as the ideal location in Europe for a depot it was, for many observers and critics of the oil industry, a cynical short-term route to higher profits,' wrote Robert Allen and Tara Jones in 1990. 'The Whiddy Island terminal would be expendable; therefore it would have to pay for itself as quickly as possible.'[95]

The main suppliers of crude oil to the terminal were Kuwait and Nigeria. The senior vice-president of Gulf Oil, Dr Jerry McAfee, said at a press conference in Dublin in April 1966 that the company had set three criteria in its search for a suitable site for its new terminal. It 'had to be built alongside very deep water offering a draft of more than 80 feet. It had to be fairly near the company's European refineries and had to be suitable for operation seven days a week and 365 days a year.'[96] Bantry Bay and Whiddy Island met all these requirements. Not only that, as the Minister for Transport and Power, Erskine Childers, pointed out, Whiddy Island was 'virtually the only location near the company's European oil refinery in a sheltered bay with sufficient draft of water to ensure all-the-year-round operation of the huge tankers which will bring the oil 11,000 miles around the Cape of Good Hope from Kuwait'.[97] And at £350 an acre, no harbour fees, and no interference from local authorities, it represented an unbelievable bargain. With Bantry Bay the Irish government held all the cards, and it had folded.

From the outset there were concerns about the environmental impact and safety of the terminal. These were brought into focus when, in March 1967, a supertanker off the coast of Britain, the *Torrey Canyon*, went aground on Seven Stones Rocks, 8 miles north of the Scilly Isles, just south of Cornwall. It was carrying around 117,000 tons of Kuwaiti crude oil, the bulk of which spilt into the sea, damaging nearly 200 miles of the coastlines of Britain and France. The clean-up operation was a disaster in itself, due to the type of chemicals used and counter-productive procedures such as burying the oil under beach sand and bombing the wreck from the air. The total cost of the damage caused by the spill was put at £2.9 million.[98] In April 1967, at the unveiling of the plans for the Whiddy Island terminal, Minister Childers said that 'the Torrey Canyon episode had been a timely reminder of the ever-growing need for greater vigilance'.[99] However, as the Irish State had given Gulf Oil effective control of Whiddy Island and Bantry Bay, the need for vigilance had no statutory backing. Gulf Oil could do as it pleased and, not surprisingly, that is what it did.

In February 1968, a deputation from Cork County Council met with the Minister for Transport and Power, Mr Patrick Lalor, in an attempt to have the government set up a port authority for Bantry Bay. They voiced their concerns that Gulf Oil had a 'virtual monopoly' which 'might tend to dissuade other companies who might otherwise investigate the possibilities of using the bay'. The deputation cited the examples of Rotterdam Europort and Milford Haven, which were able to develop off-shoot industries on the back of their respective terminals such as oil refining, petro-chemicals, plastics and fertilizers. 'A Harbour authority was needed to promote such a development as it could sell Bantry Bay to world industry,' they said.[100] The Minister, in turn, politely received and quietly dismissed the concerns of the councillors. Within seven months the first tankers arrived at the terminal, which provided direct employment for around eighty-six men. 'When the Whiddy Terminal is fully operational,' wrote *The Irish Times*, 'it will be run by three teams of twelve experienced oilmen and a group of twelve men will be employed on maintenance. A further twenty-four men will be employed on tugs, fourteen will be on standby.'[101] It was reckoned that around twenty men would be employed in ancillary industry. With just over a hundred jobs as a result of the terminal, and with no actual revenue from the terminal itself, the boon to Bantry came first of all through the construction of the terminal, and there afterwards from the wages of the employees.

During the eighteen months of its construction, the Whiddy Island project employed nearly 1,000 people, and contributed an average of £30,000 a week to Bantry's economy, making the town for that period one of the most prosperous of its size in Ireland. 'Unemployment has virtually ceased to be a problem,' wrote the journalist Dick Walsh, 'emigration has been cut, emigrants who had been away for years have come home; shops, pubs and hotels have been opened or restored.'[102] However, the locals were a lot less sanguine about the prospects offered by the terminal. 'There'll be a lot of unemployment when the construction is finished,' said one of the locals to Walsh. 'People here are keeping their fingers crossed that something else will come about.'

A pattern was forming, one that would repeat itself over the next forty years. The initial boom in construction and ancillary services caused by the arrival of Gulf Oil was followed by relatively low levels of direct and indirect employment, with equally low rates of taxation and local rate payments due from the company, which left wages, rather than secondary industry, the main contributor to the local economy. At the same time the social, economic and environmental impact of such an industrial policy helped to undermine efforts to develop indigenous industry based on the resources of the State. With regard to Whiddy Island, this was seen in the treatment of the local fishermen by Gulf Oil, and the numerous setbacks to the attempts to expand Bantry Bay's shellfish and herring industry – one that, at its height, employed more men than the terminal.

From 1968 to 1979 there were thirty-three oil spills recorded at Bantry. On 21 October 1974 over 650,000 gallons of oil were pumped into the bay after a 16-inch valve was left open for thirty minutes by a seaman on the tanker *Universe Leader*, which was loading a cargo of Persian oil for a refinery in Spain. It was, up to then, the largest ever spillage recorded by Gulf Oil, and the company waited eight days until making the story public. The terminal's stock of 20,000 gallons of dispersant was used up after four days, and one week after the spill the company said that an estimated 325,000 gallons of oil remained in the bay. The disaster led to an immediate review of procedure and thirteen new precautions were put in place to ensure that this type of accident would not happen again. 'We are going through all other procedures asking ourselves is there some way some particularly incompetent or malicious person could circumvent something or cause something to happen,' said Mr Herbert J. Goodman, chairman of Gulf Oil's trading company. 'We are going to revise our system to make that impossible.'[103] The company had announced in 1972 that in the absence of a harbour authority it was required by law to ensure safety and pollution control in the bay. It had done so in order to curtail the fishing rights of local trawlermen, but when faced with the damage of the *Leader* spillage, it found itself amenable to outside agencies. 'We will welcome any help from a government authority to help us to do our job better,' said Goodman, 'and to look over our shoulders to ensure that we are doing what we are supposed to do.'[104]

On 10 January 1975, two months after the *Universe Leader* incident, a tugboat collided with the 210,000 ton *Afran Zodiac* while the tanker was being prepared for open sea. One of the *Afran*'s side plates was fractured, releasing 115,230 gallons of heavy fuel oil into the bay. The Minister for Transport and Power, Peter Barry, immediately announced his intention to press ahead 'with all speed to form a harbour authority or conservancy board for Bantry Bay'.[105] It was finally established in October 1976. Just over two years later, on the morning of 8 January 1979, the terminal suffered its greatest disaster when the oil tanker *Betelgeuse* caught fire and exploded, with the loss of fifty lives. The salvage operation was delayed due to the toxic fumes which surrounded the wreckage. Over one million gallons of oil was subsequently released into the bay.

It was soon revealed that the much-heralded Harbour Authority had no power to enforce safety regulation in the bay, as the necessary legislation was never fully put in place by the government, despite having been passed by the Dáil. 'Only three sections of the [1976 Harbours Act] have been implemented,' wrote Frank McDonald in *The Irish Times*. 'These provisions named the members of the board, gave them power to borrow money and authority to appoint officers. But the other sections, giving the board power to charge rates for the use of the bay, enforce safety and develop the area were never implemented.'[106] Gulf Oil had been allowed to continue its self-regulation with regard to Bantry Bay, despite the oil spillages and safety concerns; it had been allowed to continue to use the bay essentially for free, and it did had done so with the blessing of successive Irish governments who had used the parliamentary authority of the Dáil as cover. The subsequent tribunal into the disaster found the

Betelgeuse's owners, the French company Total SA, as mainly responsible for the explosion, as the 'seriously weakened hull was the result of conscious and deliberate decisions taken at different times by the management of Total'.[107] The terminal, which was seriously damaged in the explosion, was not repaired, and in 1986 it was taken over by the State.

In his seminal book on Bantry Bay and the Gulf Oil terminal, *The Ruling Trinity: A Community Study of Church, State and Business in Ireland*, the Australian anthropologist Chris Eipper found direct parallels between the societal power relations which surrounded the terminal and the way that Irish society itself functioned and operated. Speaking of Bantry in the 1960s and '70s, he observed that:

> In order to compete with other countries and other areas in Ireland [the local business and community leaders] had to 'sell the area' to industry in any way they could. It was better, they said, and to the benefit of the whole town, to have low wages than no wages. It would seem that to these people the future could not be compromised, the plight of West Cork justified their turning the whole community into a commodity to be purchased by incoming industrialists at their own price.
>
> It becomes clear that among the business influentials, at least, the ideology of economic development was in practice motivated by a concern with creating a favourable climate than in providing local employment as such, with guaranteeing the profits of business more than the income, living standards or welfare of the community as a whole. This is not to imply that their concern for the good of the town, the jobless and the poor, was anything but genuine and deeply felt. In fact they believed that their way was the *only* way the community's welfare could be guaranteed and jobs created. But however they may have construed their actions to themselves, and however much others may have benefited from what they did, Bantry's capitalists badly needed to consolidate and augment the foundations of the local economy and the profit-making potential of their businesses. By successfully marshalling government, religious and popular support for their interests under the banner of development, they were able, in classic fashion, to present their specific interests as general ones.[108]

The Whiddy Island terminal is probably the most extreme example of a multinational which entered and exited Ireland with all but the tiniest of imprints on the wider economy. The motifs which were used across the State to justify tax incentives and capital expenditure on foreign investment, however, were all there: low wages are better than no wages; modest jobs are better than none; guarantee the profits and the benefits will trickle down; either way, there is no alternative. Indeed, successive Irish governments embraced each and every one of these assumptions about Irish economic life. Even when they were presented with alternative strategies and achievable goals, they simply offered to believe there were none, finding comfort in the realities of their assumptions, rather than in the reality which embraced them.

THE TELESIS REPORT

> 'It could be argued that our incentives are too generous.'[109]

In July 1980, the American consultancy firm Telesis Incorporated was commissioned by the National Economic and Social Council (NESC) to undertake a review of Ireland's industrial strategy. The objective was 'to ensure that the Irish government's industrial policy is appropriate to the creation of an internationally competitive industrial base in Ireland which will support increased employment and higher living standards'.[110] It was part of a four-stage review which was flagged by Taoiseach Charles Haughey at the Fianna Fáil Ard Fheis in February 1980. 'While our economic circumstances and general economic environment have changed over the past twenty years,' he told his party, 'the basic elements of our industrial strategy have remained almost unchanged.' He said that 'present policies have served us well, but we clearly need a comprehensive review of them in the light of the circumstances today'.[111] The chairman of the NESC, Dr Noel Whelan, told *The Irish Times* that the review 'will be a fundamental, constructively critical review of existing policies', and that the extent of foreign-owned industry would be among the major areas of examination.[112]

Telesis began its review in September 1980 and finished in March 1981. Over the previous thirty years, Ireland had been engaged in a huge effort to industrialise, and had chosen foreign investment as the main impetus and stimulus for growth – a policy that Telesis saw as modestly successful. GNP had almost tripled, for example, and living standards had risen. At the same time, it wrote, 'the income gap between [Ireland] and most other industrialised countries has seriously widened over the past twenty years; the economy has become increasingly dependent on foreign corporations for its industrial jobs; the net trade balance has deteriorated [and] the cost of State aids to industry has risen rapidly'.[113] The key finding of the Telesis Report was that in order for incomes to rise, there had to be an expansion of export-led industry that was indigenous to Ireland. The reason for this was that 'successful indigenously owned industry is, in the long run, essential for a high-income country. No country has successfully achieved high incomes without a strong base of indigenously owned resource or manufacturing companies in traded businesses.'[114] Ireland needed to expand its traded sectors – i.e. its exports – but in order to have sustainable economic growth those exports needed to be Irish made and Irish sourced.

Irish manufacture underwent a significant change in the 1970s. From 1973 to 1980, over 10,000 jobs were lost in the textiles, clothing and footwear sectors. These were offset by gains of around 12,000 in metals and engineering, food, cement and glass, and printing and packaging. And while these structural changes in manufacture 'might be interpreted as showing the successful replacement of employment in the "old" protected sectors by a generation of companies in new growth sectors' – that is, the replacement of low-wage protected industries with modern industrial engineering – the reality was somewhat different. Telesis found that in terms of indigenous manufacture, 'most traded [or export-orientated] industries have fallen from their 1973 employment levels, with some noticeable exceptions in glassware and agricultural machinery'. It went on to say that 'almost all non-traded [or domestic-orientated] industries ... have enjoyed net employment increases, e.g. packaging, cement and metal fabrication'.[115] Overall, 'the indigenous sector (defined as companies owned in majority by Irish interests) represented two-thirds of manufacturing in 1980, down from three-quarters in 1973, [while] employment in indigenous manufacturing industry grew by only 2,000'.[116] Ireland's indigenous industrial sector in the 1970s had actually moved away from export-orientated employment and towards domestic-orientated employment, with the housing and office construction sectors the dominant components. And as Telesis noted, 'growth generated by the development of non-traded opportunities can only provide a limited source of income due to the size limitation of domestic demand'.[117]

The mantra of every party in government since the 1950s had been that exports were the key to Ireland's prosperity. However, the development of exports and export markets came a very distant second to government policy of enticing exporters to the country, with the resultant need for construction on greenfield sites a powerful boost to the domestic building industry. There were 1,262 new Irish companies formed between 1973 and 1980, with a total employment figure in 1980 of 21,850. 'Most of this growth has been in non-traded businesses,' reported Telesis, 'stimulated by plant construction, agricultural investments and infrastructure expenditure.'[118] The divorce of indigenous industrial growth from the export sector was underlined by Telesis when it found that 'few of the newly created [Irish] businesses serve the sub-supply needs of the foreign firms in Ireland'. In fact, only '8 per cent of the components and sub-assemblies used by the largest foreign sector, engineering, were sourced in Ireland in 1976'.[119] This was a serious structural problem, one that was not entirely down to the kind of multinational operations which had come to Ireland. Overseas companies which were interviewed by Telesis 'frequently complained of difficulties in sourcing products in Ireland, either because of poor quality or lack of cost competitiveness'. Manufacturing companies were importing 'precision iron castings and precision moulded plastic parts due to the shortage of high-quality producers in Ireland'.[120] Meanwhile the government gave tax incentives and grants for housing and office construction, and gave away mineral, oil and gas rights with little or no concern for the working dynamics of the wider economy. The need to build had become a much more important part of government policy than the need to export.

The Telesis Report highlighted the problems with such an approach, and offered viable solutions to help the Irish economy grow on a solid, sustainable, level. And just like the Ibec Report of 1951, and Kenny Report of 1974, the findings and suggestions offered by Telesis were greeted with fanfare and followed with silence. The next innovation in Irish economic policy would not arrive until 1987, when the government decided to extend the country's corporation tax benefits to the financial sector. The era of the Irish Financial Services Sector was about to begin.

4

FINANCE

There is a continuous tension between banks and businesses over the value of money. Banks make their money through credit; businesses through trade. For banks, money is a product; for businesses, money is a lubricant. It fuels transactions, enabling products to move from seller to buyer, and it is through this activity that businesses make money and, hopefully, profit. For banks, it is a different process. Money is the product. There are internal contradictions here, integral to money itself. Banks and businesses both need each other to survive, but there is a constant tension present as both use money in different ways and for different and incompatible reasons. These tensions between business and banks, between how and why they use money, have never been resolved. The fault lines lie within the system itself.

In 1927, the Irish Free State decided to hand over monetary policy to the banks, who decided, not surprisingly, that the future of Ireland lay with a strong, value-laden, currency. Yet, this strength would not be drawn from the economic dynamics of the State, but from the Irish pound's link with sterling at parity. The government had the option to link the punt to sterling in a way that would have allowed the punt to rise or fall in value in accordance with the realities of the economy, but it did not take it. The maintenance of the parity link with sterling was kept in place regardless of the cost to the wider economy. Each time sterling devalued – such as in 1931, 1939, 1949 and 1967 – the Irish punt had to follow, with significant consequences for the State's economy. There was no central bank until 1943, and even then it declined to use the powers associated with such an institution – namely the management of the national currency. Ireland did not have an independent currency until 1979, when the country joined the European Monetary System (EMS), some fifty-seven years after independence and while sitting on a credit bubble. The parity link played no small part in the decades of poverty and emigration which were inflicted on the majority of the population.

The effect of having an economy which lacked an industrial export base, as was the case with Ireland for much of its existence, was that it gave the banks free reign to dictate monetary policy. The normal tension between banks and industry over the value and function of money was weak – so weak, in fact, that the value of the Irish pound was set at such a disproportionately high rate that it became a significant hurdle in the development of indigenous Irish industry. The move to import foreign industry to Ireland in the 1950s was influenced in part by monetary policy. The alternative – affordable credit to boost indigenous growth but a weaker Irish pound – was strenuously opposed by both Irish banks and the Department of Finance.

By the mid-1980s job growth by way of FDI had stalled. The next idea was to extend Ireland's corporation tax rate to financial businesses. This was given a boost in 1987 when the leader of the opposition, Charles Haughey, announced a proposal to establish a low-tax zone for the international financial services in Ireland. The plan was to create a designated area within the State where qualifying companies would be able 'to undertake any business in the financial services area they choose and subject to new legislation specifically passed for the centre'.[1] It would lead, he said, to 7,500 jobs over a five-year period. In the election of that year, Haughey was returned as Taoiseach and one of his first acts was to establish a committee to offer advice on the financial services centre. By the end of the year the Dublin docklands area the Irish Financial Services Centre, or IFSC, was born.

From the start, the IFSC courted controversy. Although it was envisaged as an aid to foreign investment and job growth, one of the first occupants was Allied Irish Banks (AIB). The resources given to the project were completely out of proportion to the jobs it created.

In terms of the development and dynamics of the Irish economy, however, the IFSC was not an exception. It arose from the way Irish business operated, from the lopsided attention given to the facilitation of foreign investment, be it via tax breaks or simply handing over the rights to the State's oil, gas and minerals. The sectors which benefited from the park – construction, rentiers, the financial sector, accounting and legal services – were the sectors which had benefited from industrial policy since the 1950s. Similarly, the ability of the banking sector to direct economic policy according to its needs, rather than the needs of the economy, did not arise overnight. Once again, the roots run deep.

THE FIRST BANKING COMMISSION

On 3 February 1926, the Minister for Finance, Ernest Blythe, announced to the Dáil the establishment of a commission to study the situation of banking in the Irish Free State. The terms of reference, as outlined by the Minister, stated that it was 'to consider and to report to the Minister for Finance what changes, if any, in the law relative to banking and note issue are necessary or desirable, regard being had to the altered circumstances arising from the establishment of Saorstát Éireann'.[2]

Political independence had not led to monetary independence from Britain, and although Irish banks issued their own notes, they were treated and accepted as sterling by both businesses and the public. The value of money in the Free State was dependent on the strengths and weaknesses of what was now a foreign currency. Not only that, the majority of deposits in Irish banks were held in Britain, as they had been prior to independence. This gave rise to serious issues regarding the issuing of credit and the financial tools the State had at its disposal in order to develop the economy. The government also needed to regulate the supply of legal tender within its jurisdiction, and it was under these concerns that the commission was formed.

The commission was top-heavy with bankers and financiers – six out of a total of nine members. They were joined by two representatives of the Department of Finance and by Professor Henry Parker-Willis of Columbia University, USA, who was also the chairman.[3] The leader of the opposition, Tom Johnson, queried the appointments. 'Is it not the case that a commission dealing with the possible evils of the banking system and composed of people interested in the banking system is likely to lead to a curious development?' he asked. Mr Blythe replied that 'it was not thought that inexpert opinion should be appointed to the commission' and that the appointees 'represent different interests, and it will be for them to consider any recommendations that come before them'. The idea that the government was serious about tackling the issue of banking and credit was greeted with cynicism. On 12 February 1926, Mr Michael Richard Heffernan of the Farmers' Party tabled a motion to the Dáil, which was 'of the opinion that agricultural interests in the Saorstát should have been given direct representation on the Banking Commission and that the Terms of Reference should have specifically provided for an examination of the agricultural credit problems of the Saorstát'.[4] The Dáil adjourned for two weeks, but on its return Mr Blythe assured the deputy that 'the Commission will have to keep its eye open to the whole agricultural position'.[5] Mr Heffernan was not so optimistic:

> I am not of the opinion that the whole agricultural problem of this State can be met by credit, but I am of the opinion that the question of credit is one of the problems we have in connection with agriculture, and it must be dealt with amongst other problems which the commission has to deal with.[6]

The motion was defeated, but the doubts about the interests of the commission remained. In the words of a farmer at a rally in Tullamore, the Banking Commission 'was purely a commission of bankers'.[7]

The commission held its first meeting on 9 March 1926 and on 16 April it produced its first interim report. It had heard from less than a dozen witnesses.[8] In September, it presented the second, third and fourth interim reports to the government, although these were not published until December. In January 1927, the main findings, including a majority and minority report, were finally released. 'The general public will be relieved to find that the majority report contains no revolutionary proposals,' wrote *The Irish Times*. 'A new currency system is recommended but the commissioners lay the upmost stress on the necessity of an unequivocal basis in British sterling.'[9]

The commissioners took nine months to release a report, the conclusions of which had been reached after less than six weeks. They had been able to do so, they said, because of the personnel who sat on the commission. 'Our body included within its members several bankers of long and tried experience, thoroughly familiar with local conditions, in close touch with banking and financial interests, and hence able to assure us of the view of that element of the community.' This meant that the commissioners were 'obviated [of the] necessity of lengthy hearings which might otherwise have been needful with a view to ascertaining the actual state of opinion among bankers'.[10] The commissioners, it turned out, already had all the answers. There was no need to investigate. As with Éamon de Valera, who famously said that he need only to look into his own heart to know what the Irish want, the commissioners only needed to search their own hearts to investigate Irish banking. And that's exactly what they did.

The report was quick to outline what it saw as the main strength of the Free State's currency – namely the parity link with sterling:

> In every newly organised state the fundamental problem of exchange which must be dealt with is that of a monetary or currency standard. The Saorstát has encountered no difficulties on this score ... as its monetary basis has been identical with that of Great Britain [which] has been since the close of the war by far the most sound and stable nation, speaking in a financial and monetary sense, in the European world.

The commissioners recommended the installation of a new currency in the Free State, but one which 'shall be stated in terms of sterling, thus accepting the British standard of value for Saorstát Éireann, and that it shall be convertible at par into British sterling'. It made the argument that parity was essential 'in order that there may be no interruption to the comparatively free interchange of money and notes between the two countries, and no shock to the present system of inter-communication between the two, upon a uniform currency basis or standard'.

According to the commissioners, the State had the option of tying the Irish currency to the gold standard, but this was in no way desirable because of the level of trade between the Free State and the UK:

> The Saorstát is now, and will undoubtedly long continue to be, an integral part of the economic system at the head of which stands Great Britain. As the result both of centuries of parallel development and of the natural division of labour between an area predominantly agricultural and an area predominantly industrial, the Saorstát will undoubtedly continue for an indefinite period to find the great bulk of its market for exports in Great Britain.
>
> Today more than 95 per cent of its export trade is with British territory, and while the proportion of its business going to other parts of the world will undoubtedly increase, as it should, many years must elapse before it can have with any other part of the world, or with all combined, an economic relationship at all comparable to that which it at present has with respect to Great Britain.

As we saw with the history of cattle breeding as an industry in Ireland, there was nothing 'natural' about the division of labour between industrial Britain and the agricultural Free State. Nor was sterling a particularly secure or safe currency, having been tied to the gold standard in 1925 at an overvalued rate. In May 1926 the UK experienced a ten-day general strike – the first in its history – which was caused in part by the government's moves to deflate the economy via wage restrictions on the back of the gold standard measure.

The commissioners said that the reasons to maintain parity with sterling 'need but little exposition'. There is little, if anything, in this world, however, which does not need explanation. All too often, appeals to 'common sense' or the 'self-evident' nature of an argument are simply covers for the status quo. The commissioners were reluctant to explain their reasons because it suited Irish banks with deposits in London to have an expensive currency to sell. It did not suit the national economy of a newly formed state. And the Banking Commission was supposed to have the interests of the State at heart, not just its bankers. Its recommendation to tie the Irish currency at a 1:1 ratio to the wealth creation of a foreign country, not to the wealth creation of the State, was to have serious implications for the economic development of the State over the next forty years.

The 1:1 ratio had already forced a series of deflationary budgets. The move to cut the old age pension and public sector wages in 1925 was influenced in part by monetary policy – the Banking Commission's recommendations were for a continuation of policy, after all, not innovation. In 1927, the government announced that it had accepted the commission's proposals and that year it set up a Currency Commission which was mandated to administer the parity of the Irish pound with sterling. Deflation, poverty, and emigration followed in the wake of that decision.

THE SECOND BANKING COMMISSION AND THE ESTABLISHMENT OF THE CENTRAL BANK

In 1931, less than four years after the Banking Commission had tied the Irish pound to 'the most sound and stable nation' in Europe, the UK broke from the gold standard and devalued its currency. It was not the only country to undertake such a measure during this period – Sweden, Norway, Denmark and India all abandoned the gold standard around this time. However, because of the parity link, the Free State was forced to follow sterling to its new value, regardless of the financial realities in Ireland at the time.

The leader of the Irish government, William Cosgrave, responded to the financial crisis not by disentangling the Irish pound from sterling, but by appealing to patriotism and calling on the Irish people to purchase Irish goods. 'Let us see to it that our courage and our energy are not wanting in the time of national necessity,' he told a civic carnival banquet in Limerick in October 1931, 'to keep the name of our country in the forefront for being able to meet whatever demands may be made on us in difficult times.'[11] The increase in tariffs undertaken by the government at this time was in direct response to similar moves by Britain. In order to avoid the Free State becoming a dumping ground for British goods, it needed to put a marker on imports. In 1933 the World Monetary and

Economic Conference in London passed a resolution which called on the establishment of independent central banks with powers to carry out currency and credit policy in developed countries where they did not already exist. It was becoming clear that the Free State's avoidance of a central bank was out of step with the rest of the developed world.

On 26 October 1934, the Minister for Finance, Sean McEntee, announced the appointment of a commission to inquire into banking, currency, and related matters in the Irish Free State. Its personnel represented a wide range of Irish society, 'There were five university professors, five civil servants, three bankers, two trade unionists, two agriculturists, two representatives of general business and trade interests, one Roman Catholic bishop and one foreign expert.'[12] It held over 200 meetings and took four years to produce its report. It was finally released in October 1938 and found that while a central bank should be established, parity with sterling should also be maintained, and government borrowing should be curtailed. It also rejected the suggestion that a nationalised bank should be established to provide credit for the expansion of the economy. The commission took four years to conclude that the status quo offered the best solution to the problems facing the Irish economy.

The commission also produced a minority report, which was signed by Professor O'Rahilly and the two trade union representatives, William O'Brien and Sean Campbell. They stated that they could not:

> ... acquiesce in the extraordinary view that this country, alone amongst the responsible entities of the world, should not ever have the power to make decisions, and that no apparatus or mechanism for controlling the volume and direction of credit should ever be brought into existence ... We need an organ for the issue and control of developmental credit ... That is our fundamental conclusion, and the only thing startling about it is that it was not accepted sixteen years ago.[13]

It was testimony to the power of the banks in the Free State that, after sixteen years, two commissions, and one international financial crisis, their ability to dictate the pace and direction of Irish economic growth to suit their own business agenda to the detriment of almost all other aspects of Irish economic and social life remained undaunted.

One of the main recommendations of the Second Banking Commission – the establishment of a central bank – was not implemented until 1943. A central bank, the commissioners said, 'has to ensure the maintenance of external stability, to take care of the monetary reserves of gold and foreign exchange, and have certain means of influencing the currency and credit position within the country'.[14] It undertakes these responsibilities in order to assist the development of the economy, and to act as a stabiliser between the right of banks to sell credit, and the right of businesses to trade. As far as the developed world was concerned, a central bank was not seen as a luxury but as an essential element of monetary policy. The failure of Fianna Fáil to establish a central bank led to accusations that the banks, rather than the government, were setting economic policy. 'It is all nonsense to say that we are merely creatures of the banks,' said De Valera in 1939. 'We can pass a law at any time to control the banks or to sever parity with sterling. We can do all these things. It is merely a question of whether it is wise or unwise to do them.'[15] Three years and the outbreak of a world war later, the Central Bank Bill was brought before the Dáil.

The board of the Central Bank of Ireland met for the first time on 1 February 1943. The chairman was Joseph Brennan, who was the chairman of the Currency Commission prior to its disbandment. One of the few surprises was the appointment of William O'Brien to the board. O'Brien, who had signed the minority report in 1927, was also a member of the Labour Party, which had been severely critical of the legislation which established the Central Bank. Within the year, O'Brien left the Labour Party and helped form the breakaway National Labour Party – the resulting split a boon to Fianna Fáil's electoral fortunes in 1944.

The Central Bank was given the responsibility of protecting the purchasing power of the Irish pound and regulating the issue of credit in the interests of the nation. The board made it clear that there would be no change in monetary policy. On 18 September 1949, sterling was devalued by 30 per cent. In 1951 the Ibec Report, which had provided such a succinct and devastating analysis of Irish trade, also looked at the State's monetary policy. As with the cattle trade, it found the practices of the Central Bank difficult to fathom.

The decision by the Central Bank in 1943 to continue with the policy of investing the State's currency 'primarily in British exchequer bills, with the rest of the 100 per cent coverage provided by gold bullion' was heavily criticised by Ibec.[16] It said that 'the fact that the Central Bank has made no use of its statutory power to invest its legal tender reserves in Irish government securities has handicapped the development of an active domestic capital market in Ireland which is one of the country's primary needs.' This emphasis on the purchase of sterling notes didn't make any commercial sense. Ibec noted that were the Central Bank to purchase British government securities as opposed to exchequer bills, the higher yield in interest payments afforded by the former would yield at least £500,000 a year in revenue. 'The commercial banking system of Ireland, as well, has shown a similar tendency to operate in a fashion that channels Irish deposit funds into the British market rather than retaining them in Ireland for domestic use.'[17] Ireland needed to boost its means of increasing its volume of physical capital formation. 'Unless this is done,' wrote Ibec, 'it is difficult to see how any development of Irish industry and agriculture sufficiently vigorous to keep pace with outside competition can take place.' Not only did Ireland need to increase capital formation, it had to ensure that such capital went on productive enterprises. (It may be recalled that Ireland had spent the bulk of its grants and loans from the Marshall Plan on land reclamation, rather than on specialist cattle breeding, or an expansion of indigenous export-led industry. More grazing for Shorthorns. That was the essence of the plan.)

As far as Irish banking was concerned, the move to bring foreign industry to Ireland helped to kill two birds with one stone. It would allow the economy to expand, but without any need to change monetary policy. This was because the much-needed capital formation would not come from the Irish pound. Any move to expand Irish credit on a level needed to develop the economy would put pressure on the parity link, as such capital formation would weaken the 'value' of the Irish pound. This is a necessary procedure in order to expand an economy;

credit is used to develop productive enterprises which in turn will create more value than that initially provided by the credit. However, such a move would mean the end of an expensive, and groggy, Irish pound – a sluggish currency that creaked under the weight of its sterling link.

Ibec also found that of the capital formation which did occur in Ireland, between one third and one half went towards construction, 'The major part of [the capital formation] does not flow to uses that have a direct and immediate impact upon the production of goods for the Irish market or for export.' It also found that 'shockingly low' levels of capital formation went towards agriculture, and that 'an unusually high degree' of capital formation in Ireland was 'marshalled under the auspices of government agencies'.

The role of private banks in the creation and distribution of credit in Ireland was quite limited, '[This] cannot be explained in terms of a comparative dearth of personal savings,' wrote Ibec, 'since Ireland's 1949 personal savings represent about twice as large a proportion of gross capital formation as in the United Kingdom'. Instead, it concluded that 'the disparity is clearly chargeable to the fact that an active capital market for domestic issues has never been developed in Ireland' and that 'this failure is immediately influenced by the example of government and private commercial banking agencies which consistently have channelled a very large proportion of their assets into British securities rather than securities of the home market'. Irish commercial banks were seen as directly responsible, along with government, with stymieing Irish economic growth. A reform of monetary and banking policy was needed, and as so often in Ireland when an economic power bloc was challenged, the concerns were duly noted and filed away.

There were nine joint-stock banks in Ireland in the 1950s, compared to only five in the UK. The added numbers did not lead to any competition regarding credit and charges. 'To all intents and purposes,' wrote *The Irish Times*, '[the banks] work hand in glove, and their activities are coordinated by the Joint Banks Standing Committee.'[18] There was a cartel in operation, 'and entry into retail banking was inhibited other than by way of a takeover'.[19] In 1958, the Bank of Ireland acquired the Hibernian Bank, which led *The Irish Times* to wish that the move would 'contribute, even in small measure, towards a narrowing of the gap between deposit and overdraft rates, at present so much wider here than across the Channel'.[20] There was no change in costs to bank customers, but the merger was the first of a series of such moves which took place over the following decade. In 1965, Bank of Ireland took over the Irish branches of the UK-based National Bank. Ireland was opening up its financial world to foreign investors, and the mergers could be seen as a pre-emptive move to ensure that retail banking stayed under the control of the cartel.

The largest merger, however, was that which formed Allied Irish Banks. On 22 August 1966, the Munster and Leinster Bank, the Provincial Bank of Ireland and the Royal Bank of Ireland announced their decision to amalgamate and form a new bank with total resources of £225 million. The move received much praised, as it was seen to ensure 'that control of these banks [would] remain within Ireland'.[21] It was thought that the size of the new bank – ninth largest in the British clearing bank system – would enable it to compete both internationally and within the Common Market, Ireland's membership of which was seen as all but inevitable. And in international banking, *The Irish Times* noted, 'it is size that displays fertility'.[22] The newspaper voiced its concerns over the name of the new bank. 'The directors are open to suggestions from the public,' it wrote, adding that with the title, Allied Irish Banks, 'it is unfortunate that such a deplorable name has been chosen'. In December 1966, AIB announced the formation of a merchant bank subsidiary, the Allied Irish Investment Corporation, which was a joint operation with Hambros, the London-based merchant bankers, and the State-owned Irish Life Assurance. It gave AIB a foothold in the area of Irish banking that had been opened up to foreign investment.

The increase in foreign investment in the 1960s brought with it an increase in demand for bank services, especially wholesale banking. Companies needed capital, and banks, especially American banks, were credit rich and constantly on the look-out for new markets. Ireland provided such an opportunity for expansion. At the time of the Irish bank mergers, 'there was virtually no control over the establishment of branches or subsidiaries of foreign banks that wished to concentrate on non-clearing or wholesale banking'.[23] North American banks were the first to arrive, and by the 1970s they accounted for over 5 per cent of the Irish banking market. These were followed by European banks in the aftermath of Ireland's entry to the Common Market in 1973.

On 28 September 1965, the Irish branch of the First National City Bank of New York (FNCB) was officially opened at a ceremony which was held at its Dawson Street office in Dublin. The FNCB had been in Ireland since June and employed twenty-five people. It was 'the smallest branch of the largest international bank in the world' and any credit note issued in Ireland had the full backing of the bank's $12.5 billion reserves in New York.[24] In June 1967 the bank moved to new premises at 71 St Stephen's Green, the occasion of which was marked by an appearance and speech by the Minister for Finance, Charles J. Haughey. The expansion of the FNCB took place alongside the opening of Ireland to the eurodollar market and to the opportunities such a market afforded with regard to international financial speculation. 'In developing the range of their services the Irish banks may be able to benefit from the experience of their American counterparts', Haughey told the audience. 'Such facilities as the purchase and leasing of expensive industrial equipment, long-term financing of business and residential properties and term loans are provided directly to customers by American banks.'[25]

The commercial and residential property boom which Ireland was going through was financed, in part at least, by the American banks – a boom which was assisted by government tax incentives, and which led to tens of thousands of square feet of empty premises, with more absorbed by government departments under a policy of rent rather than ownership. The government was using taxpayers' money to create a demand which didn't exist, and taxpayers' money to absorb a surplus which shouldn't have been built. American banks provided a boost to finance, allowing Irish banks to keep parity with sterling, as they did not have to produce Irish-pound-based credit to fund these loans. The banks, along with the builders, contractors and their political friends, reaped the benefits.

With the Pay As You Earn (PAYE) tax scheme introduced in 1960, the government had gained a captive, and constant, supply of income. The government's policy of funding speculation with tax breaks and absorbing speculation via office rent was in effect the wholesale transfer of wealth from the working population to builders, banks and speculators, with government as the conduit. It seems incredible that something so blatant could exist so freely, but it is only so strange when seen in isolation. Given the pattern of Ireland's economic history, from the 1920s currency commission to the 2008 bank guarantee and the creation of NAMA, the 1960s speculation boom fits securely in place.

The role of the banks in facilitating and sustaining property speculation was underlined in a 1977 study of Irish banking by N.J. Gibson. In it, he noted that while 'both the merchant banks and the North American banks have been active participants in the inter-bank money market that has developed in recent years in Dublin,' the development of this money market 'is partly a consequence of their arrival and their particular methods of operation in that they … often seek out lending business and then find the funds to finance it'.[26] He found that with the Irish merchant and North American banks, 'their liabilities within Ireland tend to be less than their assets, and so they tend to be net external borrowers'. Ireland's industrial banks dealt with hire-purchase loans for consumer goods, 'industrial loans, the finance of foreign trade and company finance', and foreign banks such as the Algemene Bank Netherland (Ireland) Ltd and Banque Nationale de Paris (Ireland) Ltd.[27]

The liberalisation of the Irish banking system also had an affect on the once-conservative building societies. In 1965 they accounted for around 7 per cent of all deposit and current accounts in the State; by 1985 that share had risen to almost 50 per cent.[28] Ostensibly concerned with the provision of affordable mortgages to members, by the late 1960s, Irish building societies had turned into full-blown property developers and speculators, overseeing the construction of office blocks and suburban estates. By 1985 the societies had total assets of £2.5 billion, around 20 per cent of the liquid assets in the State. Ten years previously, total assets stood at £250 million. It was a phenomenal growth, virtually all of it based on commercial and residential property.

The banks were bringing credit into Ireland, finding buyers, and selling it to them. With a famously 'hands-off' Central Bank and government, the purpose of this credit, and its function within the wider economy, was rarely challenged or even discussed. The Irish economy was being sold credit, and this credit was ending up in land speculation, construction and mortgages. It was not long before Ireland had a major banking crisis on its hands.

'[IT] SHOOK THE FOUNDATIONS OF THE BANKING SYSTEM IN IRELAND'

Edward Collins, Minister of State at the Department of Trade. Commerce and Tourism, 6 November 1985.

On 8 March 1985, the Taoiseach, Garret Fitzgerald, was visited at his home in Rathmines by two of his cabinet colleagues and informed of an impending banking crisis which had the potential to bring down the bank and fatally undermine the economy. His Minister for Finance, Alan Dukes, and Minister for Trade, Commerce and Tourism, John Bruton, told him that the Insurance Corporation of Ireland (ICI), which had been bought by AIB the previous year, 'had racked up massive but as of yet unknown losses by wildly underwriting high-risk businesses in the insurance market'.[29] AIB had tried to cover the losses but could no longer afford to do so. However, it made sure to tell the government that if ICI's liabilities were not met, AIB itself could fold, and the effect on the Irish economy of the collapse of the largest bank in the State would be devastating. Fitzgerald, Dukes and Bruton decided that the State would have to step in and take responsibility for ICI's liabilities, even though it had absolutely no idea as to the scale of those liabilities except that they were of such a scale as to threaten the existence of AIB. The government gave AIB a blanket guarantee. It covered everything, absolving AIB of its financial commitments to the broken insurance company. 'Clearly the bank was playing a game of who blinks first?' said a former AIB banker. 'And Fitzgerald and his ministers blinked first.'[30]

The previous year, the chairman of AIB, Niall Crowley, criticised the Tánaiste, Dick Spring, over comments he had made relating to the operations of the Irish banking system. At a party conference in Cork in May 1984, Spring told delegates that 'for too long the right of the banks to ignore any obligation except to themselves has been taken entirely for granted – and I do not think it is going too far to say that what is happening now amounts to an abuse of the people of this country'.[31] He said that the banks should contribute to the alleviation of the country's major social problems, especially during times of recession. 'To give you an example,' he told the conference, 'the Allied Irish Banks' profits last year alone would go a long way to solving the housing crisis that faces thousands of our young people.' Mr Crowley's reaction was swift. He told *The Irish Times* that the Tánaiste's speech 'showed an extraordinary lack of understanding of the principles of banking'. He pointed out that banks had a commercial responsibility to their depositors, 'If we started lashing our depositors' money around the country on enterprises totally without commercial viability we would be unable to repay the money when people wanted it back, and we would have to go out of business.'[32] Less than a year later, AIB successfully dumped its financial problems onto the shoulders of the Irish people.

The Insurance Corporation of Ireland was founded in 1935, 'for the purpose of transacting all classes of fire and general insurance'.[33] In 1946, it took over the marine underwriting business of the State-owned company Irish Shipping Ltd and in 1971 'the government appointed the company sole agents for managing export credit insurance schemes for Irish exporters'.[34] One year later, it formed the Property Corporation of Ireland, in association with Irish Shipping Ltd. Its first main venture was the construction of a 62,000 square foot office block on a one and a half acre site at Merrion Hall, Sandymount, Dublin. As with so many other commercial property ventures which were built at this time, the tenants for the offices came from the public sector. In 1974, Córas Tráchtála, the Irish export board, moved into the building along with Irish Shipping Ltd.

Seven years later, AIB secured 25 per cent of the issued share capital of ICI for £10.2 million. In 1983 it made an offer for the remaining 75 per cent, which was accepted, and ICI was fully incorporated into AIB. The entire deal cost the bank £40 million, of which only £10 million was cash, the other £30 million was made up of shares. 'Allied Irish Bank picked an ideal time to make a bid for Insurance Corporation of Ireland,' wrote Bill Murdoch in *The Irish Times* in 1983. He referred to ICI's high liquidity, and its capital and free reserves of £51.1 million, which would 'boost AIB's capital base [and] allow it to expand still further'. All in all, he concluded, 'it is a good deal for AIB'.[35]

ICI had 25 per cent of the employers' and public liability insurance market in Ireland. It was the sole agent for export credit insurance for Irish exporters, and had among its clients Aer Lingus and Córas Iompair Éireann. By the time AIB took over the company, it had on its books around '120,000 insurance policies, of which 30,000 were for motor insurance'.[36] However, the Irish insurance market was not the core of ICI's operations. Around 70 per cent of its business emanated from London, where the company was active in underwriting high-risk business – an area of insurance in which it had little experience. In 1983, it recorded losses of £63 million, £50 million of which came out of its London office. In July 1984 it was audited by the Department of Trade, Commerce and Tourism, and was found wanting. The company simply shrugged its shoulders. It said everything was fine, and that it was unhappy with the State-appointed actuaries.

By November 1984, rumours about the health of ICI began appearing in the press. At a meeting between the Department of Trade and AIB and ICI executives held that month, the government officials were told that AIB had decided to invest more money in the company in order to cover any outstanding liabilities due to losses. It put over £86 million into ICI before the plug was pulled, and AIB went to the government to tell them that the largest bank in Ireland was on the verge of collapse. They were issued with an open-ended guarantee that the Irish taxpayer would cover all of ICI's losses, whatever the cost. AIB were offered a blank cheque, and they immediately took it. By October 1985, the ICI deficit was estimated at £164 million. During a time of serious economic crisis in the country, with a hair-shirt budget and cuts in health, education and social services, the Irish government gave ICI an advance of £100 million to enable it to cover its liabilities while it was wound down. Fifteen years later, in September 2000, the £100 million was eventually repaid.

On 16 March 1985, one week after the government had stepped in to save AIB from collapse, the bank issued a statement to its shareholders and employees to reassure them that it had 'extracted itself from the Insurance Corporation debacle with its balance sheet relatively intact'. The bank was also quick to point out that 'its profits forecast for the year to 31 March will not be affected by this divestment and that AIB shareholders will be receiving an unchanged dividend out of the profits'.[37] It was an incredible statement of power and influence. On 8 March, AIB had been hours away from collapse, yet seven days later it was able to inform its shareholders that not only was it rid of ICI, it would be paying out dividends on the back of its profits. The only concession to the government was the issuing of a loan of £50 million for a period of three years on which the State would pay a lower rate of interest than normal. That was it. And the Irish State accepted it as just another day in the world of Irish finance.

The collapse of the Insurance Corporation of Ireland was not unique. In October 1983, the Private Motorists Provident Society (PMPS), a friendly society with all the trappings of a bank (it took deposits and issued loans and mortgages) was ordered to close following the crash of its parent company, the Private Motorists Protection Association (PMPA). The government had recently discovered that the PMPA did not have enough money to pay out on claims. The PMPA was using revenue from new customers to pay old customers. It was not generating enough income from its investments to cover the insurance claims of its clients. It was a classic pyramid scheme. As long as there were enough new customers to pay the previous ones, the scheme could continue. However, it needed a growth multiplier of such magnitude that the scheme eventually collapsed under its own weight. There had been rumours of irregularities within PMPA for years, and by the time the Registrar of Friendly Societies sent external accountants into PMPA to investigate, it was already too late. The company was insolvent. 'On 19 October 1983, following months of secret planning by civil servants, the government rushed emergency legislation through all stages of the Dáil in just one day, and the following day an administrator was appointed by the government to take control of the insurance company.'[38] PMPS, which was also affected, had £9.4 million in deposits, all of which was frozen before the 5,600 account holders could do anything about it.

There had been signs that there were problems with PMPS. In April 1983, the news that the bank's books were under scrutiny was leaked to the press, although the Registrar of Friendly Societies said that it was 'part of a programme of routine inspections of all societies'.[39] It was also announced that the PMPA group was awaiting a Supreme Court decision on the constitutionality 'of legislation which requires that all provident and friendly societies either cease taking deposits from the public by November [1983] or take out a full banking licence'.[40] This related to a court case between PMPS and the government over a Bill introduced in 1978 which stated that 'societies with more than £25,000 deposited would have to cease their quasi-banking activities within five years of the passing of the legislation'.[41] The purpose of the Bill was to tackle this 'fringe banking sector' which was 'in competition with the conventional banking sector'.[42] The passing of the Bill was held up by the PMPS court case; the knowledge that PMPS was outside regulated banking was not. Despite this, PMPS and PMPA were able to continue their business up until the moment they crashed.

The implosion of the PMPS pyramid scheme was predated by the collapse of the Gallagher Group and Merchant Banking, which was put into receivership on 30 April 1982 with debts of close to £50 million. The group had been founded by Matt Gallagher, father of the two joint managing directors. Matt had made his money in Britain in the 1950s, in construction, mining and plant hire. He returned to Ireland in the early 1960s and became acquainted with Seán Lemass. In the words of the journalist Simon Carswell, 'with the arrival of new multinational companies, Lemass needed someone to build homes for their workers and Matt was one of the businessmen charged with the task.[43] His bank, Merchant Banking, was first set up in February 1961, primarily as a hire-purchase business, but in the 1970s the emphasis shifted towards deposit-taking. The death of Matt Gallagher in January 1974 propelled his son Patrick to the head of the family business. He spent much of the next eight years engaging in property development and speculation. With the economic downturn in the early 1980s, Patrick turned to the cash deposits of Merchant Banking and treated them as his own.

Ireland in the 1980s not only ignored the actions of its banks, but refused to prosecute or adapt whenever criminal acts or credit crises occurred. The power of the banks was such that regulatory procedures common in other developed economies were dismissed as either uncompetitive or damaging to the economy. The IFSC entered this world with great fanfare. The age of Ireland as a tax haven for financial services was about to begin.

'IS THIS ALL BLARNEY? CAN IT REALLY BE SO PERFECT?'[44]

In April 1990 Daiwa Securities, the Japanese investment house, commenced operations in the IFSC with a £100 million open-ended foreign stock fund primarily aimed at Japanese investors. 'The global scap [*sic*] fund will be managed by ABD International Management Company and International Capital Management' wrote *The Irish Times*, 'and will be the first stock fund to operate out of Ireland.'[45] The news item finished with a quote from Daiwa's spokesman: 'Ireland levies no tax on investment trusts' he said, 'so we decided to try it instead of Luxembourg which is usually used.' The following week the UK-based newspaper, the *Guardian*, published an article on Daiwa and the IFSC, except it quoted Daiwa's spokesman as saying, 'Ireland levies no taxes on investment trusts so we decided to try it instead of Luxemburg, which is usually used as a tax haven.'[46]

It may have been unintentional, but the omission highlighted the difference between the image in Ireland of the IFSC, and the tawdry reality which surrounded it. 'The Irish are not keen on the term "tax haven", with its connotations of dubious legality and doubtful security associated with places like the Cayman Islands' wrote the *Guardian*. 'But they are keen on attracting investment, and have proved adept at using tax incentives to attract companies, despite the country's reputation for levying high taxes on its own citizens.' The newspaper said that apart from the 10 per cent corporation tax, 'companies can also benefit from 100 per cent allowances on equipment and development spending, and 200 per cent tax allowance for rental payments for 10 years.' The article ended with a quote from Eric Wallace of the accounting firm Peat Marwick, in which he outlined the key advantages the IFSC had over other tax havens: 'property and salaries are much cheaper than, for example, Luxembourg: it is much closer than the Cayman Islands: and it has the advantage over the Isle of Man or Jersey that it is in the European Community.' The Irish government talked about the IFSC in terms of investment and job creation, but the focus was firmly on allowing financial firms to maximize profit through tax avoidance. There was little by way of actual investment in the State, with the main economic stimuli taking place in areas such as accounting, rent and construction.

The contract for the development of the IFSC was awarded to a consortium of three companies: Hardwicke Ltd, McInerney Properties plc and British Land plc. The estimated cost was £250 million, and created around 3,500 temporary construction jobs. In January 1989 AIB announced that it intended to locate 'no fewer than six different activities in the centre', while in June the Sumitomo Bank of Japan confirmed its intentions to establish an office in Dublin with 'assets under management of $1 billion and capital of $250 million.'[47] By the end of the year over seventy companies had secured approval from the Minister for Finance to operate in the IFSC, but as the centre had not yet been built they were allowed to set up office in other parts of Dublin, pending completion. The IFSC was a virtual world, held together through the approval of the Minister of Finance.

The perception of the IFSC as a tax haven was challenged by the president of the Institute of Chartered Accountants in Ireland, Mr Jim Gallaher. In 1989 he said that 'the success of Dublin as a financial services centre is *not* just about increasing profits of multi-national financial conglomerates – it is about top-class professional services provided to the world by Irish men and women out of Ireland to the benefit of the whole Irish economy.'[48] One year later the managing director of Mitsubishi Trust & Banking Corporation's international banking group, Mr Tadashi Kohno, explained the bank's decision to locate to the IFSC: 'since Mitsubishi's international banking operations commenced' he said, 'we have always been on the lookout for places with as little regulation as possible and as much tax incentive as possible from which to do business [and, in relation to London,] Ireland is more profitable in terms of tax and reserve costs.'[49]

Three years after the establishment of the IFSC there were just over 400 staff employed by the various companies based at the centre.[50] By the end of 1990 over 190 projects had been approved, with a total job pledge of 2,400. This was somewhat of a shortfall on the prediction made in 1987 by the then Taoiseach Charles Haughey, when he said that the IFSC would create over 7,500 new jobs over a five-year period.

The main growth in jobs happened within service provision to the IFSC. These included accountancy and legal firms, computer software houses, builders' suppliers and engineers. Even here the actual growth generated by the Financial Centre was limited by the fact that a sizable part of the IFSC consisted of Irish firms who had simply moved from one part of the city to another, slashing their tax bill as a result. 'Well over half the office space in the IFSC is occupied by Irish companies such as AIB, Bank of Ireland, Irish Life, Smurfit Paribas and many lesser-known names' wrote the journalist Frank McDonald in 1991. 'The relocation element has been substantial – with the banks, for example, simply shifting their currency dealing operations to the Custom House docks to take advantage of the lucrative tax incentives.'[51] McDonald gave the example of the lawyer firm McCann Fitzgerald and accountants Arthur Anderson, both of whom had agreed to rent over 120,000 square feet of office space in the IFSC. They were vacating 'the buildings they had occupied for years in Pembroke Street and St. Stephen's Green, respectively.' 'It is little wonder' said, McDonald, 'that the Dublin office market is depressed.' And, as *The Irish Times* noted, 'taking account of transfers of existing jobs into the centre [by] large employers such as AIB and Bank of Ireland, the number of genuinely new [pledged] jobs is probably no more than 1,000 to 1,500 at best.'[52]

The limp employment figures for the IFSC were noted by the magazine, *Finance*. In September 1992 it reported that the centre, 'which is five years old this year, currently employs 2,000 people, considerably less than the original projections.'[53] *The Irish Times*, quoting the IDA, reported a revised figure in December of that year. It said that there were just over 1,250 people employed by around 150 companies, and that the jobs were 'a mixture of back office administration-type jobs and more senior jobs.'[54] Furthermore, 'the majority of companies are located elsewhere in Dublin, and the IFSC is more of a concept than a place at this stage.' It noted that 'because of the off-shore nature of their activities, IFSC companies may be buffered from any ups and downs in the Irish economy' – a tacit admission of the lack of investment undertaken by IFSC-based operations in the Irish economy. The international scope of its operation meant that it was a direct drain not only on Irish tax revenue – as seen by the amount of Irish institutions based within its virtual walls – but also on the tax revenue of sovereign states in Europe, Asia and the Americas.

Mr James Deeny, chairman of the International and Commercial Banks in Ireland, addressed the association's annual general meeting in April 1991. He told the assembled guests that the IFSC 'will not be a tax-avoidance haven for international financial institutions as some commentators have claimed', but rather it 'will prove to be one of the most cost-effective projects ever undertaken by the Irish government.'[55] In August *The New York Times* ran a special report on offshore banking centres. It said:

> They occupy a kind of shadowland of finance that is little understood but increasingly important. Broadly, these banking havens are places that offer customers the right to strict secrecy, few regulatory constraints and an official indifference to tax evasion. The leading havens include Switzerland, the Cayman Islands, Luxembourg, the Bahamas and the Channel Islands. Sometimes Hong Kong, Singapore and Bahrain are included as well. New entrants are crowding the field. Ireland, for example, established the International Financial Services Center three years ago as a tax haven in Dublin. Already, 170 financial institutions have set up shop there.[56]

The report highlighted the fact that the main clients of tax havens 'are international banks and corporations, seeking higher profits, not tax-dodging rich people or crooks hiding ill-gotten gains.'

In January 1992 the German authorities said that the IFSC was being used by German financial institutions to avoid tax, and that they intended to bring in new tax laws in order to counter it. They said that the IFSC and Shannon zone were little more than 'tax havens for many big foreign investment companies', in particular, Special Purpose Investment Companies which handled large amounts of funds but which had 'no real trading function, and had only located in Dublin or Shannon for their low-tax regimes.'[57] Sweden launched an investigation into the IFSC and its tax arrangements at the same time as the Germans. 'The

Swedish authorities have become unhappy about the loss of tax revenue arising from companies establishing in the centre' wrote *The Irish Times*.[58] 'The authorities believe that 20 billion Krone (£2 billion), much of it borrowed, has been placed by Swedish companies in IFSC subsidiaries which then invest in bond and equity markets. After paying 10 per cent tax on their profits to the Irish authorities, they return the rest to Sweden and avoid 30 per cent Swedish company tax.' *The Irish Times* said that Sweden was investigating whether 'the size of the money invested was being matched by real activity conducted through its centre, or whether the IFSC is being used to channel funds for tax avoidance.' Its reputation as a money-laundering centre was slowly 'gaining credence among professionals who specialized in combating the activity.'[59]

By 2005 the IFSC was frequently referenced as the 'Wild West of European finance.'[60] At the same time a litany of Irish politicians, journalists and financial experts spoke in glowing terms about the 'light touch' of the country's financial regulators and the necessity of a low corporation tax rate in order to keep its economic miracle alive. 'Light-touch regulation does not mean a free for all or the condoning of illegal or immoral practices,' wrote Séamus Mulconroy, director of policy for the Progressive Democrats. 'It does mean as Charlie McCreevy says striking the right balance between protecting the public and the integrity of the market and stifling business with burdensome regulation and unsustainable costs.'[61] An *Irish Times* editorial in August 2007, written in the wake of the near-collapse of the German bank Sachsen LB as a result of problems arising from its Irish operation, urged caution with regard to regulation. 'On the face of it, there appears to be a strong case for stricter regulation of international financial services here' wrote the paper's editor. 'In considering any such action, however, it is important to have regard to the role that the existing "light touch" regulatory regime has played in the development of a world-class [Irish] financial services industry in a few short decades.'[62] In December 2007, on the eve of the financial crisis, the chairman of the Financial Services Consultative Industry Panel which provided independent input to the Irish financial regulator, said that he would seriously doubt 'whether any of the over 10,000 funds and firms regulated by the Irish financial regulator would categorize their regulation as light touch.'[63]

He stated that 'the use by some media commentators of easy catchphrases to help describe the complex matters that have arisen equally have no place in a serious debate on these issues.'

In 2007, the *International Securitization and Finance Report* ran an article on the artificial transfer of profits procedure known as the 'Double-Irish.' This was a tax avoidance scheme undertaken by international financial corporations with little more than an address in the IFSC. Such was the scale of these sham corporations that in 2010, the economists Peter Boone and Simon Johnson wrote a post for *The New York Times*' blog 'Economix', in which they pointed out the fantastical nature of the official figures for Ireland's exports and GDP:

> It is possible to set up a corporation in Ireland, channel sales through that head office (with some highly complicated links to offshore tax havens in order to avoid paying Irish tax) and then pay a minuscule corporate profits tax. Ireland boasts a large industry of foreign 'tax minimizers' that do this, but these tax minimizers hardly employ any people. Nearly one-quarter of Irish GDP comes from the profits of these ghost corporations.[64]

The scale of these operations was a reflection of the fundamental changes which had taken place in the financial services sector at an international level. The changes in the way money and finance operated across the world influenced the IFSC as much as the Bahamas or Singapore, Munich or Madrid. In this at least, Ireland was not an island. At the same time, the physical reality of the IFSC as an international financial centre in the heart of Dublin's docklands made the land on which the docklands was built a very profitable investment indeed.

'THERE IS NO OTHER MAGIC TO IT. WE ARE A LEAN, MEAN MACHINE'[65]

In May 1996 the Minister for Finance, Ruairi Quinn, announced the creation of the Dublin Docklands Development Authority (DDDA), onto which he conferred 'overall responsibility for rejuvenating the city's redundant port area, including the Custom House Docks.'[66] It was formally established one year later, with business consultant Lar Bradshaw as its chairman. None of the outgoing members of the Custom House Docks Development Authority, which the DDDA now replaced, were incorporated into the new authority. It was seen as a clean sweep, with Mr Bradshaw in particular singled out for his 'relative youth, expertise and incredible vision.'[67]

The DDDA was eventually given extensive powers 'to grant lucrative planning permissions (known as Section 25 certificates) on lands it controlled along the city quays without the developers having to go through the transparent, if lengthy, procedures involved in facing objections and appeals from residents or city planners.'[68] By the time it presented its draft plan for the area, the DDDA had received over 200 submissions, a large number of which were from developers seeking Section 25 tax exemptions for their plans. 'If estate agents and property developers had their way' wrote Frank McDonald, 'Dublin's redundant docklands area would be peppered with tall buildings, as well as high-density apartment blocks with minimal open space and almost unlimited car-parking. And nearly every site in the area would be a tax shelter.'[69]

At the heart of these applications was Treasury Holdings, which had been formed in 1989 by two property speculators, Johnny Ronan and Richard Barrett. In 1998 they signed an agreement with the state-owned transport company, Córas Iompair Éireann (CIÉ), where Treasury Holdings were given disused rail freight marshalling yards at Spencer Dock in return for 17.5 per cent of the rental income from the completed developments. 'When these terms came public in 2002,' wrote Frank McDonald and Kathy Sheridan in their book *The Builders*, 'leading to criticism in the Dáil that [CIÉ] had been short-changed, Barrett said CIÉ stood to gain a lot more from the deal over time than it would have raised by selling the site.'[70] The deal led to the formation of the Spencer Dock Development Company. It wanted to build a national conference centre on the site, with 'a massively overblown high-rise development of offices, hotels, apartments and ancillary facilities' to help fund its construction.[71]

The development of the site was slow, mainly due to legal challenges, but it was given a boost in 2004 when the consortium secured €300 million in funding – with half of the figure coming from Anglo Irish Bank, and the balance coming from AIB and Bank of Ireland. It was billed as the 'largest and most ambitious urban development in the State's history, with an expected capital value of €3 billion.'[72] The chief executive of Anglo Irish Bank, Seán Fitzpatrick, was a member of the board of DDDA. In 2006 the property consortium Beebay formed an equity partnership with the DDDA to buy out the former Irish Glass bottle site in Ringsend for €412 million. The transaction was funded 'through a combination of new debt issued by Anglo Irish and the sale of more equity and loan stock to Beebay's current shareholders.'[73] The *Irish Times* journalist, John McManus wrote that the involvement of the DDDA in such speculative building raised all kinds of issues regarding conflicts of interest. 'What it brings to the party is the statutory power to have the developments exempted from planning, which was granted to it by the government in order to expedite its mandate to redevelop Dublin's docks.'[74] The concerns, while raised, went largely uninvestigated. One of the few journalists willing to dig deeper was Frank Connolly, who ended up paying quite a heavy price for his efforts.

In February 2005 the Centre for Public Inquiry, an independent body which set itself the task of investigating corruption in Irish society, was established in Dublin. In September of that year it published a report on the planning procedure surrounding the Trim Castle Hotel. This was quickly followed by a report on the Corrib pipeline. However, in December the centre was fatally undermined by a series of attacks on Connolly, who was the centre's executive director. These were led by the Irish Minister for Justice, Michael McDowell, who accused Connolly of association with the narco-terrorist organisation, FARC.

The accusations, read out in the Dáil under special privilege and so exempt from libel, were without foundation, but caused enough controversy as to lead the centre's financier, Chuck Feeney, to withdraw funding from the centre. In April 2006 the chairman of the Centre for Public Inquiry (CPI), retired High Court judge Fergus Flood, announced that the centre had ceased operations, that it would not publish any more reports. It had just completed an investigation into the DDDA and Anglo Irish Bank, but was unable to publish its findings due to threats of libel and a lack of financial cover should such a case be brought against them.

In an article for *Irish Central* in 2010, Connolly wrote that the CPI had come across 'minutes of specific board meetings of the DDDA where a clear conflict of interest involving Fitzpatrick and [Larry] Bradshaw was evident.' Bradshaw was chairman of the DDDA and had been appointed to the board of Anglo Irish Bank in 2004. 'Minutes seen by the CPI researchers showed that both participated in board discussions without declaring their commercial interest or 'stepping outside' when issues of potential conflict arose in decisions pertaining to the development of Spencer Dock.' Connolly said that the CPI 'got early guidance from well placed sources within the DDDA machine, public servants who were concerned at the way in which a State body was easing the path for the wealthiest business interests at the direction of one the country's most powerful bankers.'

The conflict of interest between Bradshaw and Fitzpatrick as members of the boards of Anglo Irish and the DDDA also came into play with regard to the Ringsend site, but Ireland in 2006 was not really moved by such concerns. Equally, the slowdown in the US property market in 2007, and the hard-to-follow reports which talked about subprime mortgages and asset-back securities, seemed worlds away from Ireland and its economic miracle. Indeed, during the general election campaign in May 2007 the Labour Party's campaign slogan was, 'Are you Happy?' Over the next three years the painful truth of how Ireland was actually run, and in whose interest economic and political decisions which affected the state were made, would make itself known to virtually every household in the country.

5

FROM BANK GUARANTEE TO BAILOUT

The Irish bank guarantee was the government's response to the crisis that swept the globe in the aftermath of the collapse of Lehman Brothers. However, the guarantee was not designed to protect the national economy, the State's citizens, or even the majority of Irish businesses from the effects of that crisis. Instead, its purpose was to protect that section of Irish society which drew its power, and continues to draw its power, from the very fault lines which were exposed by the crisis in the first place. The State's role as a conduit for international finance; as a tax haven for both domestic and foreign enterprises; the promotion of construction and land speculation as entrepreneurship, and the development of services to exporters rather than the development of actual exports – these were the deep-seated problems that exacerbated the crisis in Ireland.

Such was the strength of this type of comprador business and tax avoidance speculation within the Republic, that social and political resistance to its struggle for survival were frustratingly weak and ineffective. With the mainstream media and political parties on board, the only tangible forms of protest open to the Republic's citizens were street protests and the ballot box, which resulted in the collapse in support for Fianna Fáil, and its coalition partner, the Irish Green Party.

It was only in the final weeks of the government, after the arrival of an EU/IMF team in November 2010 and the imposition of a bailout package designed to support Irish bank bondholders in Europe, that the leadership of Fianna Fáil turned its attention to the survival of the party. The reasons why Brian Cowen and his cabinet took such a stance are not entirely certain, but what is known is that for decades Fianna Fáil was a party with two faces. It was a populist party with a strong working-class and public-sector base, but one that was funded by particular banking and business interests. Normally, such contradictions can co-exist once there is sufficient room for manoeuvre. With the 2008 bank crisis, however, the party's options contracted to almost zero. It could no longer sugarcoat its business-led economic policies with political gestures and tax breaks for PRSI workers. In order to get the country through the crisis, the State needed to quarantine the loans which had been used for tax avoidance measures, such as Section 23, while at the same time guaranteeing deposits. Instead, it decided to transfer responsibility for the loans onto the shoulders of the State, to cut back on funding for education, health, pensions and welfare, increase tax on personal income and expenditure, and appeal to patriotism and sense of duty. Its decision to borrow tens of billions of euros to prop up dead banks and Section 23 loans consigned the rest of the economy to freefall – the part of the economy where the jobs lay – and the party lost support as a result. It could not bail out its financial backers *and* keep its working-class and public-sector vote on board. The economic situation just wouldn't allow for such an option.

The two-year period between the bank guarantee and the EU/IMF intervention was a time when the controlling forces within Irish society revealed themselves in a way that had not been seen for decades. The scale and depth of the crisis made it impossible for the nature of their wealth to remain under the radar. The crisis brought clarity to the actual focus of the State's economic and political system. What we see during those two years are the consequences of the empowerment of financial dealers and property developers, the glorified *Maître d*'s who meet and greet multinationals as they arrive on our shores, aided and abetted by the main political parties, who are unable, or unwilling, to see any alternative.

The financial crisis was global in nature, but Ireland's almost fatal exposure to it was not a fluke or simple bad luck. Similarly, the reaction of the government was not because of moral failings, alcoholism, dysfunctional leaders, a lack of interest in the media or a lack of an 'ear for strategic political advice'.[1] On the contrary, the government's reaction to the bank crisis made sense – when viewed from the perspective that the logic was to cushion Ireland's financial vested interests from the fall, with the bank guarantee the most direct and secure way of providing that protection. At the same time, the economic and social myths which had built up over the previous fifteen years, of a prosperous land and a classless people, simply vanished. Ireland was a democracy, to be sure, with open and free elections, but it was far from governed in the interests of its people.

'FINANCIAL INNOVATION IS GREAT, BUT YOU HAVE TO HAVE SOME BASIC RULES'[2]

Sheila Bair, Federal Deposit Insurance Corporation, December 2007.

The general explanation for the 2008 global financial crisis is that its roots lay with the American housing market – more specifically with subprime mortgages, the shadow banking system, securities, and the complex, opaque system of over-the-counter derivatives. *The Irish Times* wrote that in the US, 'the combination of reckless borrowing by house purchasers and imprudent lending practices by banks and financial institutions, when set against the background of rising interest rates and falling property prices ... proved to be a lethal mixture'.[3] The Fianna Fáil TD Seán Ardagh told the Dáil in July 2008 that it began 'with subprime mortgages in the United States ... Many of these subprime mortgages suddenly became bad and thereby all of the securities based on them became bad.'[4] The monthly financial newspaper *The Banker* wrote that 'the credit crisis, triggered by the subprime mortgage meltdown in the US, produced devastating repercussions'.[5] The *Guardian* said that 'the global financial crisis has its roots in the US mortgage industry, where the sheer scale of liabilities on subprime loans is gradually becoming clear',[6] while Fiona Walsh of *The Irish Times* said that 2008 was the year when 'the credit crunch hit the high street, as the financial contagion that sprang from the subprime mortgage market in America finally spilled over into the real economy'.[7]

The destabilising effect of the subprime loan market on the wider economy was two-fold: it added to an already-expanded housing bubble, while the loans themselves entered the global bloodstream through the proliferation of Mortgage-Backed Securities (MBS). MBSs are bonds which are essentially pools of mortgages. An investor buys a share in the MBS and receives a fixed payment for the investment. There were three US government-sponsored agencies – Fannie Mae, Freddie Mac and Ginnie Mae – that used them as a way of funding the US mortgage market and expanding home ownership. The securities issued by Ginnie Mae were backed 'by the full faith and credit of the US government, [which] guarantees that investors receive timely payments',[8] whereas those issued by Fannie Mae and Freddie Mac did not have full federal backing. However, both enterprises benefited from what was called 'an implicit federal guarantee ... investors perceive a government guarantee'.[9]

In 1999, the Clinton administration put pressure on Fannie Mae to ease 'the credit requirements on loans that it will purchase from banks and other lenders'.[10] The government wanted to encourage banks 'to extend home mortgages to individuals whose credit is generally not good enough to qualify for conventional loans', and it used Fannie Mae and MBSs to do so. Essentially, Fannie Mae, the main underwriter of home mortgages in the US, was moving into subprime lending. 'In moving, even tentatively, into this new area of lending,' wrote *The New York Times* in 1999, 'Fannie May is taking on significantly more risk, which may not pose any difficulties during flush economic times. But the government-subsidized corporation may run into trouble in an economic downturn, prompting a government rescue similar to that of the savings and loan industry in the 1980s.'[11] In February 2004, the chairman of the Federal Reserve, Alan Greenspan, explained to *The New York Times* that the sizes of Fannie Mae and Freddie Mac, and the fact that they were government-sponsored enterprises, made it 'difficult for Congress to avoid a bailout in the event of a financial calamity'. 'It's basically creating an abnormality,' he said, 'which the system cannot close around, and the potential of that is a systemic risk sometime in the future, if they continue to increase at the rate at which they are.'[12] Greenspan's concerns were not with MBSs as such, but with the fact that they were concentrated within federal-protected financial institutions. His preferred solution was not the oversight of such potentially risky ventures, but the further deregulation of mortgage securities in order to let the dynamics of the free market – and its invisible hand – set the parameters of risk and, of course, to profit from that risk.

In the late 1990s, new types of MBSs were developed, this time for private banks. They were called private-label mortgage-backed securities. They lacked any form of a government guarantee – implicit or otherwise – and as such they carried greater risk. The absence of a government guarantee also meant that banks relied on private credit-rating agencies to enhance confidence in these new securities and to encourage investors. These were freely given. As one commentator put it:

> Debt holders relied on credit rating agencies such as Moody's, Standard & Poor's, and Fitch to prescribe the amount of risk associated with private label securities. These private label securities earned great ratings from the credit agencies. In fact, the vast majority of private label debt was rated AAA, the highest rating achievable, second only to debt that was government insured. The appeal to investors was a higher return as to the comparable government insured securities.[13]

The rise of these private-label mortgage-back securities, coupled with the liberalisation of lending practices in Freddie Mac and Fannie Mae, meant that 'most subprime lenders were [now] financed by investors on Wall Street' rather than 'traditional banks and thrifts, which traditionally financed their loans with deposits'.[14] Furthermore, the transactions surrounding these products were highly complex and required a strong degree of mathematical fluency to decipher them, so much so that many of the bank executives and regulators who traded and regulated the securities simply did not understand the mechanics. Such were the wage bonuses and profits generated by these products, however, that there was little desire on the part of the financial markets to question the process. Accordingly, there was an increasing reliance on computer software packages to compensate for the lack of detailed knowledge. In the words of the 2011 Financial Crisis Inquiry Commission Report:

> Financial institutions made, bought, and sold mortgage securities they never examined, did not care to examine, or knew to be defective; firms depended on tens of billions of dollars of borrowing that had to be renewed each and every night, secured by subprime mortgage securities; and major firms and investors blindly relied on credit rating agencies as their arbiters of risk.[15]

Furthermore:

> ... while the vulnerabilities that created the potential for crisis were years in the making, it was the collapse of the housing bubble – fuelled by low interest rates, easy and available credit, scant regulation, and toxic mortgages – that was the spark that ignited a string of events, which led to a full-blown crisis in the fall of 2008.
>
> Trillions of dollars in risky mortgages had become embedded throughout the financial system, as mortgage-related securities were packaged, repackaged, and sold to investors around the world.
>
> When the bubble burst, hundreds of billions of dollars in losses in mortgages and mortgage-related securities shook markets as well as financial institutions that had significant exposures to those mortgages and had borrowed heavily against them.
>
> This happened not just in the United States but around the world. The losses were magnified by derivatives such as synthetic securities.[16]

The slowdown in the US housing market in 2006 took place alongside a rise in mortgage defaults. The securitisation of mortgages, however, had become a key element of the world's financial markets. The route by which bad loans in Chicago ended up on the balance sheets of ILB

Deutsche in Düsseldorf was 'opaque and laden with short-term debt', and was facilitated by the development of the shadow banking system.[17]

'IT WAS KIND OF A FREE RIDE'[18]

Paul Volcker, former Chairman of the Federal Reserve, 11 October 2010.

The authors of the Financial Crisis Inquiry Commission Report found that the US financial system of 2008 bore little resemblance to that of their parents' generation; 'The changes in the past three decades alone,' they concluded, 'have been remarkable.'[19] In 1933, in the wake of the Wall Street Crash and Great Depression, the US legislature passed the Glass-Steagall Act. This established the Federal Deposit Insurance Corporation (FDIC), which was set up in order to avert banks runs and sharp contractions in the finance markets. It meant that 'if banks were short of cash, they could now borrow from the Federal Reserve, even when they could borrow nowhere else. The Fed, acting as lender of last resort, would ensure that banks would not fail simply from a lack of liquidity.'[20] The price of this bank guarantee was regulation. In order to lessen the chances of a bank failure, the Fed insisted on measures to avoid excessive risk. The 1933 and 1935 Banking Acts 'prohibited the payment of interest on demand deposits and authorized the Federal Reserve to set interest rates on time and savings deposits paid banks and savings and loans associations' (S&Ls or thrifts).[21] Congress moved to limit the competition for deposits, as it felt that 'competition for deposits not only reduced bank profits by raising interest expenses, but also might cause banks to acquire riskier assets with higher expected returns in attempts to limit the erosion of their profits'.[22]

The cap on interest rates came under increasing pressure in the late 1960s and early 1970s, as inflation grew and institutions such as 'Merrill Lynch, Fidelity, Vanguard and others persuaded consumers and businesses to abandon banks and thrifts for higher returns'.[23] 'These firms,' said the Financial Crisis Inquiry Report:

> ...created money market mutual funds that invested these depositors' money in short-term, safe securities such as Treasury bonds and highly rated corporate debt, and the funds paid higher interest rates than banks and thrifts were allowed to pay. The funds functioned like bank accounts, although with a different mechanism: customers bought shares redeemable daily at a stable value. In 1977, Merrill Lynch introduced something even more like a bank account: 'cash management accounts' allowed customers to write checks. Other money market mutual funds quickly followed.
>
> These funds differed from bank and thrift deposits in one important respect: they were not protected by FDIC deposit insurance. Nevertheless, consumers liked the higher interest rates, and the stature of the funds' sponsors reassured them ...
>
> Business boomed, and so was born a key player in the shadow banking industry, the less-regulated market for capital that was growing up beside the traditional banking system. Assets in money market mutual funds jumped from $3 billion in 1977 to more than $740 billion in 1995 and $1.8 trillion by 2000.[24]

The Glass-Steagall Act, along with limiting interest rates, had also 'strictly limited commercial banks' participation in the securities markets, in part to end the practices of the 1920s, when banks sold highly speculative securities to depositors'.[25] Most of these regulations were phased out in the 1980s and '90s, with the Gramm-Leach-Bliley Act in 1999 one of the final nails in the regulatory coffin. This Act 'allowed banks to affiliate for the first time since the New Deal with firms engaged in underwriting or dealing with securities'.[26] On 15 December 2000, the US Congress passed the Commodity Futures Modernization Act. This allowed for the deregulation of the Over-The-Counter (OTC) derivatives market. It also extended the 1992 pre-emption of State laws relating to derivatives, ensuring that they could not be declared as illegal or, indeed, as gambling. The Bill's promoter, Senator Phil Gramm, told Congress that:

> [The] enactment of the Commodity Futures Modernization Act of 2000 will be noted as a major achievement by the 106th Congress.

> Taken together with the Gramm-Leach-Bliley Act, the work of this Congress will be seen as a watershed, where we turned away from the out-moded, Depression-era approach to financial regulation and adopted a framework that will position our financial services industries to be world leaders into the new century.[27]

The Act 'shielded OTC derivatives from virtually all regulation or oversight'.[28] It led to a boom in the trade of these products, especially credit default swaps. These successful moves towards deregulation ensured that financial markets had such scant supervision as had not been seen since before the Wall Street Crash and Great Depression. In 2011, the Financial Crisis Inquiry Commission concluded that the Commodity Futures Modernization Act of 2000 and the rapid expansion of the derivatives market 'was a key turning point in the march towards the financial crisis'.[29]

'... TURNING THE FINANCIAL MARKETS INTO GAMBLING PARLOURS SO THAT THE CROUPIERS CAN MAKE MORE MONEY ...'

Charlie Munger, Vice-Chairman, Berkshire Hathaway Corporation, May 2008.

At its simplest, an OTC derivative is a contract between two parties which involves a transfer of risk. With regard to financial markets, risk is associated with the volatility of prices over time. Currencies change in value, for example, on a daily, hourly, even minute-by-minute basis, and are subject, in times of extreme crisis, to crashes. Similarly, the value of bonds, shares and securities are subject to fluctuations in price and the threat of bankruptcy and default on the part of the issuer. OTC derivatives are used by those who trade in financial products as a way of hedging the risk associated with financial products, of limiting exposure to risk and to the inherent market volatility of financial assets or rates. However, unlike standard derivatives (also known as 'plain vanilla' derivatives), OTC derivatives are traded outside of the regulated exchange environment. The contract is between two parties only, and remains that way. The two parties 'agree on a trade without meeting through an organised exchange'.[31] They are 'neither registered nor systematically reported to the market. Thus the full risk exposure in the system is not known until the crisis hits.'[32] OTC derivatives are custom-made to meet the risk-hedging requirements of the customer. They are the *haute couture* of the securities world – each one unique and mathematically ornate. And the construction and sale of each OTC derivative yields a handsome fee.

Derivatives as financial instruments date back centuries, but the market for them was small until 1971, when interest and currency exchange rates became highly volatile in the wake of the Nixon administration's decision to end its association with the Bretton Woods system. This system had been established in 1944, when the major industrial countries of the world agreed to adopt a common monetary policy. Each major currency maintained a fixed exchange rate with the US dollar, which acted as a reserve currency and which itself was fixed to a gold standard rate. The International Monetary Fund and World Bank were created under this system to help countries bridge temporary balances of payments. The decision in 1971, known as the 'Nixon Shock', soon saw significant fluctuations in the exchange rates between currencies – a costly and damaging process for multinational companies who dealt with multiple currencies on a daily basis. These unpredictable fluctuations in exchange rates affected costs and profits. In 1972, the Chicago Mercantile Exchange began trading futures contracts on currencies, as a way of companies limiting their exposure to the market volatility of currency prices over time. The volatility generated by the Nixon Shock offered new opportunities. 'Money could be made out of that instability using financial derivatives,' writes Dr Jan Toporowsaki of the University of London, 'and no one has yet invented a foolproof way to prevent people with money from using it to make even more money no matter how ruinous the consequences may be for society.'[33]

The sale of these contracts was given a boost in 1973, when Fisher Black of the University of Chicago and Myron Scholes of MIT published a paper in the *Journal of Political Economy* entitled 'The Pricing of Options and Corporate Liabilities'. They had developed an algorithm which advanced the way traders could price futures options in a way that limited risk exposure. It assumed 'ideal conditions' in the market for the stock and the option, and concluded that under these assumptions, 'it is possible to take a hedged position on the option, whose value will not depend on the price of the stock, but will depend only on time and the values of known constants'.[34] The algorithm was further advanced by the economist Robert C. Merton in his 1973 article 'Theory of Rational Option Pricing'.[35] This modified formula became known as the Black-Merton-Scholes model, for which Merton and Scholes received the Nobel Memorial Prize in Economic Sciences in 1997 (Black had died in 1995, and the award is not awarded posthumously).

The effect of the Black-Merton-Scholes model was to give mathematical security to risk-hedging. One way to eliminate risk is to make two bets: one that covers you if the outcome is favourable and one that covers you if the outcome is unfavourable. The trick is to work out the correct pricing so that the winning bet covers the loss of the losing bet. Black-Merton-Scholes allowed traders to perform this task. 'Almost immediately,' wrote the economist René M. Stulz, '[the model] was found useful to price, evaluate the risk of and hedge most derivatives, plain vanilla or exotic. Financial engineers could even invent new instruments and find their value with the Black-Merton-Scholes pricing method.'[36]

In 1974, Texas Instruments brought out a calculator that used the Black-Merton-Scholes model. 'Soon, every young trader, many as second-year college drop-outs fresh from their first finance classes, was using a handheld TI calculator to trade options and was making more profit in a day than the college professors made a year.'[37] The development of computers in the 1970s, and the exponential growth in speed, power and programming, made it easier not only to use Black-Merton-Scholes to price derivatives, but also to develop new and ever-more complex financial products, even to adapt them for individual clients. All of this was done with one purpose in mind: both the buyer and seller of OTC derivatives were trying to beat the market. They were trying to eliminate risk. The growth of the derivatives market also turned derivatives into financial assets in themselves. The sale of a derivative generates revenue. 'The contracts can be traded, further limiting risk but also increasing the number of parties exposed if problems occur.'[38] Furthermore, 'losses suffered because of price movements can be recouped through gains on the derivatives contract'.[39] Instead of helping to limit risk, however, 'the models were used to justify a bigger appetite for risk'.[40]

Writing in 2002, the economist Henry C.K. Liu said that although the trade in derivatives 'grew up alongside new forms of capital flows as part of an effort to better manage the risks of global investing', it also facilitated new compositions of capital flows 'by unbundling risk and redistributing it in commensurate return/risk ratios to a broad market'.[41] In other words, derivatives, particularly OTC derivatives, not only added a level of insurance to existing financial products, they facilitated the creation and expansion of new financial products by enabling risk, seemingly, to disappear. Liu continued:

> At the same time, derivatives create new systemic risks that are potentially destabilizing for both developing and advanced economies. While the risk shifting function of derivatives initially served the useful role of hedging and thereby facilitating fund flows, the prevalence of derivatives is now threatening the stability of the global economy as a whole.

This is because:

> Derivatives are unlike securities and other assets because no principle or title is exchanged. In their essence, nothing is owned but pure price exposure based on 'notional' values. They are merely pricing contracts. Their price is derived from an underlying commodity, asset, rate, index or event, and *this malleability allows them to be used to create leverage and to change the appearance of transactions* [my emphasis]. Derivatives can be used to restructure transactions so that positions can be moved off balance sheet, floating rates can be changed into fixed rates (and vice versa), currency denominations can be changed, interest or dividend income can become capital gains (and vice versa), liability can be turned into assets or revenue, payments can be moved into different periods in order to manipulate tax liabilities and earnings reports, and high-yield securities can be made to look like convention AAA investments.

OTC derivatives may appear to limit risk for the individual client, but the risk does not go away. It does not leave the system. It is merely passed on to somewhere (and someone) else. 'You as an individual can diversify your risk,' said Lawrence B. Lindsey, former Governor of the Federal Reserve. 'The system as a whole, though, cannot reduce the risk. And that's where the confusion lies.'[42] And in the case of financial markets, risk is not a by-product of the process of buying and selling, it is risk which makes the act of buying and selling financial products possible. Without risk, financial markets as constituted today would cease to exist. Nobody has an edge. There is nothing of which to take advantage.

OTC derivatives increased the amount of leverage that a bank could utilise on its assets. They allowed 'financial services firms and corporations to take more complex risks that they might otherwise avoid – for example, issuing more mortgages or corporate debt'.[43] However, OTC derivatives did not diversify risk; instead, they had the effect of concentrating systemic risk within the handful of financial firms that dealt in the issuing of these contracts. If one of those firms was to collapse, the effect on the rest of the financial markets would be devastating. In the words of Alan Greenspan, 'the very efficiency that is involved here means that if a crisis were to occur, that that crisis is transmitted at a far faster pace and with some greater virulence'.[44] Despite this, there was no oversight, no regulation, no checking of whether the insurers had the capital to cover any potential losses. When questioned on this lack of oversight, Greenspan responded that the chances of such an event occurring were extremely remote. And anyway, 'risk' he said, 'was part of life'.[45]

The power of OTC derivatives to destabilise markets showed itself, seemingly, as an anomaly, but became more frequent as the twentieth century drew to a close. The multinational firm Proctor & Gamble reported a pre-tax loss of $157 million in 1994. It stemmed from OTC derivatives sold to it by Bankers Trust. The same year, Orange County, California, filed for bankruptcy. It lost $1.5 billion speculating on derivatives. Its dealer was Merrill Lynch. The county treasurer, Robert Criton, later pleaded guilty to six felony counts. In 1996, the Japanese Sumitomo business group lost $2.6 billion on copper derivatives. The Commodity Futures Trading Commission (CFTC) later fined Merrill Lynch $15 million 'for knowingly and intentionally aiding, abetting and assisting the manipulation of copper prices'.[46] In 1995, the UK-based Barings Bank was declared insolvent after it lost $1.3 billion due to the activities of one of its derivatives dealers, Nick Leeson. In September 1998, the New York Federal Reserve organised a bailout of the hedge fund management firm Long-Term Capital Management (LTCM), which had lost €4.6 billion during the 1997 and 1998 Asian and Russian financial crises. It 'held more than 50,000 derivatives contracts with a notional sum involved in excess of $1 trillion'.[47]

The instability, lack of oversight, and toxic concentration of risk that was generated by OTC derivatives led Warren Buffet to declare, in 2003, that 'derivatives are financial weapons of mass destruction, carrying dangers that, while now latent, are potentially lethal'. By 2007, the five largest investment banks in the US – J.P. Morgan Chase, Citigroup, Bank of America, Wachovia and HSBE – were among the world's largest derivatives dealers. Goldman Sachs estimated that from 2006 to 2009, somewhere between 25 per cent and 35 per cent of its revenues were generated by derivatives. The American insurance corporation AIG had sold credit default swaps totalling $79 billion 'to investors in these new-fangled mortgage securities, helping to launch and expand the market and, in turn, to further fuel the housing bubble'.[48] In 2006 and 2007, the top underwriter of mortgage bonds in the US was Lehman Brothers. 'When housing prices fell and mortgage borrowers defaulted', said the *Financial Crisis Inquiry Report*, 'the lights began to dim on Wall Street'.[49]

'THE FUNDAMENTALS REMAIN VERY, VERY STRONG'[50]

Alan Doherty, head of AIB Corporate Finance, September 2007.

In February 2007, US stocks fell, 'as concern about the extent of the housing market's slowdown unleashed a sell-off in shares of mortgage lenders and hurt shares of big banks like Citigroup'.[51] One month later, shares in the European-based Deutsche Bank and Credit Suisse slipped by over 4 per cent, 'amid mounting concerns about their exposure to the

US subprime mortgage market'.[52] By the end of the year, the crisis was such that the Federal Reserve was 'scrambling to head off a recession'.[53]

One of the first victims of the escalating situation was the global investment bank Bear Sterns, which was a key player 'in the credit default swaps market, a prime broker to many hedge funds, a primary dealer in the bond market and a counterparty to many leading Wall Street firms'.[54] The bank had issued huge amounts of asset-backed securities and derivative financial instruments, and by the end of 2007 found itself facing a multitude of court actions, with a loan book valued at $395 billion which was supported by a net equity position of €11.1 billion. On 14 March 2008, the Federal Reserve authorised the provision of emergency funding for Bear Sterns, stating that the bank was 'too interconnected to be allowed to fail at a time when financial markets are extremely fragile'.[55] The bank was sold two days later to its one-time rival, J.P. Morgan Chase, as part of the federal funding deal. Six months later, on 7 September 2008, both Freddie Mae and Fannie Mac were placed under the conservatorship of the Federal Housing Finance Agency. The following week, Merrill Lynch, on the verge of bankruptcy, was sold to Bank of America for $50 billion, while Lehman Brothers filed for chapter 11 bankruptcy protection. The US government's decision to allow Lehman Brothers to go to the wall sent shockwaves around the world. The Irish Central Bank said that it was 'carefully monitoring the emerging developments on the global financial markets', while the Taoiseach, Brian Cowen told reporters that whatever response the government took, it was informed by the principle that it 'must do its duty in the long-term interests of the Irish people'.[56]

The next day, Michael Casey, former chief economist at the Central Bank and a former member of the IMF board, put the collapse of Lehman Brother in context. He told the readers of *The Irish Times* that although Irish banks had lent a lot of money for housing and property development, the difference between Ireland and the US was that in the US, 'several … banks were greedy, incompetently run, and that the US system of regulation failed almost completely'.[57] Furthermore, 'Irish banks have not had to raise more capital from existing shareholders; if and when they have liquidity problems, they can access funds from the European Central Bank. They can also pledge their existing mortgage assets in exchange for these funds.' In addition, Casey repeated the Central Bank's statement that 'Irish banks are virtually free of the sub-prime mortgages which have caused all the problems in the US' – as if Ireland was somehow firewalled from the international markets, MBSs, and OTC derivatives. Casey ended his piece with a fatherly reassurance:

> The Financial Regulator examines the books of all the banks regularly with a fine-tooth comb and is fully engaged in the stress-testing exercises – which hypothesise very difficult scenarios – and then assess the banks' abilities to deal with them. No one else in the country would have anything like the detailed knowledge of the financial sector. The Central Bank's and Financial Regulator's assurances are the best indicators Irish shareholders are going to get.

No mention of derivatives and leverage, no mention of the shadow banking system, no acknowledgement of the fundamental changes in financial trading in the past thirty years – the financial system that 'bears little resemblance to that of our parents' generation'.[58]

Just two weeks later, the US Congress rejected a €700 billion bailout of the country's financial system, which had been proposed by the Bush administration. The resulting panic saw markets in freefall around the world. In Ireland, 'shares in Allied Irish Banks tumbled 16.7 per cent, Bank of Ireland slid 20.2 per cent, Irish Life and Permanent sank 39.9 per cent and Anglo Irish Bank plummeted 46.2 per cent'.[59] Charlie Weston of the *Irish Independent* said that 'as a peripheral country in the middle of a property bubble burst, Ireland has been singled out unfairly as the next country likely to see a bank go bust'.[60] It was a curious comment to make, as if a country on the periphery, with a heavily leveraged banking system, in the middle of a property bubble burst, should be considered a safe, steady bet by anyone but the insane.

That same day, three European banks were rescued in State bailouts – Bradford & Bingley in the UK, Hypo Real Estate in Germany, and the Dutch-Belgian financial giant Fortis – while Irish stocks shed almost €6.5 billion in value. The Taoiseach told the press that while Ireland was officially in recession, he wished to reassure the country that these events were simply part of the economic cycle. 'We must not at any time underestimate the capacity of our own people to confront these challenges,' he said, 'to face up to them and to do whatever is necessary to protect the achievements to the greatest extent we possibly can.'[61]

The Irish Central Bank had planned for such a crisis. In April 2008, its staff members role-played a crisis simulation exercise. 'We pretend that there is a bank experiencing difficulties such as large loan defaults, a withdrawal of liquidity or false rumours' said Pat Neary, Chief Executive of the Irish Financial Services Regulatory Authority, in a conversation with *The Irish Times*.[62] 'People pretend that they are representatives of the media,' said Neary, 'or some people act as creditors who attempt to appoint an administrator ... It is quite intense.' The authority's prudential director said that the Central Bank 'first held crisis simulation exercises four years ago' and so 'there is nothing especially ominous about the fact that they have held them recently'. *The Irish Times* finished the article with the comment that 'unfortunately, the only way to judge if simulation exercises work is to see how calm the regulators are when a real crisis hits'.

On 30 September 2008, the Irish people woke up to find that the Fianna Fáil/Green coalition had put up the entire Irish State as collateral for the crushing liabilities of six private banks. The country was now liable for approximately €400 billion in leveraged loans, in a recession, while sitting on top of a slowly deflating property bubble. The Irish people were about to find out just how calm and organised the government, the Central Bank, and the Department of Finance were when it came to a real-life crisis.

'AN ELEGANT SOLUTION TO THE CRISIS OF LIQUIDITY AND CONFIDENCE FACING THE BANKING SYSTEM'[63]

Deutsche Bank in London on the Irish bank guarantee, 30 September 2008.

On 29 September 2008, a meeting to discuss the government's approach to the bank crisis took place between representatives of Bank of Ireland

and AIB, the Irish Central Bank, and the Department of Finance. It was held at Government Buildings. The details of the meeting – even who exactly was in attendance – are still subject to controversy. One thing is certain. In order to combat the problems faced by Ireland's banking system, the government moved to 'guarantee all the liabilities – the customer and interbank deposits, and also the vast majority of bonds – of the six Irish banks'.[64] Several of the major players of the Irish financial system had argued for this solution, as had the economist and journalist David McWilliams.[65] At 6.45 a.m. on Tuesday 30 September, the government released the following press statement:

> The Government has decided to put in place with immediate effect a guarantee arrangement to safeguard all deposits (retail, commercial, institutional and interbank), covered bonds, senior debt and dated subordinated debt (lower tier II), with the following banks: Allied Irish Bank, Bank of Ireland, Anglo Irish Bank, Irish Life and Permanent, Irish Nationwide Building Society and the Educational Building Society and such specific subsidiaries as may be approved by Government following consultation with the Central Bank and the Financial Regulator ... This very important initiative by the Government is designed to safeguard the Irish financial system and to remedy a serious disturbance in the economy caused by the recent turmoil in the international financial markets.[66]

Later that day, Brian Lenihan outlined in the Dáil the bare bones of the Credit Institution (Banking Support) Bill. The government would guarantee 'deposits and debts totalling €400 billion at six Irish-owned lenders in a move to protect the country's financial system ... the liabilities amounted to almost 10 times the value of the national debt of about €45 billion'.[67] The government's apparent rationale was that the Bill would allow Irish banks access to the 'short-term funding that enables Irish financial institutions to fund their day-to-day operations [and which] had become scarce in the global banking system since the collapse of US investment bank Lehman Brothers'.[68] The Bill was passed by the Dáil at 2 a.m. on the morning of Tuesday 2 October, by 124 votes to

18. The Labour Party voted against the Bill, while Sinn Féin abstained. The Seanad sat all night and passed the Bill at 7.40 a.m. It was signed into law at 3.30 p.m. by President Mary McAleese – just shy of thirty-three hours after the release of Brian Lenihan's press statement. The Minister for Defence, Willie O'Dea, told the readers of the *Sunday Independent* that weekend that, 'in the case of a problem [under the guarantee], the first call will be on the bank's funds, on its shareholders, on their assets, capital and funds. This is a very significant buffer as the estimated total assets of the six financial institutions exceed their liabilities by about €80bn.'[69]

The guarantee was commented on by a flurry of economists, columnists, agencies and experts, all clamouring to support the government's decision. The credit rating agency Fitch continued with Ireland's top triple-A ranking, saying that 'this proactive measure should help buttress confidence in the Irish financial system and limit the risks of a deeper and more prolonged than necessary recession at a time of unusual stress in global banking markets'.[70] The source of its confidence was the announcement that the government intended to charge the six institutions a fee for the cover provided by the guarantee. 'While the amount of liabilities covered by the guarantee is more than double Irish gross domestic product,' said Fitch, 'the government will receive fee income to help protect taxpayers against any potential costs relating to possible calls on the guarantee.'[71]

Dermot O'Leary, chief economist with Goodbody Stockbrokers, said that 'the innovative and timely intervention by the Department of Finance in relation to the Budget, the deposit guarantee ceiling and now wider deposit safeguards, must be applauded.'[72] Simon Carswell of *The Irish Times* said that although the size of the liabilities covered by the legislation was something the government could hardly afford, 'the guarantee would only be triggered if one of the six institutions defaulted on some of their debt, and this is regarded as unlikely'.[73] In fact, the Bill would act as a boon for the economy, as it 'will also attract foreign deposits to the Irish banks at a time of turmoil when cash is king'.

Brendan Keenan of the *Irish Independent* gave a cautious welcome to the government's plan. 'The purpose of the guarantee is to make conditions more normal for Irish banks,' he wrote, adding jokingly that now 'they can get on with the time-honoured process of bankrupting over-stretched customers, selling off their assets, writing off the resulting losses, and moving on'.[74] Keenan's banking world, however, had little in common with the twenty-first-century reality of electronic transfers and credit default swaps. His 'time-honoured' allusion was more akin to a Frank Capra movie, where the clock on the bank manager's wall still ticked and tocked, as the local children played hopscotch on chalk-scratched pavements outside. Deregulation and financial innovation; these were the brush strokes of the modern banking system. In the days after the bank guarantee, the leader of the opposition, Enda Kenny, called for 'fair play', and for the banks to stick to the rules. He did not seem to understand that in the world of derivatives and deregulation, there are no rules. That is what deregulation is all about.

The Credit Institution (Banking Support) Bill received the approval of Kenny in the Dáil, who said that 'the Fine Gael party will continue to act responsibly in opposition and our primary concern here is for the protection of the Irish economy and Irish taxpayers' interests'.[75] Yet the party by-passed the €400 billion in potential liabilities with a call for 'a freeze on bonuses and super-payments to bankers for the duration of the government guarantee', adding that 'the importance of this guarantee is that it is guaranteeing depositors'.[76] It is not known if the leader of the opposition had actually read the Bill, but, if he had, he clearly did not understand it. While the Labour Party did oppose the Bill – calling it a blank cheque for the banks – its amendments imply that the explicit danger of guaranteeing all creditors equally passed them by. The party's spokeswoman, Joan Burton, called for a cap on bank manager pay levels, saying that none should earn more than the Taoiseach or Minister for Finance. She added that with the guarantee in place, 'the banks should supply liquidity for the real economic activity of the nation: the jobs, the businesses and the firms, not the speculators and fat cats who had been making a killing in the past 10 years'.[77]

The economist and journalist David McWilliams told his readers in the *Irish Independent* that 'Finance Minister Brian Lenihan has made a wise choice. By coming up with a unique, Irish plan – guaranteeing all deposits – instead of importing a failed solution from abroad, he has installed confidence in the Irish financial system.' 'Most importantly,' he added, 'Irish banks are now safe. This is the single most crucial upshot of yesterday.'[78] McWilliams, of course, had got it wrong. The government had not guaranteed deposits: it had guaranteed deposits *and* loans – the banks' debts to investors, bondholders and other financial institutions were also covered. In the same article, McWilliams said that with the guarantee 'the chastened banks will now have to accelerate the process of writing down loans, sort out bad debts, bring developers to book, and repay the government's trust, not in their own interest, but in the national interest'.

The same day, the independent senator Shane Ross stood up in the Seanad and said:

> Let's forget about the fact that the depositors are being underwritten. The same problem is going to be there tomorrow and the banks are going to be just as insolvent tomorrow, with the same loans and the same property developers into them for huge amounts of money. How is that going to be tackled, because that's going to come up and bite us next week when we have realised that the depositors are all right.[79]

The problem was that while the expected income from these loans had collapsed – because of the commercial and residential property crash, coupled with the deepening recession in the economy – the money owed by banks to investors in bank debt was guaranteed. The gap between the money the banks could salvage from its loan portfolio and the money the banks owed to its external creditors was now the responsibility of the Irish taxpayer. This was not a case of too big to fail. It was now a case of too big to function. That which twenty-four hours previously had drowned in its own debt had been miraculously brought back to life. The Irish government had reanimated a corpse; it had created a zombie. The bank guarantee had nothing to do with ensuring liquidity in the economy and everything to do with protecting Irish banks from their creditors. Thanks to Brian Lenihan and the Fianna Fáil/Green coalition, the losses of the banks were now the losses of the people. The sins of the father had been laid upon the children.

'ONE ARGUMENT AGAINST ANY SUCH BLANKET GUARANTEE IS THAT WHEN YOU INSURE EVERYTHING, YOU INSURE NOTHING'[80]

Tom Petruno, Los Angeles Times, *October 2008.*

The government, along with bank executives, continued to reassure the public that Irish banks were well capitalised with a solid business base. The problems, they said, came from outside the country, and the banks were the innocent victims of an international crisis in confidence. 'The oxygen supply for Irish banks was being cut off and healthy banks were starting to gasp for breath,' said Denis Casey, Chief Executive of Irish Life and Permanent, 'This guarantee turns on the oxygen supply.'[81] The Taoiseach, Brian Cowen told the Dáil that it was:

> ... a question of looking at the situation that we are in, that has been caused by the turbulence of financial markets, what has been happening in Germany, the Netherlands, Belgium, the United Kingdom and the United States. A situation emerged and it was made clear to me that [the bank guarantee] was what was required.[82]

John Gormley, the leader of the Greens, spoke with satisfaction about his party's contribution to the guarantee:

> The Minister for Finance has brought forward a mechanism which minimises the cost to taxpayers but at the same time places a bedrock of State guarantee under our banking sector ... This bold move has seen commentators from around the world look on with a degree of admiration. I am very proud of the role the Green Party was able to play in providing this innovative solution.[83]

However, not everyone shared this view. There were a few who argued that the guarantee was counterproductive and that it contained within itself the seeds of its own failure.

The UCD economist Colm McCarthy called the guarantee a blank cheque, adding that 'it is entirely likely that one of the banks could have negative capital.'[84] Professor Morgan Kelly of UCD, who had warned of the impending property crash and was vilified on national television and in the print media as a result, tried to outline to the public why the bank guarantee was already a failure. 'This is the wrong solution to the wrong problem,' he said. 'It has put the Irish taxpayer at risk of considerable losses, and does nothing to solve the real problem of Irish banks, which is a shortage of capital.'[85] He explained that the 'difficulty the Irish banks had in raising funds was a symptom of the bad debts that foreign investors know have eaten up most of their capital. By treating the symptom, the Government has ignored the cause, which is the shortage of bank capital.' The professor of international financial economics at TCD, Patrick Honohan, queried the rationale of the blanket guarantee, noting that it covered 'even subordinated debt-holders, who had already been earning a premium for the explicit risks they were taking'.[86] 'There is also the somewhat worrying fact', he added, 'that official statements continue to deny any possibility of under-capitalisation of any Irish bank, despite market concern.' Honohan pointed out that, as with Kelly, his key worry was how much equity capital was actually left in Irish banks. 'If there is little or no equity left, a bank will effectively be paying the insurance premium out of the government-guaranteed deposit funds. This will increase the temptation for those controlling such a bank to gamble for resurrection.'

Two weeks later, the financial regulator, Patrick Neary, told the Oireachtas Committee on Economic Regulatory Affairs that the banks had a regulatory capital buffer of €42 billion, but that he had 'identified €15 billion of property loans as being vulnerable'.[87] Nonetheless, he maintained the view (and that of the government) that the banks were well capitalised, that the bank guarantee had proven itself to have been successful, and that international confidence in the Irish banking system had returned. 'The only people who have confidence in you are the banks and the property developers,' replied Senator Shane Ross. This was no surprise, as they were the section of society for whom the guarantee was designed to protect. The scale and depth of the crisis may have been new, but the attitude and approach was not. Ireland remained a place where bankers and builders wielded the most power.

On 28 November 2008, the Central Bank and financial regulator submitted a report to Brian Lenihan on the financial position of the six institutions covered by the guarantee. It stated that the 'capital position of each of the institutions reviewed is in excess of regulatory requirements as at 30 September 2008 [and] that even in certain stress scenarios the capital levels in the financial institutions will remain within regulatory requirements in the period to 2011'.[88] Lenihan added to the optimism of the report, saying that the guarantee scheme had been successful in 'safeguarding the stability of the Irish banking sector and in restoring its liquidity position'. He did concede, though, that in 'certain institutions the need for additional capital may be very modest, whereas for others the need may be greater'. These capital funding needs would be provided by the markets, although 'in certain circumstances it would be appropriate for the State, through the National Pensions Reserve Fund or otherwise, to consider supplementing private investment with State participation, where in doing so the aim of securing the financial system can be better met.'

The message the Minister sent out was confused and contradictory. He said that the banks were fine and well capitalised up to at least 2011 – except in cases where they weren't – but that was ok because private financiers will step in to provide the gaps in capital funding – which according to the Central Bank and financial regulator didn't exist – but in any case the pension reserve fund could always be used to shore up the capital funding needs of the banks, if the banks needed shoring up – which they don't – but if they did the money is there – but they don't, so none of that matters – everything is ok.

Not surprisingly, no one believed such a jumbled message. It was clear that behind the 'nothing to see here' waving of hands by Lenihan and the Taoiseach Brian Cowen the Irish banks were structurally unsound. It was only ten weeks old, and already the rationale of a guarantee for all deposits, covered bonds, senior debt and dated subordinated debt, was falling apart. The shock for many was not that the government's plan was not working, but that it decided to keep on digging. The idea that the government's response was an economic one (however ill thought out) still held sway among the majority of citizens, commentators and journalists. Here, as so often, Morgan Kelly proved to be the public exception. In late October 2008, he wrote:

> … three weeks ago … Brian Lenihan was faced with a choice between rescuing two banks [Anglo Irish Bank and Irish Nationwide Building Society] and the handful of developers through whom they placed real estate bets, or recapitalising the financial infrastructure on which the other four million of us depend. He chose the former.[89]

The obvious conclusion as to the reasons behind the government's actions – that a tiny but powerful section of Irish society was doing everything it could to protect itself, even if that meant the financial collapse of the State – seemed almost impossible for most people to accept. It did not take long, however, for that sentiment to change.

On 14 December 2008, after weeks of speculation, the government announced that it was supporting a recapitalisation programme of up to €10 billion for the State's credit institutions. It was doing so because 'in current market conditions even fundamentally sound banks may require additional capital to respond to widespread market perception that higher capital ratios are appropriate for the sector internationally'.[90] The National Reserve Pension Fund was opened up to help finance the operation. In order to assuage any fears the public may have had on such a move, the government declared that it was committed to fully safeguarding the interests of the taxpayer:

> State investment will be assessed on a case-by-case basis in an objective and non-discriminatory manner, having regard to the systemic importance of the institution, the importance of maintaining the stability of the financial system of the State, and the most effective and economical use of resources available to the State and each credit institution's particular requirement for capital.[91]

It was reported that Irish banks had 'lost more than €56 billion of their market capitalisation since the stock market peaked in February 2007'.[92]

At first, the banks were reluctant to support recapitalisation. However, with international financial investors demanding that banks hold more capital, this resistance soon dimmed. As Shane Ross put it:

> The alternative to State bailouts was a takeover by private equity groups, which were hovering over the carcasses of the Irish banks. If the private equity groups were allowed inside the door, the board, staff, and culture of the banks would have been filleted. Recapitalisation suddenly seemed a trifle more appetising.[93]

Michael Casey, former chief economist with the Central Bank and a board member of the IMF, made a similar observation:

> Politicians and senior public officials (including former central bankers and regulators) are regularly invited on to the boards of banks. It is also the case that the children and other relatives of politicians and senior officials are employed by the banks via an inside track. If foreign banks took over, would these perks continue?[94]

The government's handling of the crisis had all the hallmarks of a state doing everything it could to save individuals within a broken system, rather than trying to fix the system itself.

In its first round of recapitalisation, the government gave €2 billion each to AIB and Bank of Ireland. It also gave €1.5 billion to Anglo Irish. 'The fact that Anglo Irish Bank is deemed to pose a systemic threat is surprising,' wrote Michael Casey in *The Irish Times*, 'clearly the government's Christmas spirit knows no bounds'.[95] The value of Anglo Irish shares in December 2008 amounted to €266 million; twelve months previously they were worth over €8 billion. In the days after the capitalisation was first announced, it was revealed that the chairman of Anglo Irish Bank, Seánie Fitzpatrick, had temporarily transferred loans worth €87 million that were in his name to Irish Nationwide Building Society. This was done in the days before the group's 30 September year-end audit, and was undertaken in order to avoid disclosing the loans to the group's shareholders. The loans were transferred back a few weeks later. Fitzpatrick had done this every September for the past eight years. He was forced to resign in light of the revelations.

Anglo Irish Bank was not of systemic importance to the Irish economy. In January 2009, the Department of Finance, in a report to the EU Commission, said that the bank operated within a 'niche market rather than [the] broad market'.[96] That niche was property speculation. On 15 January 2009, Brian Lenihan announced that Anglo Irish Bank would be placed under public ownership. The financial management and advisory company Merrill Lynch, in a report that cost the government €7.4 million, said that the bank was 'fundamentally sound'.[97] 'The proposed Anglo nationalisation marks a decisive watershed in Irish democracy' wrote Morgan Kelly. 'With it, an Irish government has coolly looked its citizens in the eye and said: "Sorry, but your priorities are not ours."'[98] This had always been the case, of course, going as far back as the 1927 Banking Commission. The scale and depth of the banking crisis was such that, for the first time in a generation, there were active, critical voices coming from within the mainstream. They were not used to being ignored, but then again, neither were they used to finding themselves out of step with the economic consensus. Aside from the occasional article in the socially liberal but economically right-wing *Irish Times*, and maybe a two-minute Q&A on *Morning Ireland* or *Prime Time*, they continued to be shouted down and marginalised.

The creation of the National Assets Management Agency (NAMA) in 2009, in the face of almost unanimous opposition across the country, brought home to the educated, conservative, middle classes that, in spite of what they had been telling themselves for years, their opinion, quite frankly, did not matter. The Irish middle classes honestly believed that the country's housing market had been driven by a property-owning gene unique to the Celts, one forged after the famine and shaped like a semi-detached in suburbia, instead of seeing it for what it was: a speculative bubble fuelled by deregulated finance and Section 23-induced tax havens. The myths about our history, culture and economic success, to which the middle classes had clung for so long, were now being eroded. And the middle classes were not happy.

'PEOPLE ARE SITTING DOWN, I KNOW, AND SAYING HOW CAN WE ALL SHARE THIS BURDEN OF ADJUSTMENT?'[99]

An Taoiseach Brian Cowen, 4 February 2009.

On 18 February 2009, the National Treasury Management Agency (NTMA) appointed the economist Dr Peter Bacon as a special advisor reporting directly to the Minister for Finance. He was given a three-month contract and was hired in order to 'enhance the agency's team during the recapitalisation process'.[100] His remit was to 'access the possibility of creating a "bad bank" or risk insurance scheme to take so-called toxic debts off the banks' balance sheets in a bid to free up new lending'.[101]

The previous week, the Minister for Finance had announced a €7 billion recapitalisation of AIB and Bank of Ireland. He stressed that the government had no desire to take control of the banks, nor would it hold ordinary shares. 'The Irish financial institutions have little or no exposure to the sort of complex financial instruments which are weighing on the balance sheets of many banks internationally,' he said. 'However, Irish institutions have engaged in lending for land and property development, which exposes them to specific risk at a time of falling property prices and difficult economic conditions.'[102] (Lenihan neglected to mention that the complex financial instruments he talked about had allowed Irish banks to leverage their capital to the type of levels to which it was now exposed, ensuring that capitalisation was now a core issue.) He said that the government was prepared to discuss schemes for assessing and eliminating such risk, and Dr Bacon's appointment was seen as part of this process.

The news that the government was contemplating a 'bad bank' for toxic assets drew the attention of Karl Whelan. In an opinion piece for *The Irish Times*, published on 27 February, he said that the 'removal of toxic assets is not the key issue: banks could remove these assets themselves by simply writing down these loans to zero'. Instead, Whelan explained, 'the relevant question is: what price does the government pay for these assets?' The government, and its advocates in the press, claimed that the 'bad bank' scenario was a tried and tested way of dealing with banking crises. However, the proposals talked about by the Department of Finance and NTMA differed in crucial ways from what had gone before. Whelan explained:

> Previous bad banks were state asset management companies that worked to obtain the best sales price for assets that governments inherited from insolvent banks that had been nationalised. The current proposal, which involves paying over the odds for assets to keep insolvent banks in private hands, has not been tried before.

The government wanted to recapitalise the banks by paying more for assets than they were worth. Not only that, it was entirely feasible 'to imagine a scenario where banks struggled with weak capital bases even after a bad bank scheme has been put in place'. Whelan concluded that the bad bank and risk insurance proposals were 'unlikely to produce a clean solution to the problem of undercapitalised banks'.

The minister, however, wanted a solution which was unique to Ireland, one that would involve 'moving impaired assets – property loans and the properties securing them – into a separate property company ... which could be capitalised and attract investment in due course'.[103] It was in order to explore the practicalities of this idea – a toxic property company rather than a bad bank – that the Minister hired Dr Bacon. On 8 April 2009, a press conference took place in Dublin, at which the result of these efforts, NAMA, was presented to the people. The minister said that although NAMA would not be a bank, it would be managed like a bank, ensuring that 'optiminal value for money is obtained for the taxpayer'. It would purchase property portfolios from the banks at a discount, and these portfolios would consist of both good and bad loans. At this early stage it was estimated that NAMA would buy loans totalling €80 billion to €90 billion, at a price yet to be decided. It was reckoned that 'among the loans to be transferred are about €60 billion of land and property loans. The remaining €20 to €30 billion of loans are secured on investment properties – office blocks, shops and hotels – which have been provided as security for the speculative loans drawn by developers.'[104]

When asked as to how much of a discount the government would seek on the toxic loans, Lenihan replied, 'we cannot in this particular exercise show you our set of cards today. We wait to see their [the banks'] position but we have to protect the taxpayer in the interest of the State.'[105] Davy Stockbrokers suggested a discount of 15 per cent on the book value. 'This would involve the State paying €76.5 billion for €90 billion in bank loans,' said *The Irish Times*, 'or roughly 1.4 times the national debt of the State.' In the Dáil, Enda Kenny asked 'how much does the government expect the Irish taxpayer to have to pay for the acquisition of dodgy debts to banks? ... The government is asking us to give it another blank cheque.'

Shares in both AIB and Bank of Ireland fell sharply on news of the NAMA plan, while the credit rating agency Fitch stripped Ireland of its top AAA rating, 'citing the heavy toll on the public finances from the economic downturn'. Ireland's GNP contracted by an unprecedented 11.9 per cent in 2009, while GDP contract by 7.1 per cent. Yet the Minister's focus was on ensuring that speculators got a good deal for their loans, and that the banks remained in private hands.

One week after the NAMA announcement, an article appeared in *The Irish Times* which was signed by twenty economists working in Irish universities.[106] Entitled, 'Nationalising banks is the best option', it set out to challenge the logic behind NAMA and to propose an alternative solution to the banking crisis. The economists noted that international financial regulations require that banks hold certain levels of capital in order to stay in business. The deepening recession meant that the amount of bad loans on the banks' books would increase, thereby requiring the banks to attain capital in order to keep regulatory levels of capital in place. 'The highest grade and most desirable form of capital is ordinary share capital', wrote the economists, 'and in the current circumstances the Irish government is the only conceivable investor willing to provide this capital.'

The NAMA proposal – to buy loans at a discounted price as a means of recapitalising the banks – has been suggested to carry an inherent contradiction. The larger the discount on the loans, the greater the need to recapitalise the banks. Every cent it saved on the loans was simply one more cent to inject into the banks via State (rather than NAMA) recapitalisation. 'There is thus a fundamental contradiction in the government's current position,' read the article. 'The government is claiming that it can simultaneously: (a) purchase the bad loans at a discount reflecting their true market value; (b) keep the banks well or adequately capitalised; and (c) keep them out of State ownership. These three outcomes are simply incompatible.' Furthermore, by trying to achieve all three at once, it would end up achieving none:

> A Government that needs to be seen to purchase the bad debts at a reasonable discount and that does not want to take up too high an ownership share may end up skimping on the size of the recapitalisation programme. Thus, rather than create fully healthy banks capable of functioning without help from the State, the process may continue to leave us with zombie banks that still require the state-sponsored life-support machine that is the liability guarantee.

The economists proposed an alternative: the nationalisation of the banking system. 'We do not make this recommendation from any ideological position,' they said, lest it be thought that they harboured any left-wing views. 'In normal circumstances, none of us would recommend a nationalised banking system ... However, these are far from normal times, and we believe that in the current circumstances, nationalisation has become the best option open to the government.' They believed that nationalisation would bring transparency to the banks, mainly because 'the Government would own both the [asset agency] and the banks, so the price would hardly matter'. There would be no need to rob Peter to pay Paul. The separation of toxic assets from the banking system was defended by Dr Bacon and the government as necessary in order to keep stock market listing and market monitoring functions in place. However, as the economists pointed out, 'the experience of recent years is one that would have to cast doubt on the ability of markets to effectively monitor financial institutions'.

Towards the end of the article, the economists touched upon what they probably believed to be the real reason behind NAMA, but were too cautious to explicitly state out loud. 'The Government's plans seem likely to keep in place the current management at our biggest banks,' they said. 'It would be difficult to avoid claims of crony capitalism and golden circles were billions of State monies to be placed into the banks with minimal changes in their governance structure.' Nationalisation, on the other hand, would provide a clean break with the dubious practices of the past:

> Nationalisation provides the opportunity for a fresh start for Irish banking. The State should run the temporarily nationalised banks as independent semi-state operations headed by highly independent boards of senior figures of the upmost integrity. Executives for these banks should be sourced through an international search, and remunerated accordingly.
>
> These executive boards should be charged with a clear mandate to improve risk management practices, restore the brand image of Irish banking and finance, and return the banks to private ownership in a reasonably short time frame, for as high a stock price as possible.
>
> This would certainly see substantial changes in senior management and board members in these banks, and allow for a rebuilding of the reputational capital of these institutions.

Therein lay the rub. Whatever its inherent contradictions, and the way that those contradictions damned it to failure even before it began, NAMA would achieve one thing: the decisions surrounding Irish banks would remain the preserve of Irish bankers. This was a gentlemen's club, one that had used the Irish economy as it had seen fit for the past eighty years, and it was not about to be dictated to by anyone. This was about power; those who had it had no desire to hand it over, and the Fianna Fáil/Green coalition ensured that there was no need to do so. The parties of government were in open collusion with a tiny section of society, against the needs of both the state and the wider economy. And even though it had existed for decades, and crossed party lines, the sheer nakedness of the relationship between government, bankers and speculators was a shock to many.

'WE WILL HAVE PLENTY OF TIME TO DISCUSS NAMA, WHICH IS THE ONLY SHOW IN TOWN'[107]

Brian Lenihan speaking in Dáil Éireann, 16 June 2009.

On 7 April 2009, the government published *NAMA: Frequently Asked Questions*, as part of the documents relating to the supplementary budget which was passed that month.[108] 'NAMA is firstly an asset management company dealing with assets transferred from banks,' it said. 'NAMA will not be a bank as it will not be taking deposits from the public and will not have a banking licence.' It also stated that, contrary to public speculation, Anglo Irish Bank would not be turned into a 'bad bank', but instead 'will remain as a going concern operating at arm's length from Government'. The initial documents in April 2009 mentioned that NAMA may have recourse to use a Special Purpose Vehicle (SPV) – a financial practice which allows companies to place risky loans off their balance sheets. Enron had used it to hide losses before it filed for bankruptcy in November 2001. The government said that 'in order to achieve the optimal return, some property loans sold to NAMA will be capable of being transferred into NAMA SPVs which will be capable of being worked out and disposed of in an orderly manner with private equity partners'.[109] When the NAMA legislation was presented to the Dáil, 'some property loans' had become all of the loans earmarked for purchase by NAMA.

On 22 September 2009, Bill Keating, assistant director general of the Macroeconomics Statistics Division, Central Statistics Office (CSO), sent a letter to Eurostat regarding the classification of NAMA and its borrowings. It wanted to know whether these borrowings could be excluded from the national debt. The CSO explained that once NAMA was established, it planned to create 'a separate Special Purpose Vehicle to purchase certain assets from participating institutions [and that] most of these assets will be loans associated with property development'.[110] This SPV, known as the Master SPV, would be responsible for the purchase, management and disposal of NAMA's loan book. It would be a separate legal entity, with 51 per cent of its shares held by private investors, and

49 per cent held by the Irish government, which would have a veto over all decisions taken by the SPV. In addition, the Master SPV would have the authority to create a number of subsidiary SPVs, 'each of which will be responsible for the loan book of an individual financial institution'. Keating said that as the Bill to establish NAMA was currently before the Dáil, he would be grateful if Eurostat could give him an answer as soon as possible. On 13 October 2009, staff from the CSO, the Department of Finance, and NAMA travelled to Eurostat in Luxembourg in order to provide further information. Three days later, Eurostat gave its answer. 'Based on the preliminary information provided,' it said, 'Eurostat agrees with the CSO's analysis that NAMA should be classified inside the general government sector, and that the Master SPV should be classified in the financial corporations sector.'[111] Essentially, the solution to the problem presented by NAMA was to call NAMA something else.

Brian Lenihan welcomed Eurostat's decision, adding that it meant that the toxic loans due to be purchased by the NAMA SPV 'will not increase the general government debt ratio and neither will our budget balance be directly affected by the NAMA initiative'.[112] Not everyone, however, was convinced by such a desperate scramble to reposition the reality of Ireland's banking debacle. The head of global economics at Fitch Ratings, Brian Coulton, said that 'NAMA loans will still count as national debt regardless of Eurostat's accounting, and stripping out the debt will not improve the way Fitch rates Ireland's creditworthiness.'[113] He added that NAMA would put Ireland's debt ratio to 110 per cent of GDP – the third-highest in the eurozone.

The reaction of the opposition parties was equally dismissive. Sean Barrett of Fine Gael called the SPV 'a con job', while Labour's finance spokesperson, Joan Burton, said that it was 'extraordinary the NAMA Bill could have got as far as committee stage without the SPV architecture being set out in detail'. And even though the CSO, the Department of Finance, NAMA and Eurostat had been discussing the possibility of a NAMA SPV for weeks, the Dáil had not been told about the scheme, and only found out about it with the release of Eurostat's preliminary judgement. The Bill marched on through committee stage regardless, and was signed into law by President McAleese on 22 November 2009.

The Irish government had arranged to buy the loans subject to the control of NAMA for €68 billion. Twelve months later, Ireland was forced to accept a joint EU/IMF bailout of €67.5 billion, after fears of contagion swept the European Union.

'CUTS DON'T EQUAL SAVINGS'[114]

Michael Burke, economist, 16 October 2009.

The Irish government brought in three budgets in the wake of the banking crisis. Each one had a deflationary impact on the Irish economy. The first of these budgets was put to parliament on 14 October 2008, less than two weeks after the bank guarantee was signed into law. Normally, Irish budgets are put before the Dáil during the first week in December. Brian Lenihan said that the decision to move the budget forward by two months was made so that the government could 'seize the initiative [and provide] political leadership in the time of changed economic realities'.[115] He added that 'while the strength of the economy in the past decade has given us some room for manoeuvre, we cannot put our reputation for fiscal responsibility in jeopardy'. With this in mind, Lenihan told the Dáil that the government planned 'to reduce public expenditure as much as possible on the current side and as much as is sensible on the capital side'. Lenihan said that the choices made in the budget did not serve any vested interest. 'Rather,' he said, 'it provides an opportunity for us all to pull together and play our part according to our means so that we can secure the gains which have been the achievement of the men and women of this country.' He ended the speech by saying that the budget was 'no less than a call to patriotic action' – thus proving that while patriotism may be the last refuge of a scoundrel, it's the first port of call for a government minister under pressure.

In April 2009, the government passed a supplementary budget in order to provide a correction to the 'unexpected' deterioration in the state's finances. Once again, draconian cuts were made in an effort to stabilise the deficit, and once again the effect was to further shrink the economy.

On 9 December 2009, Brian Lenihan presented his third budget to the Dáil, but before doing so he commented on his previous two efforts:

> The government over the past 18 months has made budgetary adjustments of more than €8 billion for this year [2009]. Had we not done so, the deficit would have ballooned to 20 per cent of GDP ... Because of these decisive actions, we are now in a position to stabilise the deficit.

He announced that the government planned to make cuts of €4 billion for 2010, despite the fact that the EU Commission had given Ireland some leeway in meeting its target of a deficit of 3 per cent of GDP. 'We welcome this revision,' said Lenihan, 'but it does not change what needs to be done in this budget. €4 billion is still the right target. Our strategy is on track.'

Three months later, a letter appeared in *The Irish Times* which was signed by twenty-eight leading economists, social scientists and analysts. Entitled, 'All the wrong options have been pursued', it set out to explain why the government's deflationary policies were counterproductive, and what the government could do to help, rather than hinder, growth.[116] The letter was the initiative of the independent think-tank TASC. 'Budgetary policies have been short-termist and reactive,' it read. 'Instead of cutting real waste in the public sector by increasing productivity and efficiency, the Government has cut public services and the living standards of those who can least afford it, further reducing domestic demand and, thus, employment.' The signatories argued that the only way to combat debt is to outgrow it. Borrowings should be used to enhance and modernise the country's infrastructure, as such investments lower business costs for all in the long-term, and they stimulate growth and increase tax revenue in the process. 'It may seem astonishing that we face ... economic and social deficits after 15 years of boom,' they said, 'but these are the consequences of pursuing a failed low-tax, low-spend model which sought short-term gains from the speculative activity of a small but powerful golden circle.' The Irish government was borrowing billions of euro to soak up toxic property debt, while the real economy lay dying of thirst beside the fountain. 'Embedding investment, rather than debt, into the economy,' they said, 'while restructuring taxation and expenditure in a progressive and expansionary manner to ensure a job-rich recovery – this, and not the current deflationary strategy, is the road to success.' The idea that the road to recovery is paved with cuts – that cuts are identical to savings – was so embedded at this stage that the TASC initiative was ridiculed as madness. The government insisted it was on the right path; the logical, sane and sober path to recovery, and for the most part Ireland's media agreed with them. Meanwhile, the economy continued to contract.

The debt obligations bestowed on the State by the banks and speculators, however, had become almost impossible to bear. In May 2010, Greece was forced to accept EU/IMF funding in return for a series of austerity budgets. It was reckoned that either Ireland or Portugal was next. The pathological rush to deflate the Irish economy, the obvious instability of the Irish banking system, and the announcement that the government intended cutting a further €15 billion from its budget, saw the State slouch towards its endgame. On 18 November 2011, a delegation from the IMF and EU arrived in Dublin to discuss a funding strategy for Ireland, despite a deluge of almost surreal denials by the government that such meetings were due to take place. By the end of the week an announcement was made that Ireland had accepted a three-year, €85 billion bailout. Ireland would contribute €17 billion from its national pension fund, while the remaining €68 billion would come from the EU, the IMF, and individual states within the European Union. The news shook the ruling Fianna Fáil/Green coalition to its core, eventually leading to a general election in February 2011. Both government parties were decimated at the polling stations. The Taoiseach-in-waiting, Enda Kenny, assured the Irish public that he would not shirk from the 'tough choices' to be made regarding cuts in social provisions. He also promised that, above all else, Ireland's corporation tax rate would remain untouched. The parties may have changed, but the approach and analysis remained the same: just keep on digging.

CONCLUSION

The 2008 banking crisis was not caused by an outbreak of moral failure or individual weakness. The significant power of Irish banks to dictate economic and monetary policy, and to protect themselves against the negative consequences of such policies, had developed over decades. The social and economic forces which fed and sustained that power run deep within Irish society. The exploration of those power dynamics, their significant strengths and structural weaknesses, has been the central theme of this book, and what follows is a brief summary of those main points.

At the time of its independence, the Irish Free State was a fully integrated part of the UK economy. Its role within that economy was primarily agricultural; more specifically, the provision of livestock for the finishing farms and slaughterhouses of England. This relationship, not surprisingly, benefitted livestock breeders and traders, who had come to prominence in the post-famine era, as land was cleared and secured for grazing rather than tillage. This became a source of conflict within Irish rural society, between small farmers and graziers. Upon independence, however, it was the graziers who were in the ascent, and Irish economic policy developed with their interests very much at heart. The end of formal political links with Westminster meant that the Free State was now an independent country without an independent economy.

In order to secure its future, it needed to expand its industrial base and develop new markets. For this it needed credit; something that a central bank based around a national currency could provide. The Irish banking system, however, was entirely focused on the London financial markets and resistant to the development of a national currency centred on the economic demands of the State. The first banking commission rejected outright any move towards fiscal independence. The need to expand agricultural and industrial output in order to provide an economic base for sustainable communities was pushed to one side. The result was increased emigration, with the Free State providing not only cattle and finance to the UK, but also a steady stream of labour. The lack of industrial growth also meant that there wasn't a sufficiently strong economic base to provide the standard of living demanded by the aspirational Irish urban middle class, who turned to the State for grants and tax relief in order to fund the type of home ownership and *petit-bourgeois* lifestyle they read about in the newspapers and watched on cinema screens.

The emergence of Fianna Fáil as a political force in 1927, followed by its rise to power in 1932, saw a change in aspects of economic policy, with greater use of tariffs to encourage industrial growth. These initiatives were soon hampered by self-inflicted blows. The party kept the parity link with sterling. It also decided to focus on the expansion of production for the home market only. The structural deficiencies within Irish agriculture (including the continued use of the Shorthorn for both dairy and beef production and the serious lack of a food-processing industry) remained untouched, as did any attempt to export to anywhere except Britain.

The second banking commission recommended the establishment of a central bank, which in its first act outlined its commitment to parity with sterling, a move which immediately undermined the very reason for its existence. Irish credit remained pitched at sterling levels, stifling growth. The demands placed on the Irish economy in order to maintain parity included periodic deflations, which were timed in line with the dynamics of the British (not Irish) economy, and an obsessive concern with inflation at home. By the end of the 1940s, the Irish State was more dependent on Britain than it had been at the time of independence, while an overweight Irish pound stood, drenched in sterling and out of breath, its hands on its knees, desperately trying to take a few more steps towards expansion before it collapsed from exhaustion.

The 1952 Ibec report was clear as to the changes in economic policy Ireland had to undertake in order to expand its economy and provide opportunities for job creation. Its authors simply could not understand why the State persisted in exporting livestock to Britain, given the potential for industrial growth which the slaughter and processing of animal produce would provide. Similarly, the practice by Irish banks of investing in British securities with the full support of the central bank and Irish government seemed bizarre, given the fundamental need for credit and investment in Ireland. Its calls for an expansionary policy, with a fully funded central bank using deposits to underwrite the Irish pound and provide credit, as well as an agricultural policy which would see the creation of a viable and profitable food-processing industry on Irish shores, were dismissed in favour of the pursuit of foreign investment. Such a move allowed the Irish State to appease the banking sector and its cheerleaders in the Department of Finance. It allowed credit and foreign investment to enter the Irish economy without a revaluation of the Irish pound – something that was needed in order for indigenous businesses to attain the level of credit needed for sustainable growth. The State was on a path to industrial expansion, but one which was centred on tax breaks and financial incentives to multinational companies, and not necessarily the development of local industry and indigenous exports.

The expansion in financial investment, construction and land sales gave rise to a particular type of Irish capitalist entrepreneur. There was money to be made by providing services to foreign investors. Construction, banking, insurance, property, road haulage, and legal services – these were the areas of commercial activity that gained a commanding presence in the Irish economy, all of which directly benefited from the influx of American, German, British and Dutch companies. At the same time, there was also money to be made by speculating on the boon to the economy which foreign investment brought. In the 1960s and '70s, the State started to provide these entrepreneurs with a similar range of grants and tax incentives as those offered to multinationals. In the case of office blocks in the 1960s, the State not only funded the speculation, it acted as tenant as well. The PAYE system, first introduced in the late 1950s, became a cash faucet for the government. The revenue generated through the direct taxation of ordinary workers was fed directly to speculators and foreign investors via the litany of tax havens which propped up these new industries. Such was the lack of concern about developing indigenous growth that the country's natural resources were sold off wholesale without a second thought. In Ireland, the handshake did not secure the deal, the handshake *was* the deal. The middleman: he is the dominant force in modern Irish capitalism. The type of local business interests which expanded on the back of foreign finance were all about making the deal happen. Construction, finance, land and law: this was the four-leaf clover, the new lucky charm for the modern Ireland of Lemass.

By the 1970s, the trick of foreign investment (and speculation on same) was running out of steam. Growth in the Irish economy relied more and more on construction, both commercial and residential. The notion that exports needed to be linked to the wider economy was paid lip service but little else. The growth in building societies and the entry of banks into the private mortgage market took place alongside moves to strangle public housing as a viable option for working people and the increased use of tax incentives to bolster owner-occupancy as the only real option open to families. Housing was increasingly portrayed as a cure for all social ills, a bulwark against inflation, a nest egg for retirement, a foolproof pension plan for the honest worker. It was also a multi-billion pound industry, where standards and security played a very minor role. The Kenny Report was shelved precisely because it threatened to upset the speculation machine. It threatened the livelihoods of the various politicians, bankers, builders and landowners who profiteered from the rezoning game. By the time the Telesis Report was published, only 8 per cent of all materials used by foreign companies in Ireland were sourced from Ireland. This was in spite of repeated calls by foreign companies for the development of secondary industries to act as feeders for production.

The Irish entrepreneur as middleman was firmly – and fatally – entrenched in the way the economy functioned. Construction and services can only work as an aid to growth; in Ireland they had become growth itself. In the late 1980s, the widening of Ireland's tax relief schemes to include financial services helped to turn the State into a glorified offshore bank. Incredibly, it became a tax haven for Irish financial and commercial businesses. Ireland had become its own tax haven. The decision by the Irish government in 2008 to guarantee almost all deposits and liabilities of the Irish banking system was everything people saw it as at the time: a bailout of well-connected bankers, speculators and builders – the dominant strands of Irish economic and political life. We need to understand why things happened the way they did, and to recognise that the old ways of doing business are not going to help us. In the words of the authors of the *Financial Crisis Inquiry Report*, it falls on us to make different choices if we want different results.

NOTES

INTRODUCTION

i Fintan O'Toole, *Ship of Fools: How Stupidity and Corruption Sank the Celtic Tiger* (London, 2009), p.219.
ii *The Irish Times*, 20 December 2008.
iii *Ibid.*, 14 February 2009; 15 June 2009.
iv Fintan O'Toole is an exception here, as he consistently highlighted the moral failings of Irish businesses and financial institutions for almost thirty years. His is no 'Road to Damascus' conversion.
v Shane Ross, *The Bankers: How the Banks Brought Ireland to its Knees* (London, 2009), p.271.

1. HOUSING

1 Ruth McManus, 'Blue Collars, "Red Forts" and Green Fields: Working-Class Housing in Ireland in the Twentieth Century', *International Labor and Working Class History*, No.64 (Fall, 2003), p.52.
2 Ebenezer Howard, *Garden Cities of Tomorrow* (London: Faber & Faber, 1965), p.49.
3 Tony Fahey, Brian Nolan and Bertrand Maître, *Housing, Poverty and Wealth in Ireland* (Dublin: Combat Poverty Agency, 2004), p.20.
4 *British Medical Journal*, 23 June 1906, p.1,494.
5 Michelle Norris, 'Housing', in Mark Callanan & Justin F. Keogan, *Local Government in Ireland Inside Out* (Dublin: Institute of Public Administration,

2003), p.169. Additional figures relating to labourers' cottages are from this source.

6 President W.T. Cosgrave, 1 April 1925.
7 *The Irish Times*, 3 May 1923.
8 *Ibid.*, 3 January 1921.
9 *Ibid.*, 26 February 1924.
10 Quoted in Ruth McManus, *Dublin 1910-1940: Shaping the City & Suburbs* (Dublin: Four Courts Press, 2002), p.359.
11 Quoted in McManus, *Dublin*, p.358.
12 McManus, *Dublin*, p.81.
13 *The Irish Times*, 24 May 1924.
14 *Ibid.*, 12 November 1924.
15 *Dáil Debates*, Vol.6, 25 January 1924, pp629-30.
16 Cathal O'Connell, *The State and Housing in Ireland: Ideology, Policy and Practice* (New York, 2007), p.25.
17 McManus, *Dublin*, p.80.
18 *The Irish Times*, 2 September 1925.
19 McManus, *Dublin*, p.182.
20 *The Irish Times*, 21 May 1925.
21 *Ibid.*, 8 June 1925.
22 *Ibid.*, 21 May 1925.
23 *Ibid.*, 26 November 1927.
24 *Ibid.*, 29 September 1926.
25 McManus, 'Red Forts', p.46.
26 Murray Fraser, John Bull's *Other Homes: State Housing and British Policy in Ireland, 1883-1922* (Liverpool, 1996), p.284.
27 Fraser, p.162.
28 *Report of Inquiry into the Housing of the Working Classes of the City of Dublin 1939/43* (Dublin, 1943), p.25.
29 *Report*, p.35.
30 McManus, *Dublin*, p.212.
31 *Ibid.*, p.220.
32 McManus, 'Red Forts', p.46.
33 *Ibid.*, p.50.
34 *The Irish Times*, 8 February 1940.
35 *Ibid.*, 30 May 1940.
36 McManus, *Dublin*, p.225.
37 Quoted in McManus, 'Red Forts', p.48.
38 *The Irish Times*, 22 January 1948.
39 *Ibid.*, 26 July 1948.
40 *Ibid.*, 21 September 1946.
41 *Ibid.*, 16 July 1949.
42 *Ibid.*, 15 October 1952.
43 *Ibid.*, 26 May 1956.

44 *Ibid.*, 24 May 1957.
45 Leo Grebler, 'National Programs for Urban Renewal in Western Europe', Land Economics, Vol.38, No.4 (November 1962), p.12.
46 *The Irish Times*, 5 October 1963.
47 *Ibid.*, 9 February 1966.
48 Norris, 'Housing', p.173.
49 Fahey, Nolan & Maître, p.21.
50 *Census '91, Volume 10: Housing* (1997), pp42-3.
51 *Housing in the Seventies* (1969), p.9.
52 *The Irish Times*, 10 February 1973.
53 *Ibid.*, 26 September 1973.
54 *Ibid.*, 26 September 1973.
55 *Ibid.*, 1 November 1974.
56 *Ibid.*, 18 February 1971; 1 November 1974; 28 August 1974.
57 *Ibid.*, 28 August 1974.
58 *Ibid.*, 13 December 1974.
59 *Ibid.*, 10 January 1975.
60 *Ibid.*, 19 March 1975.
61 *Ibid.*, 28 October 1987.
62 Minister for the Environment, John Boland, in response to a question on the £5,000 Surrender Grant Scheme, Dáil Eireann, 10 June 1986.
63 *The Irish Times*, 29 March 1985.
64 O'Connell, p.48.
65 *Ibid.*, p.48.
66 *The Irish Times*, 29 March 1985.
67 *Dáil Debates*, 10 June 1986, Vol.367, Paragraph 1,529.
68 O'Connell, p.48.
69 *Ibid.*, p.50.
70 *Ibid.*, p.50.
71 *The Irish Times*, 6 April 1987.
72 *Ibid.*, 1 April 1987.
73 O'Connell, p.47.
74 *The Irish Times*, 25 June 1988.
75 *Ibid.*, 25 June 1988.
76 Department of the Environment, Heritage, and Local Government, 'House Loans Approved and Paid by Year, House Type New or Second hand and Statistic' (accessed 15 October 2010).
77 *The Irish Times*, 26 April 1989.
78 Unnamed member of the Irish accountancy industry, quoted in *The Irish Times*, 15 August 1988.
79 *The Irish Times*, 15 August 1988.
80 *Ibid.*, 22 September 1988.
81 *Ibid.*, 25 February 1988.
82 *Ibid.*, 15 August 1988.

83 *Ibid.*, 8 December 1988.
84 *Ibid.*, 8 December 1988.
85 *Ibid.*, 24 November 1988.
86 *Ibid.*, 17 May 1989.
87 *Ibid.* 16 January 1992.
88 *Ibid.*, 24 February 1993.
89 *Ibid.*, 27 January 1994.
90 *Ibid.*, 22 July 1994.
91 *Ibid.*, 18 November 1994.
92 *Ibid.*, 2 September 1994.
93 *Ibid.*, 2 September 1994.
94 *Ibid.*, 3 September 1994.
95 *Ibid.*, 24 September 1994.
96 *Ibid.*, 24 September 1994.
97 *Ibid.*, 25 October 1994.
98 *Ibid.*, 3 February 1995.
99 Fahey, *Social Housing in Ireland* (Dublin, 1999), p.5.
100 Dermot Coates & Michelle Norris, *Supplementary Welfare Allowance, Rent Supplement: Implications for the Implementation of the Rental Accommodation Scheme* (Dublin, 2006), p.54.
101 *A House of your Own* (1967), p.7.
102 Anonymous, quoted in *The Irish Times*, 19 March 1998.
103 *The Irish Times*, 3 February 1998.
104 'McCreevy Announces Green Light For New Urban & Rural Renewal Schemes', Department of Finance press release, 23 June 1999 (accessed 21 October 2010).
105 *The Irish Times*, 7 January 1999.
106 *Ibid.*, 1 February 1999.
107 *Urban and Rural Renewal Tax Incentive Schemes* (1999), TSG 99/32, Paragraph 34
108 'An Estimate of Vacant Housing in Ireland', http://irelandafternama.wordpress.com/2010/01/18/an-estimate-of-vacant-housing-in-ireland/ (accessed 23 October 2010).
109 *The Irish Times*, 8 October 2007.
110 *Census 2002: Volume 13: Housing* (Dublin, 2004), Table 19, p.42.
111 *Eurostat Yearbook 2010*, p.332. Eurostat puts Irish home ownership at 79 per cent for 2007, whereas the 2006 census puts it at just under 75 per cent. The discrepancy appears to be due to Eurostat, which seems to have calculated the level of renting in the State (just over 20 per cent) and subtracted this figure from the total. There are a number of households which are rent-free but not owner-occupied, and this explains the difference. Even with the higher rate of home ownership in the Eurostat figures, Ireland is eighteenth out of the twenty-nine countries listed. For more detailed figures see *Europe in Figures – Eurostat Yearbook 2010: Living Conditions and Welfare (tables and graphs)*, figure 6.13.
112 *Ship of Fools*, p.102.

2. AGRICULTURE

1 An obvious exception here is concrete and other building materials. For more on this, see Chapter Three.
2 *Digest of evidence taken before Her Majesty's Commissioners of Inquiry into the state of the law and practice in respect to the occupation of land in Ireland. Part I, House of Lords, Vol. XXXV* (1847), p.73.
3 *Dáil Debates*, 19 September 1922, paragraph 443.
4 Mary E. Daly, *Industrial Development and Irish National Identity, 1922-1939* (New York, 1992), p.15.
5 *The Irish Times*, 8 March 1926. Total export sales are listed at £49,752,313, which is £1.83 million short of the figure cited by Daly. The 35 per cent figure is based on *The Irish Times* estimate.
6 Raymond Crotty, *Farming Collapse: National Opportunity* (Naas, 1990), p.5.
7 Sir William Petty, A *Treatise of Ireland* (1687), preface (accessed online, 26 July 2010 http://www.taieb.net/auteurs/Petty/pastimes1.html#00).
8 Donald Woodward, 'The Anglo-Irish Livestock Trade of the Seventeenth Century', *Irish Historical Studies*, Vol.18, No.72 (September 1973), p.514.
9 Woodward, p.490.
10 John Feehan, *Farming in Ireland: History, Heritage and Environment* (Dublin, 2003), p.111.
11 Alice Effie Murray, *A History of the Commercial and Financial Relations between England and Ireland from the Period of the Restoration* (London, 1903), p.24.
12 William J. Smyth, 'Landholding changes, kinship networks and class formation in rural Ireland: a case study from Co. Tipperary', *Irish Geography*, Vol. XXI (1983), p.20.
13 Quoted in Raymond Crotty, *Irish Agricultural Production: Its Volume and Structure* (Cork, 1966), p.16.
14 Michael Beames, *Peasants and Power: the Whiteboy Movements and Their Control in Pre-Famine Ireland* (Sussex, 1983), p.27. Tithes were taxes paid to the Church of Ireland.
15 Beames, p.27. The Whiteboys were a secret agrarian society that used violent tactics to defend the rights of tenant farmers.
16 Feehan, p.111.
17 *Ibid.*, p.112.
18 Crotty, p.53.
19 Feehan, p.121.
20 *Occupation of Land in Ireland*, p.73.
21 S.H. Cousens, 'The regional pattern of emigration during the Great Irish Famine, 1846-51', *Transactions and Papers (Institute of British Geographers)* no.28 (1960), p.121.
22 Paul Bew, *Land and the National Question in Ireland, 1858-82* (Dublin, 1978), p.9.
23 Fergus Campbell, *Land and Revolution: Nationalist Politics in the West of Ireland 1891-1921* (Oxford, 2008), pp12-13.

24 Bew, p.223.
25 Quoted in Tony Varley, 'A region of sturdy smallholders? Western nationalists and agrarian politics during the First World War', *Journal of the Galway Archaeological and Historical Society*, Vol.55 (2003), p.142, note no.2.
26 *Leitrim Observer*, 6 April 1907.
27 Campbell, p.92.
28 Paul Bew, *Conflict and Conciliation in Ireland 1890-1910: Parnellites and Radical Agrarians* (Oxford, 2002), p.140.
29 Diarmaid Ferriter, *The Transformation of Ireland, 1900-2000* (London, 2004), p.69.
30 P.L. Curran, *Kerry and Dexter Cattle* (Dublin, 1990), p.3.
31 Commission of Inquiry into the Resources and Industries of Ireland, *Report on Stock-Breeding Farms for Pure-Bred Dairy Cattle* (Dublin, 1921), p.12.
32 Quoted in *The Irish Times*, 27 August 1910.
33 *Agricultural Statistics 1847-1926: Reports and Tables (1928)*, pp88-89.
34 William J. Smyth, 'Landholding changes, kinship networks and class formation in rural Ireland: a case study from Co. Tipperary', *Irish Geography*, Vol. XVI (1983), pp27,33.
35 Daly, p.16.
36 John O'Donovan, *The Economic History of Live Stock in Ireland* (Cork, 1940), p.381.
37 *Dáil Reports*, 23 January 1924, paragraph 497.
38 Paul Rouse, *Ireland's Own Soil: Government and Agriculture in Ireland, 1945-1965* (Dublin, 2000), p.47.
39 George O'Brien, 'Patrick Hogan: Minister for Agriculture 1922-32', *Studies 25* (1936), p.355.
40 J.J. Lee, *Ireland 1912-1985: Politics and Society* (Cambridge, 1989), p.115.
41 Daly, p.17.
42 Rouse, p.9.
43 Daly, p.17.
44 *The Irish Times*, 27 January 1925. This was not the hyperbole it seems. The death rate among children under one year in the city was 116 per 1,000, or 11.6 per cent. With regard to children born to mothers covered by the Coombe clinic, Dr Crichton found the death rate to be around 193 per 1,000, or 19.3 per cent. The death rate in the trenches in the First World War was around 10 per cent.
45 *The Irish Times*, 16 January 1925.
46 *Ibid.*, 16 January 1925.
47 *Ibid.*, 18 September 1925.
48 Daly, p.19.
49 *Ibid.*, p.16.
50 *The Irish Times*, 8 April 1924.
51 Daly, p.22.
52 Lee, p.115.
53 *Ibid.*, p.117.

54 Daly, p.22.
55 *Ibid.*, p.23.
56 *Ibid.*, p.21.
57 *Ibid.*, p.37.
58 *The Irish Times*, 1 May 1930.
59 Peter Neary & Cormac Ó Gráda, 'Protection, economic war and structural change: the 1930s in Ireland,' *Irish Historical Studies*, Vol.27, No.107 (May 1991), p.254.
60 Neary & Ó Gráda, pp252-3.
61 Rouse, p.15.
62 Kieran Kennedy, Thomas Giblin & Deirdre McHugh, *The Economic Development of Ireland in the Twentieth Century* (London, 1988), p.40.
63 Quoted in Neary & Ó Gráda, p.254.
64 Daly, p.78. There is some dispute as to how many new jobs were actually created during the period 1926-1936. Daly says that 'it seems probable that up to 40,000 industrial jobs were generated in the years 1932 to 1936'. For more on this see Daly, pp75-81.
65 Neary & Ó Gráda, p.255.
66 Kennedy, Giblin & McHugh, p.44.
67 Rouse, p.16.
68 *Seanad Debates*, Vol.16, 15 December 1932, paragraph 559.
69 *Dáil Debates*, Vol.44, 10 November 1932, paragraph 1,417. Ryan also said that an increase in wheat production would mean that Ireland 'would be more secure in case food supplies were cut off for any reason, such as a shipping strike, a war, or anything of that sort'. See paragraphs 1,399-1,400.
70 Rouse, p.16.
71 Crotty, pp146-7.
72 *Ibid.*, p.146.
73 Rouse, p.17.
74 *Dáil Debates*, Vol.41, 11 May 1932, paragraph 1,463.
75 Rouse, p.17.
76 *Ibid.*, p.17.
77 Foster, *Modern Ireland*, p.541.
78 Rouse, p.124.
79 De Valera in a speech to small farmers and labourers in Sligo. See *The Irish Times*, 7 July 1930.
80 *Dáil Debates*, Vol.41, 11 May 1932, paragraph 1,463.
81 Rouse, pp55-56.
82 *Ibid.*, p.56.
83 *Ibid.*, p.59.
84 *Ibid.*, p.50.
85 *Ibid.*, p.95. The following account of Irish agriculture from 1945 to 1957 draws heavily from Ireland's Own Soil, pp50-118, and all quotes used are from this source, unless otherwise stated.

86 Ibec Technical Services Corporation, *An Appraisal of Ireland's Industrial Potentials* (New York: 1952), p.70. All subsequent quotes from the cattle section of *Appraisal* are taken from pp70-8.
87 *The Irish Times*, 12 November 1958.
88 *Ibid.*, 28 September 1957.

3. INDUSTRY

1 *The Irish Times*, 4 August 2007.
2 Figures taken from website of the National Treasury Management Agency, http://www.ntma.ie/NationalDebt/levelOfDebt.php (accessed 20 August 2010).
3 'Ireland is in Top 10 Exporters of Services in 2009', 'Progressive Economy Blog', http://www.progressive-economy.ie/2010/05/ireland-is-in-top-10-exporters-of.html (Accessed 20 August 2010).
4 *The Irish Times*, 24 February 2007.
5 *Ibid.*, 8 June 2007.
6 *Ibid.*, 10 December 2007.
7 'Statement on the Budget by the Taoiseach Mr Brian Cowen TD', Dáil Éireann, Thursday 10 December 2009, at 11 a.m.
8 IDA Annual Report 2009 (2010), p.20.
9 IDA, p.19; *Bloomberg*, 'Ireland's Economy Resumes Growth After Two-Year Recession as Exports Jump,' http://www.bloomberg.com/news/2010-06-30/irish-economy-resumes-growth-after-two-year-recession-as-exports-jump.html (accessed 23 August 2010).
10 Bernadette Whelan, 'The New World and the Old: American Marshall Planners in Ireland, 1947-57', *Irish Studies in International Affairs*, Vol.12 (2001), p.180.
11 Whelan, p.180.
12 *Ibid.*, p.188.
13 *Ibid.*, p.187.
14 *The Irish Times*, 26 January 1956.
15 *Ibid.*, 8 February 1956.
16 *Ibid.*, 9 August 1955.
17 *Ibid.*, 8 February 1956.
18 *Ibid.*, 8 November 1955.
19 *Ibid.*, 31 January 1956.
20 *Dáil Debates*, 2 July 1957, Vol.163, paragraph 453.
21 *The Irish Times*, 19 January 1955.
22 *Ibid.*, 10 April 1957.
23 *Ibid.*, 22 November 1958.
24 *Second Programme for Economic Expansion: Laid by the Government before each House of the Oireachtas, August, 1963* (1963), p.19.
25 Kevin C. Kearns, 'Industrialization and Regional Development in Ireland, 1958-72', *American Journal of Economics and Sociology*, Vol.33 (July 1974), p.302.
26 *The Irish Times*, 7 May 1965.

27 Patrick O'Farrell, *Regional Industrial Development Trends in Ireland, 1960-1973* (Dublin, 1975), p.52.
28 O'Farrell, p.14. Total costs for the period 1960–1973 have been indexed at 1973 values.
29 O'Farrell, p.37.
30 *The Irish Times*, 15 November 1966.
31 *Ibid.*, 15 November 1966.
32 *New Scientist*, 10 June 1971, p.608.
33 *Ibid.*, 13 August 1987, p.48.
34 *Ibid.*, 13 August 1987, p.48.
35 *Ibid.*, 13 August 1987, p.48.
36 *The Irish Times*, 10 January 1961.
37 Andrew MacLaran, Patrick Malone & Cecil Beamish, *Property and the Urban Environment: Dublin* (Dublin, 1985), p.68.
38 *The Irish Times*, 29 May 1968.
39 *Ibid.*, 17 September 1968.
40 *Ibid.*, 29 May 1968.
41 *Ibid.*, 28 May 1969.
42 *Ibid.*, 2 January 1969.
43 *Ibid.*, 2 January 1969.
44 *Dáil Debates*, 25 February 1969, Vol.238, paragraphs 1,542–1,558. The figures are my calculations, based on the Minister's reply.
45 MacLaran Malone & Beamish, p.53.
46 *Dáil Debates*, 25 February 1969, Vol.238, paragraph 1,558.
47 *The Irish Times*, 5 January 1962.
48 *Ibid.*, 10 June 1969.
49 Kieran Allen, *Fianna Fáil and Irish Labour: 1926 to the Present* (London, 1997), p.138
50 Rosita Sweetman, *On Our Knees: Ireland 1972* (London, 1972), pp30–31.
51 Committee on the Price of Building Land, *Report to the Minister for Local Government (Dublin: Government Publications*, 1974), p.4. All subsequent quotes from the Kenny Report are from his publication.
52 *Ibid.*, p.11.
53 *Ibid.*, p.24.
54 *Ibid.*, p.36.
55 *Ibid.*, p.40.
56 *Ibid.*, p.94.
57 *The Irish Times*, 26 January 1974.
58 *Ibid.*
59 *Ibid.*
60 'End Foot-dragging on Kenny Report Law?' Press statement issued on 16 February 2007, http://www.greenparty.ie/en/news/latest_news/end_foot_dragging_on_kenny_report_law_sargent (accessed 2 September 2010).
61 There is a scanned copy of the Kenny Report available online via the Dublin Opinion blog (http://dublinopinion.com/2009/05/15/committee-on-the-

price-of-building-land-report-to-the-minister-for-local-government-robert-molloy-chairman-mr-justice-j-kenny-dublin1974/).

62 *The Irish Times*, 26 August 1955.

63 *Ibid.*

64 *Ibid.*, 14 December 1955.

65 *Ibid.*

66 Kevin C. Kearns, 'Ireland's Mining Boom: Development and Impact', *American Journal of Economics and Sociology*, Vol.35, No.3 (July 1976), p.253.

67 *Resources Study Group, Irish Mining – The Need for Action. A Case Study of Exploration* (Dublin, 1971), pp5-6.

68 C.R. Aldwell, 'Some examples of mining in Ireland and its impact on the environment', *Environmental Geology*, Vol.15, No.2 (1990), p.145.

69 Irish Mining, p.11.

70 Kearns, p.254.

71 *Dáil Debates*, 11 April 1967, Vol.227, paragraphs 1,276-77.

72 Kearns, p.260.

73 Resources Study Group, *Navan and Irish Mining: Documentation of an £850,000,000, Robbery* (Dublin, 1972), p.3

74 *The Irish Times*, 5 November 1970.

75 *Ibid.*, 31 August 1971.

76 *Ibid.*, 27 February 1974.

77 *Ibid.*, 23 March 1993.

78 Boliden website, 'Facts and Figures', http://www.boliden.com/www/BolidenSE.nsf/ (accessed 9 September 2010).

79 *The Irish Times*, 23 March 1993.

80 Quote from Justin Keating, *Minister for Industry and Commerce*, December 1973. Quoted in *Research Section: Sinn Féin, The Great Irish Oil and Gas Robbery: A Case Study of Monopoly Capital* (Dublin, c.1975), p.27.

81 *The Irish Times*, 6 February 1974.

82 *Great Oil and Gas Robbery*, p.14.

83 *Ibid.*, p.15; *The Irish Times*, 28 July 1977.

84 *The Irish Times*, 28 July 1977.

85 *Ibid.*, 8 February 1974.

86 *Ibid.*

87 *Ibid.*

88 *Ibid.*, 10 April 1974.

89 'Marathon Oil Corporation Announces Sale of Irish Subsidiary', Press release, 17 December 2008, http://www.marathon.com/News/Press_Releases/Press_Release/?id=1237225 (accessed 14 September 2010).

90 *The Irish Times*, 28 July 1977.

91 Robert Allen & Tara Jones, *Guests of the Nation: People of Ireland Versus the Multinationals* (London, 1990), p.7.

92 *The Irish Times*, 7 May 1969.

93 *Guests of the Nation*, p.20.

94 *The Irish Times*, 7 April 1967.
95 *Guests of the Nation*, p.14.
96 *The Irish Times*, 27 April 1966.
97 *Ibid.*, 7 April 1967.
98 *Ibid.*, 12 November 1969.
99 *Ibid.*, 7 April 1967.
100 *Ibid.*, 22 February 1968.
101 *Ibid.*, 30 October 1968.
102 *Ibid.*, 1 October 1968.
103 *Ibid.*, 1 November 1974.
104 *Ibid.*
105 *Ibid.*, 13 January 1975.
106 *Ibid.*, 10 January 1979.
107 *Guests of the Nation*, p.22.
108 Chris Eipper, *The Ruling Trinity: A Community Study of Church, State and Business in Ireland* (Aldershot, 1986), pp50–1.
109 Mr Niall Crowley, Chairman of Allied Irish Banks, *The Irish Times*, 25 March 1982.
110 National Economic and Social Council, *A Review of Industrial Policy: A Report Prepared by the Telesis Consultancy Group* (Dublin: NESC, 1983), p.3. This report is commonly referred to as the *Telesis Report.*
111 *The Irish Times*, 19 May 1980.
112 *Ibid.*
113 *Telesis Report*, p.3.
114 *Ibid.*, p.26.
115 *Ibid.*, p.12.
116 *Ibid.*
117 *Ibid.*
118 *Ibid.*, p.15.
119 *Ibid.*, p.16.
120 *Ibid.*

4. FINANCE

1 *The Irish Times*, 14 February 1987.
2 *Dáil Report*, 3 February 1926, Vol.14, paragraph 325.
3 Originally there were eight members, but they were later joined by Mr J.L. Lynd of the Department of Finance. See *The Irish Times*, 4 February 1926; 22 January 1927.
4 *Dáil Report*, 12 February 1926, Vol.14, paragraph 844.
5 *Dáil Report*, 24 February 1926, Vol.14, paragraph 1,042.
6 *Dáil Report*, 24 February 1926, Vol.14, paragraph 1,050.
7 *The Irish Times*, 15 February 1926.
8 *Ibid.*, 24 April 1926.

9 *Ibid.*, 22 January 1927.
10 *Ibid.*, 22 January 1927. This edition contained a reprint of the main report and all quotes relating to the report are from this source.
11 *Ibid.*, 3 October 1931.
12 *Ibid.*, 27 October 1934.
13 *Ibid.*, 9 August 1938.
14 *Ibid.*, 8 August 1938.
15 *Dáil Report*, 7 July 1939, Vol.76, paragraph 2,164.
16 Ibec Technical Services Corporation, *An Appraisal of Ireland's Industrial Potentials* (New York, 1952), p.20. All subsequent quotes from the capital finance section of Appraisal are taken from pp20–27.
17 The authors noted that this practice 'may reflect the choice of individual investors rather than bank initiatives'. The fact that the practise was systemic, though – well over half of all bank assets were held outside Ireland – would suggest a banking policy than a random convergence of events.
18 *The Irish Times*, 28 August 1958.
19 Padraig McGowan, *Money and Banking in Ireland: Origins, Development and Future* (Dublin, 1990), p.55.
20 *The Irish Times*, 28 August 1958.
21 *Ibid.*, 23 August 1966.
22 *Ibid.*
23 McGowan, p.55.
24 *The Irish Times*, 30 June 1967.
25 *Ibid.*, 29 September 1965.
26 N.J. Gibson, 'The Banking System,' in Norman J. Gibson & John E. Spenser (eds), *Economic Activity in Ireland: A Study of Two Open Economies* (Dublin, 1977), p.230.
27 *Ibid.*
28 McGowan, p.60.
29 Simon Carswell, *Something Rotten: Irish Banking Scandals* (Dublin, 2006), p.67.
30 *Ibid.*
31 *The Irish Times*, 26 May 1984.
32 *Ibid.*
33 *Ibid.*, 28 February 1935.
34 *Ibid.*, 16 March 1985.
35 *Ibid.*, 8 August 1983.
36 Carswell, p.68. The following account of ICI and the AIB bailout of 1985 draws heavily from his source, especially pp66–87.
37 *The Irish Times*, 16 March 1985.
38 Carswell, p.48.
39 *The Irish Times*, 16 April 1983.
40 *Ibid.*
41 *Ibid.*, 5 October 1978.
42 *Ibid.*, 2 November 1978.
43 Carswell, p.25.

44 US investor at the Pensions 2000 Conference, Dublin, September 1996, reported in *The Irish Times*, 21 September 1996.
45 *The Irish Times*, 13 April 1990.
46 *Guardian*, 14 April 1990.
47 *The Irish Times*, 4 January 1989; 14 June 1989.
48 *Ibid.*, 3 November 1989.
49 *Ibid.*, 31 October 1990.
50 *Ibid.*, 16 March 1990.
51 *Ibid.*, 25 September 1991.
52 *Ibid.*, 28 December 1990.
53 *Ibid.*, 11 September 1992.
54 *Ibid.*, 29 December 1992.
55 *Ibid.*, 25 April 1991.
56 Peter Murray, chairman, Anglo Irish Bank, 24 January 2003, reported in *The New York Times*, 11 August 1991.
57 *The Irish Times*, 14 November 1992.
58 *Ibid.*, 1 June 1992.
59 *Ibid.*, 24 January 1998.
60 *The New York Times*, 1 April 2005.
61 *The Irish Times*, 20 January 2006.
62 *Ibid.*, 25 August 2007.
63 *Ibid.*, 4 September 2007.
64 *The New York Times*, 'Economix', 2 September 2010.
65 *The Irish Times*, 21 September 1996.
66 *Ibid.*, 6 May 1996.
67 *Ibid.*, 3 May 1997.
68 Frank Connolly, 'Ireland's Property Crash Could Have Been Avoided', *Irish Central*, 23 August 2010. http://www.irishcentral.com/news/-Irelands-property-crash-could-have-been-avoided-101287479.html. Accessed 27 February 2011. All subsequent quotes relating to this article are from this source.
69 *The Irish Times*, 10 December 1997.
70 Frank McDonand & Kathy Sheridan, *The Builders: how a small group of property developers fuelled the building boom and transformed Ireland* (Dublin, 2008), p.165.
71 *The Builders*, p.165.
72 *The Irish Times*, 16 October 2004.
73 *Ibid.*, 11 November 2006.
74 *Ibid.*, 4 December 2006.

5. FROM BANK GUARANTEE TO BAILOUT

1 *The Irish Times*, 22 January 2011; *Sunday Independent*, 23 January 2011
2 *The New York Times*, 18 December 2008.
3 *The Irish Times*, 4 September 2007.

4 *Dáil Debates*, 9 July 2008, Vol.659, No.2, paragraph 628.
5 *The Banker*, 1 July 2009.
6 *The Guardian,* 8 October 2008.
7 *The Irish Times*, 2 January 2009.
8 US Securities and Exchange Commission, *Mortgage-Backed Securities*, http://www.sec.gov/answers/mortgagesecurities.htm (Accessed 29 January 2011).
9 J. Kevin Corder & Susan M. Hoffmann, 'Privatizing Federal Credit Programs: why Sallie Mae?', *Public Administration Review*, Vol.64, No.2 (March-April 2004), p.182.
10 *The New York Times*, 30 September 1999.
11 *Ibid.*
12 *Ibid.*, 25 February 2004.
13 'Private-Label Mortgage Back Securities', *Understanding Mortgage Securitization*, http://securitization.weebly.com/private-label-mbs.html (Accessed 27 January 2011).
14 *The New York Times*, 18 December 2007.
15 The Financial Crisis Inquiry Commission, *The Financial Crisis Inquiry Report: Final Report of the National Committee on the Causes of the Financial and Economic Crisis in the United States* (Washington DC: 2011), p.xvii.
16 *Financial Crisis*, p.xvi.
17 *Ibid.*, p.xx.
18 *Ibid.*, p.33.
19 *Ibid.*, p.xvi.
20 *Ibid.*, p.29.
21 R. Alton Gilbert, 'Requiem for Regulation Q: what it did and why it passed away', *Federal Reserve Bank of St Louis Review*, Vol.68, No.2 (February 1986), p.22.
22 'Requiem', p.23.
23 *Financial Crisis*, p.29.
24 *Ibid.*, p.30.
25 *Ibid.*, p.32.
26 *Ibid.*, p.446.
27 *Congressional Record*, V.146, Pt.18, 15 December 2000, pp271-77.
28 *Financial Crisis*, p.48.
29 *Ibid.*, p.xxiv.
30 'Back to Basics', *The Irish Times*, 12 May 2008.
31 René M. Stulz, 'Should we fear derivatives?', *Journal of Economic Perspectives*, Vol.18, No.3 (Summer, 2004), p.177.
32 Henry C.K. Liu, 'The dangers of derivatives', *Asia Times Online*, 23 May 2002, http://www.atimes.com/global-econ/DE23Dj01.html (Accessed 6 February 2011). All subsequent quotes from Liu are from this source.
33 Jan Toporowski, *Why the World Needs a Financial Crash and Other Critical Essays on Finance and Financial Economics* (London, 2010), p.31.
34 Fisher Black & Myron Scholes, 'The pricing of options and corporate liabilities', *Journal of Political Economy*, Vol.81, No.3 (May-June, 1973), p.641.

35 Robert C. Merton, 'Theory of rational option pricing', *The Bell Journal of Economics and Management Science*, Vol.4, No.1 (Spring, 1973), pp141–183.
36 René M. Stulz, 'Should We Fear Derivatives?', *Journal of Economic Perspectives*, Vol.18, No.3 (Summer, 2004), p.177.
37 Henry C.K. Liu, 'Derivative Market Reform Part 1: The Folly of Deregulation', *Asia Times Online*, 3 December 2009, http://atimes.com/atimes/Global_Economy/KL03Dj02.html (Accessed 7 February 2011).
38 *The New York Times*, 8 October 2008.
39 *Financial Crisis*, p.46.
40 Chelsea Wald, 'Crazy Money', *Science*, 12 December 2008.
41 Henry C.K. Liu, 'The dangers of derivatives', *Asia Times Online*, 23 May 2002. All subsequent quotes from Liu are from this source.
42 *Financial Crisis*, p.45.
43 *The New York Times*, 8 October 2008.
44 *Ibid.*
45 *Ibid.*
46 *Financial Crisis*, p.47.
47 Andrew Glyn, *Capitalism Unleashed: Finance, Globalization and Welfare* (Oxford, 2007), p.71.
48 *Financial Crisis*, p.xxiv.
49 *Ibid.*, p.xxiii.
50 *The Irish Times*, 21 September 2007.51 The Irish Times, 9 February 2007.
52 *Ibid.*, 17 March 2007.
53 *The New York Times*, 18 December 2007.
54 *The Irish Times*, 15 March 2008.
55 *Ibid.*
56 *Irish Independent*, 16 September 2008.
57 *The Irish Times*, 16 September 2008. All subsequent quotes from Casey in this paragraph are from this source.
58 *Financial Crisis*, p.xvi.
59 *Irish Independent*, 30 September 2008.
60 *Ibid.*
61 *The Irish Times*, 30 September 2008. All subsequent quotes are taken from this article.
62 *Ibid*, 29 April 2008.
63 *Irish Independent*, 1 October 2008.
64 Shane Ross, *The Bankers: How the Banks Brought Ireland to its Knees* (London: Penguin, 2009), p.193.
65 *Ibid.*
66 Department of the Taoiseach, 'Government Decision to Safeguard Irish Banking System', 30 September 2008, http://www.taoiseach.gov.ie/eng/Government_Press_Office/Government_Press_Releases_2008/Government_Decision_to_Safeguard_Irish_Banking_System.html (Accessed 13 February 2011).
67 *The Irish Times*, 1 October 2008.

68 *Ibid.*
69 *Sunday Independent*, 5 October 2008.
70 *The Irish Times*, 1 October 2008.
71 *Ibid.*
72 *Irish Independent*, 2 October 2008.
73 *The Irish Times*, 1 October 2008.
74 *Irish Independent*, 1 October 2008.
75 *The Irish Times*, 1 October 2008.
76 *Ibid.*
77 *Ibid.*
78 *Irish Independent*, 1 October 2008.
79 *The Irish Times*, 1 October 2008.
80 *Irish Independent*, 2 October 2008.
81 *The Irish Times*, 2 October 2008.
82 *Dáil Debates*, 30 September 2008, Vol.662, No.1, paragraph 22.
83 *Dáil Debates*, 30 September 2008, Vol.662, No.1, paragraph 44.
84 *Sunday Independent*, 5 October 2008.
85 *The Irish Times*, 2 October 2008. All subsequent quotes from this article are from this source.
86 *The Irish Times*, 4 October 2008.
87 *Ibid.*, 15 October 2008.
88 *Announcement in Relation to Covered Institutions, Department of Finance* press release, 28 November 2008, http://finance.gov.ie/viewdoc.asp?DocID=5553&CatID=1&StartDate=01+January+2008 (Accessed 14 February 2008).
89 *The Irish Times*, 24 October 2008.
90 *Statement by the Government on the Recapitalisation of Credit Institutions*, Department of Finance press release, 14 December 2008, http://www.finance.gov.ie/viewdoc.asp?DocID=5604 (Accessed 13 February 2011).
91 *Ibid.*
92 *The Irish Times*, 15 December 2008.
93 *The Bankers*, p.207.
94 *The Irish Times*, 27 December 2008.
95 *Ibid.*
96 *Dáil Debates*, 4 November 2009, Vol.693, No.2, paragraph 619.
97 *Irish Independent*, 5 November 2009.
98 *The Irish Times*, 20 January 2009.
99 *Ibid.*, 6 February 2009.
100 *Ibid.*, 19 February 2009.
101 *Ibid.*, 20 February 2009.
102 *Recapitalisation of Allied Irish Bank and Bank of Ireland*, Department of Finance press release, 11 February 2009, http://www.finance.gov.ie/viewdoc.asp?DocID=5669&CatID=1&StartDate=01+January+2009 (Accessed 17 February 2011).
103 *The Irish Times*, 10 March 2009.
104 *Ibid.*, 9 April 2009.

105 *Ibid.*

106 *Ibid.*, 17 April 2009. All subsequent quotes from this article are from this source. The twenty signatories were: Karl Whelan, professor of economics, Department of Economics, UCD; John Cotter, associate professor of finance, Smurfit School, UCD; Don Bredin, senior lecturer in finance, Smurfit School, UCD; Elaine Hutson, lecturer in finance, UCD; Cal Muckley, lecturer in finance, Smurfit School, UCD; Shane Whelan, senior lecturer in actuarial studies, School of Mathematics, UCD; Kevin O'Rourke, professor of economics, TCD; Frank Barry, professor of international business and development, School of Business, TCD; Pearse Colbert, professor of accounting, School of Business, TCD; Brian Lucey, associate professor of finance, School of Business, TCD; Patrick McCabe, senior lecturer in accounting, School of Business, TCD; Alex Savic, lecturer in finance, School of Business, TCD; Constantin Gurdgiev, lecturer in finance, School of Business, TCD; Valerio Poti, lecturer in finance, DCU Business School; Jennifer Berrill, lecturer in finance, DCU Business School; Ciarán Mac an Bhaird, lecturer in finance, Fiontar, DCU; Gregory Connor, professor of finance, Department of Economics, Finance and Accounting, NUI Maynooth; Rowena Pecchenino, professor of economics, Dept of Economics, Finance and Accounting, NUI Maynooth; James Deegan, professor of economics, Kemmy School of Business, Limerick; Cormac Ó Gráda, professor of economics, UCD.

107 *Dáil Debates*, 16 June 2009, Vol.684, No.5, paragraph 800.

108 *Nama: Frequently Asked Questions*, Annex I, Supplementary Budget, April 2009, http://www.budget.gov.ie/Budgets/2009Supp/2009Supp.aspx (Accessed 19 February 2011).

109 *NAMA Indicative Term Sheet – Proposed Asset Management Company*, Annex H, Supplementary Budget, April 2009, http://www.budget.gov.ie/Budgets/2009Supp/2009Supp.aspx (Accessed 19 February 2011).

110 *Annex 2: Methological Paper for Eurostat on Classification of NAMA and SPV*, Eurostat advice provided, 2009, http://epp.eurostat.ec.europa.eu/portal/page/portal/government_finance_statistics/documents/Annex%202_Methodological%20paper%20for%20Eurostat%20on%20classificat.pdf (Accessed 20 February 2011).

111 *Preliminary view on the ESA95 accounting treatment of the National Asset Management Agency (NAMA) and related majority privately owned SPV*, Eurostat advice provided, 2009, http://epp.eurostat.ec.europa.eu/portal/page/portal/government_finance_statistics/documents/Irish_letter_19_10_2009.pdf (Accessed 20 February 2011).

112 *Eurostat Preliminary View on the Operations of the National Asset Management Agency in the National Accounts*, Deparment of Finance press release, 20 October 2009, http://www.finance.gov.ie/viewdoc.asp?DocID=6025&CatID=1&StartDate=01+January+2009 (Accessed 20 February 2011).

113 'Eurostat Number-crunching Fails to Impress Fitch', *Sunday Tribune*, 25 October 2009.

114 'Impact of TASC budget proposals', *Progressive Economy*, 15 October 2009, Comment No.8, http://www.progressive-economy.ie/2010/10/impact-of-tasc-budget-proposals.html?showComment=1287226868232#c8610633249622185368 (Accessed 20 February 2011).

115 *The Irish Times*, 15 October 2008. Subsequent quotes from the minister's speech are taken from this source.

116 *Ibid.*, 8 March 2010. The twenty-eight signatories were: Prof. Terrence McDonough, Department of Economics, NUI Galway; Prof. Ray Kinsella, Smurfit Business School, UCD; Prof. David Jacobson, Dublin City University Business School; Prof. Paul Teague, School of Management and Economics, Queen's University Belfast; Prof. Peadar Kirby, Department of Politics and Public Administration, University of Limerick; Prof. Rob Kitchin, National Institute for Regional and Spatial Analysis, NUI Maynooth; Prof. James Wickham, Department of Sociology, Trinity College Dublin (TCD); Prof. Seán Ó Riain, Department of Sociology, NUI Maynooth; Prof. Mark Boyle, Department of Geography, NUI Maynooth; Dr Jim Stewart, senior lecturer in finance, School of Business, TCD; Dr Joe Wallace, Kemmy School of Business, University of Limerick; Dr Michelle OSullivan, Kemmy School of Business, University of Limerick; Dr Daryl D'Art, Dublin City University Business School; Dr Roland Erne, UCD School of Business; Dr Proinnsias Breathnach, Department of Geography, NUI Maynooth; Dr Mary Murphy, Department of Sociology, NUI Maynooth; Dr Colm O'Doherty, Department of Applied Social Studies, Tralee Institute of Technology; Paul Sweeney, economic adviser, the Irish Congress of Trade Unions; Sinéad Pentony, head of policy, TASC; Dr Nat O'Connor, TASC; Tom O'Connor, lecturer in economics, Cork Institute of Technology; Rory O'Farrell, European Trade Union Institute (Brussels); John Corcoran, lecturer in economics, Limerick Institute of Technology; Michael Burke, economic consultant (London); Peter Connell, TCD; Patrick Kinsella, DIT, and Tony Moriarty and Michael Taft, Unite Trade Union.

CONCLUSION

1 For more on corruption in Irish life, see Sinn Féin/the Workers' Party, *The Banks* (Dublin: Sinn Féin, 1976); Gene Kerrigan & Pat Brennan, *This Great Little Nation; The A-Z of Irish Scandals & Controversies* (Dublin: Gill & Macmillan, 1999); Paul Cullen, *With a Little Help from my Friends: Planning Corruption in Ireland* (Dublin: Gill & Macmillan, 2002); Colm Kenna, *The Ansbacher Conspiracy* (Dublin: Gill & Macmillan, 2003), and Simon Carswell, *Something Rotten: Irish Banking Scandals* (Dublin: Gill & Macmillan, 2006).

BIBLOGRAPHY

OFFICIAL PUBLICATIONS

A House of your Own (1967)
Agricultural Statistics 1847-1926: Reports and Tables (1928)
Census '91, Volume 10: Housing (1997)
Census 2002, Volume 13: Housing (2004)
Commission of Inquiry into the Resources and Industries of Ireland, Report on Stock-Breeding Farms for Pure-Bred Dairy Cattle (1921)
Committee on the Price of Building Land, Report to the Minister for Local Government (1974)
Digest of evidence taken before Her Majesty's Commissioners of Inquiry into the state of the law and practice in respect to the occupation of land in Ireland. Part I, House of Lords, Vol.XXXV (1847)
Eurostat Yearbook 2010
Housing in the Seventies (1969)
IDA Annual Report 2009 (2010)
Urban and Rural Renewal Tax Incentive Schemes (1999)
Report of Inquiry into the Housing of the Working Classes of the City of Dublin 1939/43 (1943)
Second Programme for Economic Expansion: Laid by the Government before each House of the Oireachtas, August 1963 (1963)

JOURNALS, NEWSPAPERS AND ONLINE PUBLICATIONS

Asia Times Online
Bloomberg
British Medical Journal
Economix
Financial Times
Ireland After Nama
Irish Independent
Irish Left Review
The Irish Times
Leitrim Observer
The New York Times
New Scientist
Progressive Economy
Science
Sunday Independent
Sunday Tribune
The Banker
Guardian

ARTICLES AND BOOKS

Aldwell, C.R., 'Some Examples of Mining in Ireland and its Impact on the Environment,' *Environmental Geology*, Vol.15, No.2 (1990).
Allen, Kieran, *Fianna Fáil and Irish Labour: 1926 to the Present* (London: 1997).
Allen, Robert & Jones, Tara, *Guests of the Nation: People of Ireland Versus the Multinationals* (London: 1990).
Beames, Michael, *Peasants and Power: The Whiteboy Movements and Their Control in Pre-Famine Ireland* (Sussex: 1983).
Bew, Paul, *Conflict and Conciliation in Ireland 1890-1910: Parnellites and Radical Agrarians* (Oxford: 1987).
Bew, Paul, *Land and the National Question in Ireland, 1858-82* (Dublin: 1978).
Black, Fisher & Scholes, Myron, 'The pricing of options and corporate liabilities', *Journal of Political Economy* Vol.81, No.3 (May-June, 1973).
Campbell, Fergus, *Land and Revolution: Nationalist Politics in the West of Ireland 1891-1921* (Oxford: 2008).
Carswell, Simon, *Something Rotten: Irish Banking Scandals* (Dublin: 2006).
Coates, Dermot & Norris, Michelle, *Supplementary Welfare Allowance, Rent Supplement: Implications for the Implementation of the Rental Accommodation Scheme* (Dublin: 2006).

Cooper, Matt, *Who Really Runs Ireland? The Story of the Elite Who Led Ireland from Bust to Boom ... and Back Again* (London: 2009).

Corder, Kevin J. & Hoffmann, Susan M., 'Privatizing federal credit programs: why Sallie Mae?', *Public Administration Review* Vol.64, No.2 (March-April, 2004).

Cousens, S.H., 'The Regional Pattern of Emigration During the Great Irish Famine, 1846-51', *Transactions and Papers, Institute of British Geographers*, No.28 (1960).

Crotty, Raymond, *Farming Collapse: National Opportunity* (Naas: 1990).

Crotty, Raymond, *Irish Agricultural Production: Its Volume and Structure* (Cork: 1966).

Cullen, Paul, *With a Little Help from my Friends: Planning Corruption in Ireland* (Dublin: 2002).

Curran, P.L., *Kerry and Dexter Cattle* (Dublin: 1990).

Daly, Mary E., *Industrial Development and Irish National Identity, 1922-1939* (New York: 1992).

Eipper, Chris, *The Ruling Trinity: A Community Study of Church, State and Business in Ireland* (Aldershot: 1986).

Fahey, Tony, *Social Housing in Ireland* (Dublin: 1999).

Fahey, Tony, Nolan, Brian & Maître, Bertrand, *Housing, Poverty and Wealth in Ireland* (Dublin: 2004).

Feehan, John, *Farming in Ireland: History, Heritage and Environment* (Dublin: 2003).

Ferriter, Diarmaid, *The Transformation of Ireland, 1900-2000* (London: 2004).

Financial Crisis Inquiry Commission, *The Financial Crisis Inquiry Report: Final Report of the National Committee on the Causes of the Financial and Economic Crisis in the United States* (Washington DC: 2011).

Fraser, Murray, *John Bull's Other Homes: State Housing and British Policy in Ireland, 1883-1922* (Liverpool: 1996).

Gibson, N.J., 'The Banking System', in Norman J. Gobson & John E. Spenser (eds), *Economic Activity in Ireland: A Study of Two Open Economies* (Dublin: 1977).

Gilbert, R. Alton, 'Requiem for Regulation Q: What it Did and Why it Passed Away', *Federal Reserve Bank of St Louis Review* 68, No.2 (February, 1986).

Glyn, Andrew, *Capitalism Unleashed: Finance, Globalization and Welfare* (Oxford: 2007).

Grebler, Leo, 'National Programs for Urban Renewal in Western Europe', *Land Economics*, Vol.38, No.4 (November, 1962).

Howard, Ebenezer, *Garden Cities of Tomorrow* (London: 1965).

Ibec Technical Services Corporation, *An Appraisal of Ireland's Industrial Potentials* (New York: 1952).

Kearns, Kevin C., 'Industrialization and Regional Development in Ireland, 1958-72,' *American Journal of Economics and Sociology*, Vol.33 (July, 1974).

Kearns, Kevin C., 'Ireland's Mining Boom: Development and Impact,' *American Journal of Economics and Sociology*, Vol.35, No.3 (July, 1976).

Kenna, Colm, *The Ansbacher Conspiracy* (Dublin: 2003).

Kennedy, Kieran, Giblin, Thomas & McHugh, Deirdre, *The Economic Development of Ireland in the Twentieth Century* (London: 1988).

Kerrigan, Gene & Brennan, Pat, *This Great Little Nation; The A-Z of Irish Scandals & Controversies* (Dublin: 1999).
Lee, Joe, *Ireland 1912-1985: Politics and Society* (Cambridge: 1989).
MacLaran, Andrew, Malone, Patrick & Beamish, Cecil, *Property and the Urban Environment: Dublin* (Dublin: 1985).
McGowan, Padraig, *Money and Banking in Ireland: Origins, Development and Future* (Dublin: 1990).
McManus, Ruth, 'Blue Collars, "Red Forts" and Green Fields: Working-Class Housing in Ireland in the Twentieth Century', *International Labor and Working Class History* (Fall, 2003).
McManus, Ruth, *Dublin 1910-1940: Shaping the City & Suburbs* (Dublin: 2002).
Merton, Robert C., 'Theory of rational option pricing', *The Bell Journal of Economics and Management Science*, Vol.4, No.1 (Spring, 1973).
Murray, Alice Effie, *A History of the Commercial and Financial Relations between England and Ireland from the Period of the Restoration* (London: 1903).
National Economic and Social Council, *A Review of Industrial Policy: A Report Prepared by the Telesis Consultancy Group* (Dubin: 1983).
Neary, Peter & Ó Gráda, Cormac, 'Protection, Economic War and Structural Change: The 1930s in Ireland,' *Irish Historical Studies* Vol.27, No.107 (May, 1991).
Norris, Michelle, 'Housing', in Mark Callanan & Justin F. Keogan, *Local Government in Ireland Inside Out* (Dublin: 2003).
O'Brien, George, 'Patrick Hogan: Minister for Agriculture 1922-32', *Studies 25* (1936).
O'Connell, Cathal, *The State and Housing in Ireland: Ideology, Policy and Practice* (New York: 2007).
O'Donovan, John, *The Economic History of Live Stock in Ireland* (Cork: 1940).
O'Farrell, Patrick, *Regional Industrial Development Trends in Ireland, 1960-1973* (Dublin: 1975).
O'Toole, Fintan, *Ship of Fools: How Stupidity and Corruption Sank the Celtic Tiger* (London: 2009).
Petty, Sir William, *A Treatise of Ireland* (1687).
Resources Study Group, *Irish Mining – The Need for Action. A Case Study of Exploration* (Dublin: 1971).
Resources Study Group, *Navan and Irish Mining: Documentation of an £850,000,000, Robbery* (Dublin: 1972).
Ross, Shane, *The Bankers: How the Banks Brought Ireland to its Knees* (London: 2009).
Rouse, Paul, *Ireland's Own Soil: Government and Agriculture in Ireland, 1945-1965* (Dublin: 2000).
Sinn Féin/The Workers' Party, *The Banks* (Dublin: 1976).
Sinn Féin, *The Great Irish Oil and Gas Robbery: A Case Study of Monopoly Capital* (Dublin: *c.*1975).
Smyth, William J., 'Landholding changes, kinship networks and class formation in rural Ireland: a case study from Co. Tipperary', *Irish Geography* Vol.XVI (1983).

Stulz, René M., 'Should We Fear Derivatives?', *Journal of Economic Perspectives*, Vol.18, No.3 (Summer, 2004).
Sweetman, Rosita, *On Our Knees: Ireland, 1972* (London: 1972).
Toporowski, Jan, *Why the World Needs a Financial Crash and Other Critical Essays on Finance and Financial Economics* (London: 2010).
Varley, Tony, 'A Region of Sturdy Smallholders? Western Nationalists and Agrarian Politics during the First World War', *Journal of the Galway Archaeological and Historical Society*, Vol.55 (2003).
Whelan, Bernadette, 'The New World and the Old: American Marshall Planners in Ireland, 1947-57', *Irish Studies in International Affairs*, Vol.12 (2001).
Woodward, Donald, 'The Anglo-Irish Livestock Trade of the Seventeenth Century', *Irish Historical Studies* Vol.18, No.72 (September, 1973).

INDEX